THE
Age Care
SOURCEBOOK

*A Resource Guide for the Aging
and Their Families*

Jean Crichton

A Fireside Book
Published by Simon & Schuster, Inc.
New York

FIRESIDE and colophon are registered trademarks of Simon & Schuster, Inc.
Designed by Irving Perkins Associates
Manufactured in the United States of America

10   9   8   7   6   5   4   3   2   1

Library of Congress Cataloging in Publication Data
Crichton, Jean.
    The age care sourcebook.

    "A Fireside book."
    Bibliography: p.
    Includes index.
    1. Parents, Aged—Care—United States—Handbooks.
manuals, etc.   2. Aged—Services for—United States—
Handbooks, manuals, etc.   I. Title. [DNLM: 1. Aged.
2. Geriatrics.   3. Health Services for the Aged—
United States.   4. Home Care Services—United States.
5. Nursing Homes—United States.   WT 30 C934a]
HQ1063.6.C74   1987   362.8'2   87-1169
ISBN: 0-671-61148-8

    Excerpts from "Money Management and the Cost of Health Care: Options
for the Elderly and Disabled," by Ellice Fatoullah and David E. Frazer, are
reprinted with permission of Ellice Fatoullah.
    Photographs from the book *Let Me Hear Your Voice: Portraits of Aging Immigrant
Jews* by Mimi E. Handlin and Marilyn Smith Layton (University of Washington
Press, Seattle and London, 1983) are reprinted with permission of the
photographer, Rochelle Casserd.
    We thank Fern and Floyd Bryant, Phyllis Drakulich, Lowe McIntyre, Lucy
McIntyre, Roberta Werry, Nancy Vermeer, Sadie S. Frank, and the McClure
family for permission to reprint photographs of themselves.

For My Father and Mother

Contents

Preface

Old age can be a time for rejoicing, especially when a landmark birthday, like the 100th, can be celebrated in good health and spirits. Today, with lengthened life expectancies, 100-year-olds are hardly uncommon—more than 32,000 Americans were 100 years old or older in 1982, and about 210 more pass the centennial threshold each week.

Even so, the invitation to the 100th birthday celebration of Sadie S. Frank came as a thrill. Mrs. Frank took care of me and my brother Alan when we were youngsters. Since that time (more than 35 years ago), she has never missed sending us birthday and Christmas cards, adding newsy notes in her strong, rounded handwriting.

Today, she lives in Sun City, California, with her daughter and son-in-law, Roberta and John Werry, who are themselves great-grandparents. For the four hours of her gala party on August 28, 1986, Mrs. Frank smiled and greeted more than 100 of us from all over the country. Despite poor hearing, she clearly enjoyed the event, especially the performance by a barbershop quartet that included her handsome, blond great-grandson John Goebel. To thank her guests for attending, she gave everyone at the party a chocolate chip cookie she had baked herself.

Delightful as such celebrations are, they cannot counteract the stark realities of aging that confront many elderly people and their children at one time or another—failing health, inadequate income, feelings of uselessness and loneliness, unsuitable housing or the eventual need for long-term care.

In doing the research for this book, many people shared their expertise about the opportunities and hardships of the aging process. In addition, nearly all of them told stories of anguish and frustration at not being able to care for their own aging parents better. In many cases, professionals in the field—social workers or nursing home administrators—seemed to suffer as much as or more than those with no special training.

A lot of the pain resulted from the physical indignities their aging parents were subjected to—poor hearing and vision, arthritis, heart and respiratory problems, and Alzheimer's Disease, among others.

But, in many more cases, the ache came from the bureaucratic morass that characterizes our country's health and long-term care system. Confusing Medicare forms, premature hospital discharges, impoverishment because of high medical bills, Medicaid discrimination, nursing home neglect—even those knowledgeable about the system can be stymied by these dilemmas.

The Age Care Sourcebook is intended as an aid in negotiating the obstacle course of aging. Its goal is to describe the resources available, so that elderly people and their children can lay claim to all the services they are entitled to. A bibliography of useful books is provided, along with the phone numbers and addresses of state and area agencies on aging all over the country, so that readers can get help in solving their own particular problems.

The book is addressed specifically to the children of older people, but it is also meant for those who provide care for an aunt or uncle, a cousin, a brother or sister, or an older friend.

Most of the examples tell the stories of people I talked to in the course of my research. In some—but not all—cases, the names are changed. Some of the examples are composites of a number of actual situations.

So many people have helped me make this book a reality that I will never be able to express my gratitude to each one individually. But special thanks go to Pam Doty of the Health Care Financing Agency; Sara White, David Schulke, and other staff members of the Senate Special Committee on Aging; Frances Humphreys, Washington, D.C., representative of the Gray Panthers; attorney Ellice Fatoullah of New York City; Herbert M. Kuschner, a certified public accountant of New Rochelle, New York; Leo Baldwin, a housing consultant to the American Association of Retired Persons; Jane Sutton of Youngtown, Arizona; Elaine Serpico of King's Row congregate living center in Middletown, New Jersey; Maria Hickman of Leisure Village West, New Jersey; Bernice Shepard of Shepard Personal Services, New York City; Kathy Rutkowsky and Martha Berman of the Visiting Nurse Service of New York City; and the many people at Metropolitan Jewish Geriatric Center in Brooklyn who generously gave of their time—among them Jim Pizzili, assistant director of outreach; Dr. William Liss-Levinson, hospice director; and

Sadie S. Frank (seated) with her three children (from left to right), Lowe McIntyre, Roberta Werry, and Phyllis Drakulich. (PHOTO BY JEAN CRICHTON)

Rhonda K. Soberman, chief social worker for the long-term home health-care program.

I would also like to thank those who spent hours talking with me during a research trip in Pennsylvania—Arthur A. Ankeny, executive director of the Senior Activity Centers of Cambria County; R. Alan Smith, administrator of the Huntington/Bedford/Fulton Area Agency on Aging; Carol Freeman and John Waterstram of the Cambria County Area Agency on Aging; staff and residents of Laurel Crest Manor in Ebensburg; and the following Johnstowners: social workers Gene Myers of Conemaugh Valley Memorial Hospital, Bernice Adams of Lee Hospital, and Susan Mayer of Mercy Hospital; nursing home administrators Leah Williams of the Presbyterian Home, Robert Miller of the Allegheny Lutheran Home, and Rev. Don Sease of the Arbutus Manor Retirement Community, and Susan B. Holmes, director of the Parkview Adult Day Care Center.

The book would not have been possible without the suggestions and encouragement of my agent, Ken Davis; my publisher, Cathy Hemming; and my editors, Tim McGinnis and Laura Yorke of Simon & Schuster.

I would also like to thank Bea Danziger, Phyllis Marshall, Meg Capeci, Joan Finn, Jane Naylor, Mary Cunningham, Sue Van der Eb Green, Winky Lane Van der Hoeven, Dr. Joseph T. Sobieski, Betsy Haggerty, Marilee

Hartley, Joanna Kyd, Mary Edith and Frank Mardis, Alan and Lorna Crichton, and Will Sahlein.

A round of applause as well for the generosity of my older relatives and friends who have brought me many hours of pleasure throughout my life—Genevieve and Roy Bittinger, Margaret and William Kerr, Lydia Reese, William Crichton III, Olwen Bruckner, Jennie Boyer Williams, and Sadie S. Frank.

CHAPTER I

The Age Care Sourcebook: An Introduction

Profile of a Growing Generation • The Need to Know

A well-off suburban wife and mother, Heather Peterson had to become a parent to her mother-in-law and then to her own father when poor health made independent living impossible for them. Only gradually did she find the resources that could help her cope.

When her husband's widowed mother, Ethel, was diagnosed with cancer, the elderly woman moved from Nebraska to live with Heather and her family in California. Despite several operations, Ethel never regained her strength and soon needed help with bathing, dressing, and walking. Heather tried to shoulder the burden alone but soon found herself overwhelmed, since she often had to miss work and felt she was neglecting her three children and husband.

"We finally hired a nurse to come in each weekday," Heather said. "It was expensive, and I didn't like having another person in the house, but it took some of the pressure off me."

Ethel died two years later. Then, about a year afterward, Heather's father suffered a severe stroke. "I felt from the experience with Dan's mother that we couldn't have him live with us, so I had to look for other alternatives," Heather said. "Dad never really asked, but I knew from his face that he was disappointed."

After months in a rehabilitation center, the 76-year-old man moved into his own apartment near Heather's house. "Rather than a private duty nurse, we hired nurse's aides to be there every day, but he complained about being lonely. He just moved into a nursing home. It's supposed to be a good one, and I hope this will be the solution."

* * *

Betsey Lonnigan's parents had had a tumultuous marriage, but even so, her mother, Lucille, could not seem to recover from her husband's death. Only 60, Lucille sold her small house in Brooklyn and bought a new one in an Arizona retirement community where a sister and brother-in-law lived. But she never felt comfortable in the West and disliked mixing with couples as a single woman. After a year and a half, she moved to another retirement community in New Jersey.

Betsey was unmarried and living in a small Manhattan efficiency, so she felt she could not invite her mother to live with her. Besides the shortage of space, she and her mother generally began arguing after a visit of more than a weekend. Betsey kept in touch by telephone and visited often, especially when her mother, a stubborn smoker, was hospitalized with emphysema. One weekend, she phoned several times and got no answer.

"I persuaded myself she was visiting friends or that she was out shopping," Betsey recalled sadly. "I just can't forgive myself." Her mother had suffered a stroke and was not found until Monday morning, when Betsey alerted security guards to break into the house. Lucille never regained consciousness and died a few days later. "Since then, I've heard about telephone reassurance services. I couldn't call every hour of every day, but surely there was some resource that might have helped."

* * *

Alan Daniels's widowed mother, Margaret, retired ten years ago as headmistress of a respected private girls' school near Boston and prides herself on her independence. But on a recent visit, Alan noticed that his mother didn't seem able to keep her house clean. Her worsening arthritis and poor eyesight made her driving perilous. Always a good cook, she seemed to have no interest in food. Alan suspected she was living on cereal, tea, and toast.

Even so, Margaret flatly refused all offers of help. She became angry when Alan asked her to move in with his family—or into an apartment of her own—in the small Alabama town where they lived.

"She insists she'll never be a burden on her children," said Alan, "but it would be easier if she moved closer to us. This way I feel I have to visit at least once a month to get any idea of what's going on—sometimes I think we're subsidizing the airlines. She might accept a live-in housekeeper, but I don't know how to find someone reliable who would keep me posted on her health problems."

* * *

Martha Wright was only 55 when her husband, Ben, retired and the two moved to an attractive condominium complex in Florida. The Ohio natives made friends on the golf course and enjoyed occasional visits from their three daughters and five grandchildren.

"The whole set-up seemed ideal," said Linda Easton, the couple's oldest daughter, who lived in Milwaukee with her husband and baby son. "They both got part-time jobs and really began to get established."

A year after the move, Martha became severely confused, got lost several times on shopping trips, and had trouble even ordering from a menu. The family physician diagnosed the problem as Alzheimer's Disease. Ben suddenly had to learn to cook, clean house, and tend to his wife's most personal needs 24 hours a day. Linda and her sisters tried to visit often to help him, but, finally, Martha was placed in a nursing home. Within a year, Ben died of a heart attack.

"Dad visited mother every day, but he just couldn't adjust," Linda recalled later. "He stopped eating, lost a lot of weight, and began to drink too much. We thought he would be relieved when Mother went into the home, but I think he was depressed. He needed something, but what?" *After his death, Linda went to Florida, sold the apartment, and moved her Mother to a nursing home in Wisconsin, where she can visit more easily.*

* * *

Old age is as much a part of life as childhood, but most of us don't think much about it, as we struggle to earn a living, find a mate, and raise our children. The first brush with the realities of old age is likely to occur when we first notice our parents growing old.

For some, the discovery comes with a shock and can't be ignored—your mother may have broken her hip or your father may have unexpectedly had his driver's license revoked. For others, the light dawns gradually, after a long period of suspicion that something is amiss—your parents may stop visiting you; they may take a month or more to recover from a cold; their forgetfulness may turn into disorientation.

Traditionally, the onset of old age came with retirement. Men worked at their jobs until they could no longer do so. They retired and often died soon after. Today, however, most 65-year-olds are in thriving health and full of plans for hobbies and travel after their working days are over. As older people begin to live into their 80s and 90s, their children may be over 65 themselves by the time they are called on to address the problems of aging parents.

No matter what your age and experience, you probably feel overwhelmed by the challenge of helping your parents help themselves. If your mother and dad have always been *your* mainstay, the shift in roles may be bewildering. Your once-confident mother may be asking for help, but what does she really need? What resources are available to help her? Where do you go to find them? What if you and your husband or wife need help of your own at the same time?

This book was written to suggest answers to these questions. It is a practical guide to the often-complex realities that affect older Americans in the 1980s. Of course, no book can tell *you* exactly what to do, since your relationship with your parents comes complete with its own individual emotional demands. But up-to-date and accurate information can help you navigate the often-murky waters so your parents can make the most of their older years.

PROFILE OF A GROWING GENERATION

Knowing something about your parents' generation can provide an insight into the task of helping care for them. Older Americans are difficult to generalize about because they are so diverse, and statistics can be dry. Even so, you may be surprised to find that some of your parents' problems stem from characteristics they and their contemporaries have in common.

Increasing Numbers   People over 65 now number more than 28 million, according to U.S. Census figures, and about one of every eight Americans is elderly. More older people are alive today than ever before, and the numbers are growing. By the year 2000, less than 15 years from now, an estimated 35 million people will be 65 or older. By 2030, when most of the baby boomers are gray, more than one in five Americans will be over 65.

Longer Lives   As any casual newspaper reader knows, America's elderly tend to live longer than they used to. At 65, a man can expect to live 14 more years, until 79 years of age, while a woman of the same age can look forward to 18 more years of life, until 83.

America's elderly are living longer, giving older generations the pleasure of spending more time with much younger family members—sometimes even great-great-grandchildren! Here, Lindsay Rose McClure (left) sits with her grandmother, Nany Vermeer (center), and Nancy's grandmother, Sadie S. Frank (right). (PHOTO BY JEAN CRICHTON)

Many older people outlive the estimates, however. Americans over 85—all 2.6 million of them—became the fastest growing age group in the country in 1984. This group is expected to triple in size between 1980 and 2020, meaning that many more health and social services will be needed in the years to come.

Earlier Retirement   At the same time that the elderly are living longer, people are retiring younger. Two out of three Americans now retire before 65 and can expect to spend 20% of their total lifetime in retirement. Most, though not all, people retiring at 55 or 60 are in good health physically. But their lower Social Security benefits may not provide them with an adequate standard of living, and they may be forced back into the job market. Older people often meet illegal discrimination in looking for work, and the part-time jobs they prefer are in short supply.

Older Women Predominate and Tend to Be Widowed   Most elderly Americans are women. There are three women over 65 for every two men. Among those over 85, women outnumber men five to two.

Older women tend to be widows. Of older Americans over 75, two out of every three women are widowed, yet two out of every three men are married. In this age group, nearly half the women live alone, compared to only one in five men.

Elderly Women Are Poorer   Older women have lower incomes than older men. In 1984, the median income of women over 65 was $6,020, roughly half that of the $10,450 median for elderly men.

Health Care Still a Problem   Two out of three older Americans describe their health as good or excellent, and more than half of those over 85 have no disability at all. Even so, about one in five Americans over 65—about 5.3 million individuals—are disabled to some extent or other, and the likelihood of disability increases with age. After 70 or 75, health problems can be expected.

Health care can be very costly. Even though Medicare pays billions of dollars a year in hospital and medical expenses for people over 65, the elderly continue to spend the same amount of money out-of-pocket for health care as before Medicare and Medicaid were established—an average of $1,059 in 1984. And that figure does not include premiums for Medicare Part B and Medicare-supplementary insurance.

Illness like cancer, stroke, and Alzheimer's Disease can be financially devastating, especially when the condition requires prolonged nursing home care. Only about 5% of Americans over 65 are nursing home residents, but after the age of 85, nursing home care becomes far more common—with one in five Americans occupying beds. Surprisingly to many, Medicare covers only a tiny fraction of an individual's nursing home stay, and, to qualify for nursing home benefits under Medicaid, the only other government resource, older people often must impoverish themselves. Medicare and Medicaid policies, as well as ways to augment coverage, are thoroughly discussed in this book.

THE NEED TO KNOW

You may already be providing substantial care and support for your elderly parents, or you may be trying to prepare for the time when you may have to do so. Yet, you may know little about the resources available to aid the elderly. This guide is designed to provide information on a variety of subjects *before* problems arise.

The book deals with nine areas of age care and suggests ways of answering the following kinds of questions:

Financial Planning   Have your parents planned adequately for the financial realities of retirement? Do they know what income they will receive from Social Security, pensions, and investments? Are they taking advantage of all tax benefits for older people? Do they need to hire a financial planner?

Retirement Housing   Where will your parents live after retirement? If they stay in their current home, as most older people do, do they know the pros and cons of sharing the space with another older person or installing an accessory apartment? Can they arrange to draw income from their house through a home equity conversion program?

What are the pros and cons of selling their house and moving to an apartment near you or to a retirement resort? What should they look out for in selecting a continuing care community or a congregate living complex? Who qualifies for federally subsidized housing?

Community Services   What public programs are provided for older people? Are retirees discriminated against in looking for a job? What volunteer programs can they join? What about furthering their education? Are there advantages in joining associations especially for the elderly?

Health Care   What does Medicare cover, and how does it work? How can a Medicare payment decision be appealed? What about other health insurance options: group insurance, Medicare-supplementary policies, long-term care insurance, Health Maintenance Organizations (HMOs), and Medicaid?

Long-Term Care When does your parent need long-term care? Where should you turn for information on diseases associated with aging? What does a caregiver do? When do you need case management? When would your parent need adult day care?

Home Health Care Is there a practical way to outfit your parents' house for home health care? Can telephone reassurance or emergency response systems help? What home health care is covered by Medicare and Medicaid? Can you afford to hire home workers on your own? If care is needed on a 24-hour basis, can you realistically expect to provide it at home—even with the help of nurses and aides?

Nursing Homes How do you decide whether your parents need a nursing home? Is a non-profit home better than one operated by a huge corporation? How effective are state inspections and other consumer watchdogs? What should you look for in choosing a home for your mother or father? How do you pay the bill? Exactly what does Medicare and Medicaid cover? How can you help your parents adjust to nursing home life? How can you be sure they are getting good care?

If Parents Are Unable to Handle Resources If your parents can't handle their own financial affairs, what are your options?

Facing Death How should you talk to your parents about making wills for estate planning or living wills so they have a voice in their future health care? At what point in a terminal illness should a family consider a hospice program? What aspects of funeral planning should you discuss with your parents?

Major Nationwide Resources

Each section of the book lists specific resources dealing with the subjects discussed. The last section of this guide gives a listing, state by state, of area agencies on aging.

CHAPTER II

Financial Planning

Sizing Up Resources and Setting Goals • Social Security • Pensions • Another Source of Income • Special Tax Considerations • Individual Retirement Accounts (IRAs) • Why Hire a Financial Planner?

In the United States, elderly people have always had to struggle economically once they ended their working days. Many suffer in silence rather than worry others, especially their children. True, Social Security benefits have increased recently, and more people are qualifying for pensions, but the economic crunch continues to take new retirees by surprise.

Older people who rely solely on Social Security are, of course, the worst off. If your parents have other resources, you may feel they will be comfortable. But retirement sometimes presents economic problems for those with higher incomes, even former executives (or their widows). An income of $20,000 may be adequate if your parents are used to living modestly, but it can cripple their lifestyle if they are accustomed to getting—and spending—$50,000 or $75,000 a year.

A financial consultant in Boston described the impact on his clients, most of whom are in the upper income group. "I know it's hard to feel sympathy for someone with two houses—one in Wellesley and the other in Cape Cod—but these people are used to living very well. It's very unsettling to them to realize they aren't going to be able to maintain their standard."

In preparing for retirement, sound financial planning plays a crucial role. Your parents may already have begun the planning process, figuring their assets and likely retirement income against the expenses they foresee for the future. And they may have discussed their situation with you.

More likely, however, you have no specific idea of your parent's resources and whether they have planned their retirement adequately. If your parents have always lived comfortably, there has probably never been a reason to ask. And when you do try, you may find your parents resistant.

"Especially when it comes to estate planning, it's very tough to talk to parents about finances," said Carla Gordon of Constructive Financial Planning in Chicago. "The children may feel they're being greedy while the parents may feel used."

Even so, your input can be important. Because life expectancies have increased sharply since the turn of the century, people retiring today must provide not just for a decade but for 15 or 20 years or more. In 1983, men and women of 65 could expect to live to be 80 and 84 respectively, according to statistics compiled by the National Center for Health Statistics.

Older people also must take inflation into account. Inflation has been reduced sharply over the past few years from the 13.5% yearly average in 1980. But even if the rate remains at 4% for the next 20 years, it will then take $2.19 to buy what $1 buys today.

The future poses many other unknowns for the elderly. Social Security, for 50 years the financial safety net of the retired, has been under the threat of bankruptcy, though Congress now claims to have insured the program's health into the 21st century. As for other government assistance programs, only the poorest of the poor can qualify. Pensions, the other main source of retirement income, go to less than one-third of American retirees, and some people have lost pension benefits altogether through corporate bankruptcies.

You can't, of course, expect to protect your parents from the nation's financial insecurities. But you may be able to help them wend their way through this thicket of economic options, if you are aware of the financial realities of retirement.

SIZING UP RESOURCES AND SETTING GOALS

Financial planning for retirement is usually seen as a process similar to preparing for a trip. The first step is to take a careful look at the starting place and create a personal financial statement of assets and retirement income.

Assessing Resources

A personal financial statement includes a survey of retirement income, current assets, and existing debts. The following checklist could be a guide for you or your parents:

FIXED INCOME

Monthly Income

Social Security _____

Pension _____

Profit Sharing Plan _____

Annuity _____

Other _____

Total _____

ASSETS THAT PRODUCE INCOME

	Estimated Value*	% Earned (if any)	Yearly Income (if any)
Checking Accounts			
Savings Accounts			
Certificates of Deposit			
U.S. Notes and Bonds			
Money Market Accounts			
Stocks (list each)			
Bonds (list each)			
Mutual Fund			
Real Estate (resale value and rents, if any)			
Family Home			
Other Property			
Life Insurance (cash value)			
Businesses You Own			
Total			

(Divide yearly income by 12 to get monthly average.)

* Stocks, bonds, and other investments including real estate should be valued at market price the day the calculation is made, but this figure obviously is subject to change.

The cash value of a life insurance policy corresponds to the total premiums already paid plus the interest earned. The owner of a life insurance policy (not the beneficiary) can borrow the cash value at a low interest rate. Repayment of the loan and interest can be postponed until the policy owner dies with the total to be subtracted from the beneficiary's face value amount.

PAYMENTS

	Unpaid Balance	*Monthly Payment*
Unpaid Bills		
Mortgage		
Bank Loan		
Auto Loan		
Other		
Total		

After recording the totals in all appropriate categories, subtract the total monthly payments from total income to get a rough estimate of the money available for retirement living expenses.

Retirement Needs

Your parents should expect to see living costs decline after retirement. The home mortgage may be paid off, so those monthly payments end. Without a job, your father and/or mother will save money once needed for commuting, lunch, and a workplace wardrobe. Many office workers—both men and women—never need to buy another suit once they retire. Their income tax rate will decline along with income and, after 65, there is an additional standard deduction in addition to other tax advantages.

Unfortunately, other expenses rise after retirement, especially those for health care. Many people believe that Medicare has freed the elderly from worries about medical bills, but a federal study showed that in 1984, direct out-of-pocket health costs averaged 15% of their income, the same as before Medicare was enacted. Most of these medical bills were for prescription drugs, eyeglasses, and other services covered neither by Medicare nor private insurance.

To estimate retirement living expenses, this checklist may help:

MONTHLY LIVING EXPENSES

	Current Costs	Estimated Costs After Retirement*
Food		
Utilities		
Electricity		
Phone		
Heating		
Gas, Water, Trash, etc.		
Shelter		
Taxes		
Federal		
State		
Local		
Medical (including drugs, eyeglasses, doctor bills)		
Insurance premiums (including Medicare Part B, other health insurance, life, home and auto)		
Transportation		
Clothing		
Savings and Investments		
Grooming (haircuts, cleaners, etc.)		
Books, Newspapers, Education		
Travel		
Entertainment		
Gifts and Contributions		
Other		
Total		

Most people will be surprised to see how high their retirement expenses are likely to be. What's more, even a modest rate of inflation means less spending power for those on a fixed income. No estimate can accurately predict the future, but a thoughtful look at the realities can help.

* Financial planning for retirement is discussed in books and pamphlets available free or at a nominal cost from banks, retirement associations, and other groups. Any of these publications could help you and your parents begin the planning process.

SOCIAL SECURITY

The single largest source of money income for the elderly is Social Security, which now goes to more than 90% of older Americans. Many retirees find their monthly checks disappointingly low, but, even so, more than one-third of the country's elderly rely on Social Security for 80% or more of their income, according to the Senate Special Committee on Aging.

Social Security benefits now average $478 a month, or $5,736 a year, but some people, especially those who have had an irregular job history, get checks as low as $20 or $30 monthly. Even so, Social Security has been expanded over the years since it began issuing benefits in 1937. It now covers farmers, doctors, and other self-employed people who were not included initially. Benefits have increased, particularly since 1972, when cost of living adjustments were added. As a result, wage earners retiring in 1986 were able to collect maximum payments of $760 a month, or $9,120 a year, depending on their lifetime contributions.

In planning for retirement, your parents need to find out what their monthly Social Security checks will total. To be eligible for Social Security, your father and/or mother must have worked a certain number of calendar quarters in jobs where both they and their employers contributed to a Social Security account in their names. Neither you nor your parents have to rely on your own records to determine the number of quarters, because Social Security keeps track, but, for those born before 1929, the number of quarters varies by birthdate. Forty quarters are required for retirees born in 1929 or thereafter. If the required contributions were *not* made for the minimum period of time, your parents will not receive any benefits at all.

In general, the higher the contribution, the higher the check, but benefits are limited, because there has always been a limit on the amount of wages taxed by Social Security.

How Benefits Are Calculated

Benefits are calculated by computer at the central headquarters of the Social Security Administration in Baltimore. When your father and mother turn 60, their earnings figures to date go on line and, after that time, they can call or visit their local office to get an estimate of what their benefit will be as of their desired retirement date.

Benefit amounts are determined as follows:

Your father (the primary wage earner in most families) retires with full benefits if he works until the current retirement age of 65. Benefits are based on earnings over his working life, corrected for inflation and with his lowest five-year earnings period deducted.

Retiring at 62   More and more people are choosing to retire early, from age 62 on. If they do, benefits are permanently reduced, because of the longer period during which they will be collected. At 62, retirees get 80% of the full benefit, with the amount rising for each month they continue working until 65.

Full retirement age has been 65 since Social Security began, but the age is now being increased gradually and eventually, it will hit 67. It will still be possible to retire at 62, but the benefit reduction will be even greater than it now is.

Your mother   If your mother followed tradition and stayed home to raise children, her check for a dependent's benefit will amount to half your father's. She begins collecting when your father retires if she is 62 or older by then; she cannot begin collecting until she is 62.

If she held a job, she may choose either her own benefits or a check for half of your father's, whichever is higher. Since many women worked part-time and at lower wages than men, their benefits as dependents are often higher than the ones they would get on their own.

If your parents are divorced after a marriage of ten years or more, your mother will get the regular dependent's benefit—one-half your father's—once he begins collecting. She gets the check regardless of whether your father remarries, and she gets widow's benefits if he dies.

If the marriage lasted less than ten years, your mother will have to depend on whatever Social Security contributions she made on her own. Her benefit may be quite small, depending on whether she was able to work continuously. If she remarries, she may become the dependent of her new husband.

Widows may begin collecting at 60, though benefits will be higher if they wait until 62 or 65. Your widowed mother receives 100% of your father's benefit if he died before beginning to collect Social Security or if he died after retiring at 65. If your father retired early and was receiving a reduced benefit, your mother's check will be reduced accordingly.

If your widowed mother remarries after the age of 60, she may continue to collect her widow's benefit or she may begin receiving a dependent's check for half of her new husband's benefit—whichever is greater. If she collects her own benefits, she can also choose to receive that check if it is to her advantage.

Until recently, widows who remarried had to give up all claim to their widow's benefit, since Social Security then regarded them as dependents of their new husband. This usually reduced the new couple's joint income. As a result, many older couples either scrapped remarriage plans or decided to live together without marrying at all, a difficult choice for a generation dedicated to traditional ideas. New legislation eliminated this problem.

Income Sharing   Social Security benefits are computed on the earnings of the higher-paid spouse (usually the husband), so the only way a wife's earnings are reflected in the couple's benefit is if her salary was greater than her husband's. Otherwise, her earnings are, in effect, ignored in the calculations.

Advocates for elderly women say it is no longer appropriate to calculate Social Security benefits this way, since more than 60% of American women now work outside the home. Benefits should be based, they say, on the combined earnings of husband and wife, especially when a woman's earnings total almost as much as her husband's.

Efforts are under way in Congress to correct this inequity through a system called earnings-sharing. Under this proposal, credit for a couple's earnings would be shared equally during a marriage. Rep. Mary Rose Oakar (D-Ohio) has led the fight for the earnings-sharing proposal, but the measure remains in obscurity. While more equitable, the earnings sharing system could result in *lower* benefits for some people, especially widows and divorcees, according to a 650-page report on the subject by the Social Security Administration.

Working Past 65   Your parents may not want to retire at 65. Choosing to go on working (and not filing for Social Security) can increase their eventual benefits by 3% for each year worked until the age of 70. As an added incentive for people to continue contributing to the Social Security fund, the delayed retirement credit is being increased gradually over the next 20 years. By 2009, every year worked past the basic retirement age will add 8% to the eventual benefit.

Part-Time Work   Your father and mother may also choose to work part-time after retirement to supplement their income. If so, their monthly checks will begin to be cut after a point; for example, in 1986 it was as soon as earnings totaled more than $7,800 for those 65 or over, or $5,760 for retirees under 65. By the age of 70, the restriction on earnings is lifted, but by that time many people may not be able to find a job.

Applying for Social Security

People 62 and older should apply for benefits at least three months before they want to begin collecting. Even if they continue working, an application

This man did not want to retire at 65. He is an active tie salesman—at the age of 100. (PHOTO BY ROCHELLE CASSERD)

should be filed two or three months before either spouse turns 65 to assure Medicare coverage. (Private health insurance should not be canceled until the month Medicare coverage actually begins.)

To apply, potential retirees should call or visit their local Social Security office. To qualify, they must be interviewed and must present their Social Security number and proof of their birthdate—either with a birth certificate or a baptismal record. Applicants are also asked to submit W-2 forms (or, if they're self-employed, tax returns) for the two years before retirement.

During the interview, your parents are entitled to look at the earnings records Social Security used to compute their benefit. If they notice an inacuracy or if the benefit seems too low, they may appeal the finding. To win the appeal, however, there must be evidence—either from their own financial records or from an employer.

The first check should arrive in the mail about the third of the month after your father (or the primary wage earner) turns 65. If he or she retires earlier, checks are not issued until applicants have been retired for an entire month. Call the local Social Security office if the check doesn't come by the sixth of the month.

No one should sign a Social Security check until he or she is with the bank teller or cashier who will cash it. Urge your parents to have their checks deposited directly to their bank accounts, so they don't have to go to the bank and run the risk of being mugged on the way.

If the check *is* lost or stolen, the Social Security office should be notified promptly. The check can be replaced, but it will take time.

PENSIONS

Pension benefits today provide a relatively small portion of the total income received by the elderly. While about half of the *current* American workforce is covered under a pension plan, only 25% of the over-65 population gets pension benefits, many of them retired government workers.

Some of these pension programs, especially those from large corporations, provide a generous standard of living when combined with Social Security. Many, however, do not. A study of recent retirees covered by private pension plans estimated median benefits at about $225 a month, less than half of the average Social Security check.

Even if your father worked for a company with a pension plan, he may not be covered if he didn't work there long enough to begin "vesting" or if the company went out of business. Vesting is the right to receive benefits. It usually requires employment at a given company for ten years or more. But in today's labor force, males have less than a 50-50 chance of remaining with a single company for a decade.

Workers sometimes lose pension benefits altogether if their companies fail. To protect them, Congress passed the Employment Retirement Income Security Act (ERISA) in 1974 to guarantee and pay benefits. Before that, pension plans were sometimes canceled in corporate financial crises, despite the fact that workers had contributed their own money during their working years.

ERISA has improved the situation, but problems remain for workers who have changed jobs often or who were fired just before retirement. Other workers erroneously assume that their vested pension benefits will continue to support their wives in case of their death. Whether this is true depends on the pension plan.

In other cases, workers receive large, lump-sum payments of pension money long before retirement, from pension plans terminated as part of a corporate merger. These funds must be invested wisely if the money is to be conserved for retirement.

If your father or mother has questions about what to expect from a pension plan, the best source of information is the employer's pension department.

To find out about a pension plan covered by ERISA and how to file for benefits, contact

Office of Reports and Disclosures
 Pension and Welfare Benefit Programs
 Department of Labor
 200 Constitution Ave., N.W.
 Washington, D.C. 20216
 (202) 523-8771

If a pension plan is terminated, beneficiaries may be covered by the Pension Benefit Guaranty Corporation. For information, write or call

Pension Benefit Guaranty Corporation
 2020 K St., N.W.
 Washington, D.C. 20006
 (202) 254-4817

ANOTHER SOURCE OF INCOME

SSI   If your parents' income is very low, they may qualify for another program handled by the Social Security Administration: Supplemental Security Income (SSI). Established in 1972, SSI goes to the aged and to needy, blind, or disabled people of any age with low-enough incomes. SSI can be paid to those over 65 whether or not they get Social Security.

Each state has its own SSI program, but most use the federal minimum-income guidelines. In 1986, the amounts were $336 a month, or $4,032 yearly, for an individual and $504 a month, or $6,048 a year, for a couple. The SSI amount is both a maximum payment and an income ceiling. If your parents' monthly income is less, SSI will pay only enough to bring them up to that standard.

Unlike Social Security, SSI is based on a means test that takes both income and total resources into account. Income may not exceed the basic benefit amount. Certain assets—including bank accounts, stocks, bonds, and other property—could not exceed $1,700 for an individual and $2,550 for a couple in 1986. The assets limit is being raised gradually under current legislation. By 1989, assets may total up to $2,000 for an individual and $3,000 for a couple to be permitted to qualify.

Owning a home or a car does not disqualify a person for SSI. The family home, no matter how valuable, is never counted in figuring assets. A car counts only if its market value is more than $4,500.

In 16 states and the District of Columbia, monthly supplements of varying sizes, ranging from $10 in Maine to $164 in California, are added directly to SSI checks. Other states providing supplements are Delaware, Hawaii, Iowa, Massachusetts, Michigan, Montana, Nevada, New Jersey, New York, Pennsylvania, Rhode Island, Vermont, Washington, and Wisconsin.

Still other states grant supplements to SSI beneficiaries out of state funds, but these extra amounts are not added to SSI checks. To qualify for these supplements, your parents will need to apply to the appropriate state agency—in most states, the Department of Welfare.

SSI payments are reduced by one-third for people living with their families or in some other household where they receive support and maintenance from another person.

Many elderly people qualify for SSI, but the government estimates that about half do not collect. One reason may be that SSI income is so low— only about 75% of the poverty level—that many feel the benefits aren't worth the trouble of applying. Other older people are too proud and self-reliant to want to subject themselves to a means test for what they think of as welfare.

SSI checks *are* low, but an important reason to enter the assistance system is the added advantage of Food Stamps and Medicaid eligibility. Guidelines for the three programs are usually similar. Your parents' local Social Security office has details for the state they live in.

Food Stamps are redeemable coupons good for buying basic foods, and those eligible can receive an amount for up to 30% of their monthly income. Medicaid, a health-care program for low-income people of all ages, provides more liberal benefits than Medicare, including continuing coverage for long-term nursing home care. It will be discussed in later sections.

SPECIAL TAX CONSIDERATIONS

To help offset their economic difficulties, older Americans get certain breaks on federal income tax burdens:

One-Time Tax Exclusion on Sale of Home   When selling the family home, people 55 and over need not pay income tax on the first $125,000 of any profit realized—on a one-time-only basis. This tax break is most important in parts of the country where real estate prices have soared over the years since a home was purchased. The provision remains under the 1986 Tax Reform Act.

In figuring the cost basis, sellers may add the cost of capital improvements to the original purchase price. The exclusion may be taken only once, no matter how many times older people sell houses. If a person who has used the exclusion remarries, he or she may not take it again, even if the new spouse has never done so.

Extra Standard Deduction for Those Over 65 In figuring federal income tax, all taxpayers are entitled to a standard deduction with the amount depending on marital status. The 1986 Tax Reform Act gives elderly or blind people an additional standard deduction. Those who are elderly *and* blind can take the additional deduction twice.

In 1987 and 1988, the additional standard deduction is $750 for a single taxpayer over 65 ($1,500 for a single person who is elderly *and* blind) and $600 for each married person ($1,200 for a spouse who is both elderly and blind). Beginning in 1989, the additional deduction will be indexed for inflation.

Credit for the Care of a Disabled Spouse or Parent If one of your parents is physically or mentally unable to care for himself or herself, an aide may be needed while the other parent goes out to work. Taxpayers with adjusted gross incomes over $28,000 may be able to deduct 20% of their expenses, up to $480, from taxes. If you provide more than half the support for a disabled parent and you are employed, you may be eligible for the credit.

Taxation of Social Security Benefits

Under the original provisions of the Social Security Act, benefits were not taxable. But in 1983, when legislation was passed to rescue the Social Security system, up to one-half of yearly benefits were made subject to taxation if retirees had total incomes over $32,000 for a couple or $25,000 for an individual.

In figuring total income under these guidelines, the IRS counts interest from nontaxable government bonds and half of the Social Security income, plus dividends, other interest, rents, and pensions. The tax is levied either on half the yearly Social Security payment or on half the income over $32,000 for a couple or $25,000 for an individual, whichever is less.

In addition, if your parents filed individual income tax returns after living together for any part of the year, they will have to pay income tax on one-half of their Social Security benefits regardless of their income.

Since 1983, some states have also begun taxing Social Security benefits as income because their tax structures are tied to the federal system. In other states, Social Security checks continue to be tax-free. For further information, check the state tax department in your parents' state.

Filing Estimates

Many older people do not realize that when they retire, they may have to file an estimated return along with their regular 1040 form in April. If so, they must pay taxes to the IRS four times a year, an unpleasant surprise after having had most income tax withheld from salary.

In retirement, much of your parents' income may come from pensions, interest, dividends, or capital gains, which are not generally subject to withholding. They must file estimated tax returns if their previous year's taxable income exceeded $500.

The quarterly installments on the estimated tax are due on April 15, June 15, September 15, and January 15. Together the four payments must total at least 90% of the current year's tax or 100% of the previous year's, whichever is less.

Arriving at the estimate need not be difficult, especially if your parents' income comes from regular pension payments or interest checks, but it may require more calculation than they are used to. In this case, they may need help from you or a professional tax practitioner.

Those who fail to file and make the quarterly payments are subject to a penalty equivalent to the interest due on the taxes that should have been paid. In 1979, about 313,000 taxpayers, many of them older people, were assessed the penalties, primarily because of taxable pensions.

Over the past few years, Congress has tried to ease the situation, directing the IRS to withhold tax from pension annuities so that fewer people need to file estimates. But pension recipients may choose not to have the taxes withheld, in order to maximize their cash income.

To help elderly people make the shift from withholding to estimating, Congress authorized the IRS in 1984 to waive the penalty for failing to file an estimated return in the first two years after a taxpayer turns 62 (or becomes disabled) and in other situations where the penalty would be inequitable.

Waiting to pay the entire tax at the end of the year poses its own financial hardship, however, so the sooner elderly taxpayers catch on to the new arrangement the better.

Itemizing

Many working-age people avoid itemizing on income tax returns, since the standard deduction is sufficient. Some elderly people continue this practice after retirement with the result that the elderly tend to pay slightly higher taxes per capita than younger people despite having lower gross incomes, according to a 1984 report by the Senate Special Committee on Aging.

This is because older people tend to have more deductible expenses than when they were younger, especially when bills for doctors and medications begin to mount. According to the Senate report, average deductions for medical expenses and charitable contributions claimed by elderly people who did itemize were more than twice those claimed by those under 65.

Taxpayers should itemize if their total deductions exceed the standard deduction listed on the tax table. In 1987, standard deductions total $2,540 for single persons and heads of household, $3,760 for married couples filing jointly, and $1,880 for married individuals filing separately. In 1988, the figures are $3,000 for single persons, $4,400 for household heads, and $2,500 each for couples whether they file jointly or not.

The Tax Reform Act of 1986, with its more generous standard deductions, "has real advantages for older people," said Herbert M. Kuschner, a certified public accountant in New Rochelle, New York. "My older clients generally don't make big charitable contributions or have big mortgage deductions, so few may now have to itemize."

Under the 1986 Tax Reform Act, medical expenses can be deducted only if they exceed 7.5% of gross income and only by the amount over the 7.5%. Deductible medical and dental expenses include bills paid for doctors, dentists, medical insurance premiums including Medicare Part B, prescription drugs, and other prescription items like glasses and hearing aids. Transportation to and from doctors' and dentists' offices is also deductible.

Other expenses to itemize include state and local real estate taxes, mortgage interest paid out on loans for up to two homes (and interest on other loans incurred for educational or medical purposes), contributions to churches or other charities, and transportation at nine cents a mile for doing volunteer work for a church or charity.

In order to itemize, the long Form 1040 must be used, rather than the short Forms 1040A or 1040EZ. Form 1040 is also required for reporting interest and dividend income over $400, income over $400 from self-employment, capital gains and losses, and pension income (with Schedule E).

State Taxes

When people retire to a new state, they may face new tax laws that will affect their financial affairs. Some states have high income, inheritance, and capital gains taxes, while other states have none of those. Sometimes, retirees moving from one state to another can take advantage of the differences.

A recent *Wall Street Journal* article told about an advertising executive from Minnesota who saved $20,000 in taxes by retiring to Wyoming where the proceeds of a pension and profit-sharing plan weren't taxable. To take advantage of the Wyoming law, the man delayed distribution of the money until he had established his new residence.

There can be other tax advantages of moving from one state to another. A Connecticut resident moving to Florida may want to establish Florida residency before selling an investment property in Connecticut. In that northeastern state, non-residents are exempt from state capital gains tax, while Florida has no income, capital gains, or inheritance tax.

For further information about taxes in various states, your parents should check with tax preparers or financial planners in the states they consider moving to. Another source of information is, *Your Retirement State Tax Guide,* a "better retirement" book from the American Association of Retired Persons (AARP).

Tax Information

For further information about federal income tax questions, the IRS has recorded Tele-Tax messages on about 150 topics that are available by phone. Some are in Spanish as well as English.

Tele-Tax phone numbers are not toll-free, but they can be reached by local calls in several hundred cities nationwide. In some cities, the numbers can be dialed only from touch-tone phones, while in others both dial and touch-tone phones can be used. Automated information on the status of an individual's refund is also available in selected locations.

The Tele-Tax numbers are listed in telephone directories under the Internal Revenue Service. Tele-Tax phone numbers and topics are listed in the IRS instruction booklet issued with Federal Income Tax Form 1040.

The Tax-Aide Program

The American Association of Retired Persons assists thousands of people each year in completing and filing federal and state tax returns through its Tax-Aide program. In 1986, more than 25,000 volunteers counseled more than a million people at no charge at 9,000 centers set up in shopping centers and community centers across the country. Many of them retired accountants, the volunteers are trained by the AARP in cooperation with the Internal Revenue Service.

To find a Tax-Aide or tax counseling site, call the nearest IRS office. To find out more about this AARP project, contact

Tax-Aide Program
AARP
1909 K St., N.W.
Washington, D.C. 20049
(202) 872-4700

INDIVIDUAL RETIREMENT ACCOUNTS (IRAs)

Individual Retirement Accounts, or IRAs, were established with great fanfare in 1981 as tax shelters for average wage earners. Under the terms of the Economic Recovery Tax Act, up to $2,000 of annual earnings (or $2,250 for couples with one wage earner) could be invested in IRA accounts and deducted from taxable income in the same year.

At the time, IRAs were touted as an important incentive for people to save for retirement, so participants were forbidden to draw on their investments (without paying a 10% penalty) until they became 59½, with the invested funds collecting tax-protected interest over the years.

Investors are *permitted* to begin withdrawing IRA funds at 59½ but are *required* to begin withdrawals by the time they reach 70½. Retirees are taxed on the withdrawals, but probably at a lower rate than they would have been, since their tax bracket is likely to be lower than during their working years.

Banks, credit unions, brokerage houses, and mutual funds ardently courted IRA investors, promising bonanzas if funds were left in place for 20 or 30 years. At the height of the promotional furor, a New York bank listed the results of "what your IRA will be worth," assuming an average annual interest rate of 10%, as follows:

Annual Contribution	10 years	20 years	30 years
$500	$9,028	$33,569	$100,279
$1,000	$18,056	$67,138	$200,557
$2,000	$36,113	$134,277	$401,114

Financial watchdogs warned that interest rates have never remained as high as 10% for a substantial period at any time in U.S. history, and in fact, rates dropped substantially by 1986. Nevertheless, the mere act of saving money over a long timespan was regarded as a positive step, and millions of people invested in the tax shelters.

IRAs became far less attractive under the Tax Reform Act of 1986. Contributors currently can continue to invest money in their IRAs, and taxes are still deferred on earnings or interest accrued over the years until the time of withdrawal. But fewer people can take the deductions, since the benefit is limited for those covered by certain pension plans through their employers.

Some people may choose to invest in IRAs even without the deductions, but the changes will probably reduce the number of people making future contributions. Even so, your parents and others who have already built up an IRA fund still have to know how to time their withdrawals.

Withdrawing from the IRA

Under the Tax Reform Act, investors still may begin withdrawing money from their IRAs at the age of 59½, taking out virtually as much money as they want each year until the age of 70½, when they *must* begin withdrawing. They will have to pay ordinary income tax on whatever contributions were tax-deductible and on the income, which was tax-deferred.

Under the 1986 tax reforms, however, penalties for withdrawals before 59½ are waived if the money is withdrawn in equal installments over a lifetime, such as through an annuity.

Deciding how much money to withdraw each year will depend on a person's tax situation and need for income, financial experts say. "In some cases, we have advised dipping into capital if an IRA is working well and then drawing the IRA down later," said Claire S. Longden, a certified financial planner with the brokerage firm of Butcher & Singer in New York.

The reason for this is tax liability. Your parents obviously would have no tax liability from spending money they have on deposit in regular savings accounts, though interest on the savings would be taxed each year. But all IRA withdrawals are liable to tax (except if the contributions were made on a non-deductible basis under the 1986 tax law).

There are rigid rules for how much money must be taken out of an IRA after the age of 70½. The money may be withdrawn in a lump sum or in yearly amounts corresponding to the older person's life expectancy, which is longer for women than men. The minimums are indicated on a table available from the IRS. If your parents fail to withdraw the minimum, a 50% penalty is imposed on the amount not removed.

For Further Information

Further information about IRAs is available from the IRS and from accountants, tax preparers, and financial advisers.

WHY HIRE A FINANCIAL PLANNER?

You may wonder whether it's realistic to try to help your parents with financial planning. First, there may be very little you can do, especially if your mother and dad's entire income comes from fixed sources like Social Security or a pension. Second, your parents may regard your interest as an unnecessary intrusion if, for example, they are financially sophisticated or have played the stock market successfully in the years before retirement.

Your input may be essential, however, if an unanticipated windfall tumbles into your parents' lap. A lump-sum pension distribution or an inheritance from a brother or sister may necessitate important investment decisions without much time for research. This need for advice may be especially acute if one parent dies, leaving the other solely responsible for a host of new investment decisions. Financial planners say older women often feel particularly unprepared.

"Many married women handle the checking accounts during a marriage, but their husbands more than likely handled the investment side," said Arthur D. Ullrich, a vice president of United Investment Counsel Inc., of Boston. "As a widow, this woman may be left all of a sudden with no idea how much money she needs, let alone how to manage her investments."

Financial experts offer a number of practical suggestions for people who want to help their parents manage retirement income. Among the ideas are the following:

Keep accurate records in an accessible place. Urge your parents to keep good records of investment amounts and dates, insurance policies, and other business matters in a secure but convenient place in their home. This will benefit them as well as you, especially if you must manage their affairs in the case of sickness or some other emergency.

Analyze insurance coverage. Suggest that your parents evaluate all their insurance policies to be sure of exactly what situations are covered and what benefits will be paid. If an insurance policy provides an outmoded level of benefits, consider upgrading or replacing it. Ask for help from an accountant or some other independent financial expert with no stake in the outcome, as an insurance agent would have.

Shift savings to earn the most interest. Urge your parents to check that all bank accounts and other investments are earning the best available interest rates.

Shop for interest-bearing NOW (Negotiated Order of Withdrawal) checking accounts by picking the best combination of features for your situation. Take note of annual interest rates, monthly charges (if any), minimum deposits to open accounts, required balances to earn interest or avoid charges, and canceled check policies.

Consolidate holdings. Many people acquire a wide-ranging portfolio of small investments during their working lives. They may be holding on to old bonds or certificates of deposit with low interest rates and may even have lost track of old savings accounts, IRAs, or stock purchases. Encourage your parents to cash in their small holdings so as to simplify recordkeeping and upgrade income.

Financial Planners

Everybody can profit from clear-headed thinking about financial matters, but not everyone needs to hire a financial planner, especially people whose retirement livelihood comes primarily from fixed sources like Social Security and pensions.

A financial planner specializes in analyzing the financial needs and resources of clients and targeting investment alternatives that will reap the best earnings possible. A good financial planner knows the fine points of tax law and can give comprehensive advice about the full range of financial options. In addition, planners should be able to weigh such psychological issues as a client's tolerance for risk. "This is especially important for the elderly," said Carol Schuder of the International Association for Financial Planning. "Older people are very risk averse."

Who needs a financial planner? People who have been able to set aside a substantial amount of savings during their working years. They may have put the money in the bank or in stocks, bonds, IRAs, or real estate. In planning for retirement, however, a different combination of investments may serve their purposes better.

"An elderly couple needs to maximize income," said Claire S. Longden, the New York planner. "They need to try to get their capital to do more for them, but without tremendous risk because the money can't be replaced since they're no longer working."

Hiring a financial planner can require a substantial investment in and of itself, however. Fees range from $150 to $5,000 and more, depending on the planner's charges and the client's holdings.

People with lower incomes may be able to get help at little or no cost by consulting an accountant already working for them on income tax returns. Free publications on financial planning can also be a low-cost aid. In addition, churches, corporations, local colleges, and community groups, including the AARP, sometimes offer seminars on personal finances at little or no cost.

Financial experts advise that people with investments of $100,000 and up consider professional help in managing their money, but some individual help may also be needed by people with assets of $30,000 or more.

Choosing a Financial Planner

Financial planning has become a growth industry. Today, an estimated 200,000 people are in the business, compared to half that number in 1975. Some planners work in their own firms, while others are affiliated with banks, accounting firms, insurance companies, or large brokerage houses. Some may be certified public accountants (CPAs); some may also have law degrees.

Unfortunately, financial planners as such are not licensed or regulated by either the federal government or the states. No qualifying exams or minimum educational standards are required such as they are in most states for brokers in stocks, insurance, and real estate. Anyone with the money for business cards or an ad in the Yellow Pages can set up shop as a financial planner.

When looking for a financial planner, proceed as you would in choosing any other professional. "Talk to your friends, especially those in a similar financial position," advised John H. Mullen, national director of personal financial planning for KMG Main Hurdman, a major international accounting firm. "Or go to your other professional advisors. Ask your attorney for a recommendation, for example, or your accountant."

Important Issues

Once you find a planner, find out about his or her education, experience, and other qualifications. Find out whether your parents fit the income range of the planner's clientele. Ask for names and telephone numbers of past and present clients as references.

Get the specifics on how the financial planner charges. There is considerable variation. Some work on a fee-only basis—charging by the hour, on a percentage of assets or a percentage of income. Others earn money only through the commissions charged when clients make recommended investments.

Find out whether each client's financial situation is analyzed individually or through a uniform plan applicable to anyone. Request a sample plan for someone whose financial situation is similar to your parents'.

Check Qualifications

Despite the fact that there are few formal regulations for financial planners, some standards do exist. Urge your parents to ask prospective planners whether they are registered or certified by any of the following organizations:

Securities and Exchange Commission   The SEC requires investment advisors to register under terms of the Investment Advisors Act of 1940. An investment advisor is defined as a person who, for compensation, advises others as to the value of securities (i.e., stocks, bonds, and other investments). Investment newsletters and other publications that offer advice on whether to buy or sell specific stocks must also register.

The SEC lists about 12,000 investment advisors, but the actual total is well above that figure since the number includes independent practitioners as well as firms with dozens of individual advisors. Many financial planners do register.

SEC registration does not guarantee quality, since no qualifying tests or educational standards are required. But by registering as an investment advisor, a financial planner conforms with the law and discloses to the public his or her educational and business background, investment philosophy, fee schedule, and any personal interest in transactions recommended for clients.

The relevant information is listed in part 2 of the SEC's ADV forms, and registered advisors are required to provide these forms to clients. Consumers may also get copies by contacting the SEC's regional offices in New York, Boston, Atlanta, Miami, Chicago, Fort Worth, Los Angeles, and Seattle.

International Association for Financial Planning The IAFP is a professional association with more than 24,000 members. It publishes a Registry of Financial Planning Practitioners for those who pass an all-day financial-planning exam, uphold certain ethical standards, complete specific educational requirements, and work in the field at least three years.

A high percentage of IAFP members are registered as investment advisors with the SEC, either individually or through their firms. The IAFP contends the financial planning process is not adequately regulated and is urging federal and/or state regulation to protect the public from incompetent and fraudulent planners. For an IAFP kit and information about IAFP planners near you or your parents, contact

> International Association for Financial Planning
> P.O. Box 468629
> Atlanta, GA 30346
> (800) 241-2148 (toll-free)

Institute of Certified Financial Planners The 10,000 members of this professional organization must be Certified Financial Planners (CFPs), abide by a code of ethics, and participate in a continuing education program involving 45 hours of course work each year. To become a CFP, applicants must complete a tough six-part course of study through the College for Financial Planning in Denver and have three years of prior experience in financial services.

For a financial planning booklet and information about CFPs in your parents' area, write or call

> The Institute of Certified Financial Planners
> 3443 South Galena, Suite 190
> Denver, CO 80231-5093
> (303) 751-7600

American College American College is a financial-planning program established by the American Society of Chartered Life Underwriters. So far, about 12,000 persons have become Chartered Financial Consultants (ChFCs) through the college. Most are in the insurance industry.

To become ChFCs, students must complete the college's ten required courses in taxation, investments, employee benefits, and other related fields either by self-study or classroom work. They must also have three years of experience in the financial services field, meet certain ethical standards, and agree to be bound by a code of ethics.

For further information about ChFCs, contact

American College
270 Bryn Mawr Ave.
Bryn Mawr, PA 19010
(215) 896-4500

National Association of Personal Financial Advisors   Members of this nationwide organization do business on a fee-only basis and are prohibited from selling products and accepting commissions. Most of the 180 members are investment advisors registered with the SEC, according to president Michael Leonetti. Fee structures vary, but many NAPFA members charge hourly rates that range from $70 to $150 an hour. They often recommend noncommission investments like no-load mutual funds and suggest clients trade securities through discount brokers.

For further information, write

National Association of Personal Financial Advisors
c/o Leonetti and Associates
125 South Wilke, Suite 204
Arlington Heights, IL 60005

CHAPTER III

Retirement Housing

To Sell or Not to Sell • Sharing a Home • Shared Group Residences •
Accessory Apartments • Home Equity Conversion • Making a Move •
ECHO Housing • Condominiums and Cooperatives • Retirement Communities • Resort Retirement Communities • Continuing Care Communities • Congregate Care Facilities • Subsidized Housing For Seniors

Louisa Cunningham was always talking about selling the big suburban home where she had lived alone ever since her husband, Anthony, died. Her children teased her about the number of homes she had looked at on trips to Florida where her friends Ruby and Bob Fairchild lived in a retirement community. "I like Florida, and I'd probably be better off in a warm climate," she would say, "but I don't want to have to depend on Ruby for my social life."

On several occasions, the wives of young doctors new to her New Jersey town called Louisa to ask whether her home was for sale. She would ask them over for a visit, and several made good offers, but she always backed off at the last minute, saying she couldn't find another place to go.

"We all love the house too," said Janet Meyers, Louisa's daughter, who lived with her husband in Philadelphia. "But it's so much for her to take care of at 72, and it costs so much to heat in the winter. I still think she'd be better off if she sold it."

But Louisa gradually made the firm decision that her "nice, old house on Elm Street" was the best place for her to live. "I finally have this placed fixed up the way it suits me—a remodeled kitchen and a new bathroom downstairs. I have room for my weaving and my grandchildren when they visit—and I just don't have the energy to go through and get rid of all the things I've accumulated over 35 years. True, the oil bill is high, but I want to stay here as long as my health is good enough."

Like Louisa Cunningham, most elderly Americans consider making a move after retirement. Those who have spent most of their lives in the northern states may long to give up icy roads and snow shoveling for the warm climate of the Sunbelt. Older people with older, two-story houses may be lured by the "maintenance free" guarantee of a newly built, one-story ranch. Those in larger houses may yearn for an apartment.

But in the end, most older people—about 70% of the total—decide to stay put after they retire, gladly enduring hard winters rather than cut themselves off from the warmth of a familiar house and community.

Your parents will have to consider a number of options in deciding whether a retirement move stays in the realm of fantasy or becomes reality. A number of housing arrangements are available to suit a variety of retirement lifestyles. This section focuses on some of the alternatives.

TO SELL OR NOT TO SELL

In debating the pros and cons of remaining in their home for retirement, your parents will have to decide whether the house meets their continuing needs. The following issues may be important:

Housing Costs   Older people can often live most cheaply in homes they've occupied for years, because so many have paid off mortgages. More than 70% of Americans over 65 own their own homes, and of that number about 80% own the dwellings free and clear. Even so, older people often live in older homes. Your parents will have to decide whether their mortgage savings will be outweighed by the need for a costly new roof or improved insulation.

"Mother and Dad say they're saving money by staying in their big house in Cleveland," said Dave Enright. "They decided to install new storm windows to save on fuel, and Dad found he could do a lot of the work himself, now that he's retired. Of course, after all these years, he knew where to go to get the most reasonable deal on the windows themselves. With their mortgage paid off, about the only housing costs they now have are taxes and utilities."

The High Cost of Moving   Selling a house and packing up to move may involve more expenses—both in money and energy—than many older people think, especially if they have spent many years in the same home. Your parents may have to pay a broker's fee, transfer taxes, and moving charges and may find relocating expensive. It can take weeks or months of agonizing to decide which furniture and heirlooms to dispose of and which to take along.

"Sue's parents expected to save money by moving to Arizona from Minnesota," said Ted Jones. "But houses there were much more expensive than they anticipated, and moving costs really mounted up. Of course, winter heating bills are lower, but now there are other things—air conditioning in summer, long distance telephone bills, and the cost of visiting back and forth."

Attachment to the House and Neighborhood   Your parents may prefer to stay in their own home because it is familiar and because of its proximity to relatives, long-time neighbors, doctors, and place of worship. Enjoying these relationships can be part of the pleasure of retirement, especially as long as your parents are in good health.

Evelyn and Dick Long were perfectly happy in their small Victorian home in a Pennsylvania town after their only child, Margaret, left home to attend college. After Dick retired, he and Evelyn visited Margaret for several weeks every winter in the Atlanta home she shared with her husband and children. But the couple was always eager to return home.

"Mother is active in the garden club, and Dad's a deacon at church," said Margaret. "I'd like to see them live closer to us, but they just don't want to move. The only problem is that so many of their old friends are moving or don't drive anymore. They told me the other day that their couples group is down to five from the 20 original members."

Sense of Security   People who have not traveled much during their working years rarely feel inclined to pick up and move after they retire. "Our son Dick just got a job in southern California, and he suggested we move into a retirement community out there," said Harry Murray, a retired steelworker from Buffalo. "We went for a visit, but I was really relieved to come back home after two weeks. The freeways were crazy, the smog affected my asthma, and I just couldn't imagine myself in some garden apartment with no job or friends. How in the world would Blanche and I meet people our age?"

Emotional Stability   In the panicky weeks immediately after the death of a mate—or after a long-postponed retirement—an older person may want to get out of the family house and leave painful memories behind. Counselors to the elderly advise against hasty decisions at a time of grief.

"Mother called a few days after Dad's funeral to say she was calling the real estate agent," said Naome Davis, a Seattle kindergarten teacher. "She was so lonely, and she missed Dad so much. I invited her to come here for a couple of weeks, and we talked about her alternatives."

Naome's mother returned to Iowa City and decided to keep her home at least for a time. "But several years later after a winter of furnace problems, she decided to sell the house and move nearer to us. By that time, I felt she knew what she wanted much better."

Making the Decision

In deciding whether (or when) to sell their home, your parents will have to consider the following kinds of questions:

CHECKLIST FOR MOVING

Financial

1. Run an informal audit of housing costs by adding the amounts for each kind of expense and comparing them to the estimated costs of various retirement options. To make estimates, ask residents of the communities your parents are considering. Real estate agents can also be good resources.

If home is owned:

Monthly Expenses	*Own Home*	*New Home*
Mortgage Payment (if any)		
Electricity		
Heat		
Garbage Collection		
Other Fees (water, etc.)		
Yard, Lawn Care		
Insurance (on monthly basis)		
Property Taxes (on monthly basis)		
Total		

If home is rented:

Monthly Expenses	*Own Home*	*New Home*
Monthly Rent		
Electricity		
Heat		
Garbage Collection		
Other Fees (water, etc.)		
Insurance		
Total		

2. How much income is spent on housing? No specific percentage applies to everyone, but more than 25–30% of retirement income is usually considered too much.

3. How do purchase prices, property taxes, and rents compare in the current home state to those in the states under consideration for retirement?

4. Are increased expenditures expected for:

—home repairs, painting, or maintenance?

—real estate taxes?

—city or county assessments for roads or streetlights?

—insurance premiums?

—heating fuel or utilities?

THE HOUSE

1. How attached are your parents to their home? How well are they likely to adapt to a smaller house or apartment? Can they handle the upheaval of moving?

2. Are they near family, old friends, church or synagogue, and shopping areas?

3. How easily will they find new doctors, hospitals, lawyers, and other needed professionals?

4. Would a warmer climate aid your parents' spirits and health?

5. Is their neighborhood safe, or is it deteriorating?

6. In case of illness or disability, would their current home be safe and easy to navigate, in terms of stairs and location of bathrooms, storage places, and laundry?

7. Could the family home be shared with a renter? Could an accessory apartment be built onto or within the house for rental?

NEED FOR ASSISTANCE OR MEDICAL CARE

1. Do your parents need to drive to get to shopping, doctors, and their church or synagogue? Do they drive? Is public transportation available and reasonably priced?

2. Can parents prepare meals, do housekeeping and home maintenance? Can they hire outside help if need be?

3. Are you or another relative nearby to help in case of problems?

4. Can both parents handle eating, walking, bathing, and personal care in their current home? If not, can one help the other, or can affordable outside help be found?

5. Even if parents are currently self-sufficient, is it likely that some outside help will be needed in the near future?

SHARING A HOME

Marcella Steinberg slipped on an icy pavement and broke her leg. Living alone, the 71-year-old widow had no one to take care of her when she got out of the hospital, so she spent three months in a local nursing home. Her family was afraid she would have to sell her house.

"But even before Mother recovered, an old friend came to visit her, and the two of them got to talking about living together," said Marcella's daughter Winifred. "Anna Marie was a retired schoolteacher who'd lived in her own apartment for years. Mother's house has three bedrooms, and Anna Marie moved her own things into one of them."

The two old friends share utilities and living expenses. They shop, cook, and eat together nearly every night. "Mother never complained about being lonely in the years after Father died," said Winifred, "but seeing how well she and Anna Marie get along, I'm sure she's much happier now."

Older people who have lived for years in their own houses or apartments may regard high utility and heating bills as relatively minor concerns, compared to isolation and loneliness. Even a beloved homestead filled with warm memories may gradually begin to generate worries after the death of a spouse. Was that late-night noise a prowler breaking in? Was it a loose shutter that should be fixed? How much will the carpenter charge to repair it?

Sharing the family home may be a solution. Years ago, it was traditional for children to live with older parents, or vice versa. Today, older people may also share living space with friends. They may find a housemate through the estimated 350 home-sharing programs across the country.

"Our programs mostly serve the elderly," said Mary Gildea, clearinghouse coordinator for the National Shared Housing Resource Center. "Most are looking for companionship and have a difficult financial situation. Those are the two main reasons people share. A third is security, especially in urban areas. All of these things are concerns of the elderly."

The clearinghouse lists both match-up services and shared group residences where a small number of people share common living areas but have private bedrooms. Some match-up services are non-profit agencies that charge no fee, but others are commercial roommate-finding firms.

Most candidates for home sharing are individuals living on their own with limited incomes. Many programs encourage intergenerational home sharing, with both young and old men and women living together. "We find that it often works better with the very young, college students, for example, and the very old," said Juanita Luster, a housing counselor at Project Match in San Jose, California. "Students are especially good because they have to spend evening hours studying."

Same-sex shares are the most frequent but not the rule. At Project Match, Mrs. Luster said, "older women prefer men because they feel more secure, and they feel the men will help them with heavy work around the house."

House Matching

The most common form of house sharing is probably the most traditional: "taking in a boarder." In most such arrangements, a person with a house or apartment rents out a bedroom to another individual, providing meals or kitchen privileges. The renter may have a private bathroom or may have to share.

Other formats also exist. Two friends may decide to share a house, cooking, and virtually all living costs. A single mother may agree to cook meals and do laundry in exchange for room and board for herself and a small child. A retired widower may share his mobile home with a grandson in college.

Some shares get started through mutual friends or personal referrals. Other sharers find each other through a church or supermarket bulletin

By sharing their homes, older people can gain companionship and the care they need to stay out of a nursing home. Morris Gittleson was able to leave a nursing home when Project Home found him a live-in companion, Anna Pagac. She does his cooking and cleaning, monitors his medicine, and helps tend his garden. (PHOTO BY STAN KIRSCHNER, COURTESY OF PROJECT HOME, CHITTENDEN COUNTY, VT)

board. In lieu of such informal methods, home-matching programs may help.

Project Home, a home-matching service set up to serve elderly residents of the Burlington, Vermont, area, listed 87 ongoing match-ups, including a number of live-in companion situations, as of May 1986. "We provide a service to keep older homeowners in their own homes as long as possible," said Helen Ginsburg, a volunteer interviewer/counselor who is a homesharer herself.

Homeseekers in the Vermont program range in age from college students to middle-aged men and women. Some may be paid a salary to render specific services, while others pay rent or exchange less-demanding duties. Project Home also maintains a clearinghouse for temporary caregivers who provide respite for live-in companions.

Successful home sharing requires careful thought about what each person needs in a housemate. A cooperative attitude is essential, since privacy may be reduced. Lifestyles may have to be altered, at least to some extent.

Most match-up services request references and then conduct extensive interviews of both homeowners and prospective sharers. Questions may cover cooking and eating preferences, pets, favorite television shows, musical tastes, and whether overnight guests (of either sex) will be permitted.

"We ask about drinking, smoking, driving, and whether a person needs a driver," said Mrs. Ginsburg. "We even match cats and dogs. One time, we placed a woman with three cats."

A homeowner and a seeker who appear to be compatible are then introduced. If the two get along and decide their needs mesh, they decide together on what money and/or services will be exchanged. Many match-up programs recommend the two parties draw up and sign written agreements.

Home-sharing set-ups may last a month, a year, or more, depending on the compatibility and changing needs of the partners. College students may move out when they graduate and get a job. Elderly homeowners may decide to sell their houses and move into smaller quarters.

If your parents are considering a home-sharing arrangement, remember these potential disadvantages:

1. Rent received may increase the homeowner's income enough to end eligibility for SSI, food stamps, or Medicaid.
2. Zoning ordinances in the homeowner's neighborhood may prohibit two or more unrelated persons from living in a single residential dwelling. Elderly people are sometimes exempted from these restrictions, however.
3. Most home-matching services expect a private bedroom for a housesharer. Your mother or father's home may not be large enough for a share situation.

4. Some match-up programs ask seekers to submit driver's licenses and personal references but leave it up to housing providers to check the references out. As they would with anyone who has a key and access to their home, your parents (or you) should be sure all references are checked and that the prospective sharer is recommended.

5. Problems can arise when either homeowners or guests don't agree beforehand on their respective needs for privacy. Some may want to share meals and leisure time, while others may expect to cook, eat, and watch TV alone.

6. Renters may want to change the way things are done in the house, and a homeowner may resent it. Sharing a bathroom and kitchen may be difficult when you own the house. Such issues should be considered and discussed in advance, if possible.

SHARED GROUP RESIDENCES

Some shared housing is created when non-profit housing organizations buy or lease a home or building and convert it into a dwelling for three to 25 people. Each resident usually has a private bedroom but shares bathrooms, living and dining areas, kitchen, and laundry.

Some shared group residences provide a staff person to help with cooking and housekeeping, while in others, individual residents cook for themselves and divide other household chores. Many residences call for occupants to share one or more common meals a week.

The National Shared Housing Resource Center in Philadelphia lists 175 shared group residences nationwide and classifies them into three groups according to the level of services. In a Level 1 house, all day-to-day chores are done by residents. Level 2 indicates that some services are provided, but not by live-in employees. Level 3 houses are staff-intensive with a live-in staff and possibly a relief staff.

"The group residences serve some frail elderly, the higher the level, the more frail," said Mary Gildea of the National Shared Housing Resource Center. "But they provide no nursing, and there is no one to administer medications or help with bathing or other personal care."

Among the intergenerational group residences are two run by Boston Aging Concerns, a non-profit agency set up to help the elderly. At least 70% of the residents at the Shared Living House and the Mary Delay House must be 50 or older. The others range in age from college students on up.

Another Level 1 residence, St. Peter's House, opened in early 1986 in the Germantown area of Philadelphia, under the sponsorship of the National Shared Housing Resource Center and Episcopal Community Services. Four men and four women, ranging in age from 32 to 74, share common living space while renting private bedrooms for $185–$195 a month, depending on room size and access.

Each week, residents are required to meet and eat one meal together. They handle all household chores, but the sponsors initially provided a facilitator for 10 to 15 hours a week to help iron out problems. "At the last meeting, they asked us (the facilitators) in effect to buzz off," said Mary Gildea of the Resource Center. "They eat and meet together so often, they felt a formal get-together wasn't necessary."

Unfortunately, relatively few shared group residences exist across the country, but interest in them is growing, especially because they can be sustained by rents once they are established. The Ohio Department of Aging is concentrating its housing efforts on bringing together private and public development funds to set up this kind of shared housing.

Finding a Sharer

Call the local Area Agency on Aging to find out about match-up programs or group residences in your parents' area. For a number of booklets on home sharing and further information about programs in various parts of the country, contact

> The National Shared Housing Resource Center
> 6344 Greene St.
> Philadelphia, PA 19144
> (215) 848-1220

CHECKLIST FOR HOME SHARING

1. What do you expect to gain by a home-sharing arrangement? What is most important?

2. Does the homeowner feel the rent is adequate? Can the housesharer afford it? Who pays utilities and taxes? If household chores are being exchanged for a room, can the housesharer reasonably handle them?

3. How much space is available? May a sharer bring his or her own belongings? Is there a private bathroom and some storage space?

4. Does either party object to overnight guests—grandchildren, adult children, or members of the opposite sex?

5. How will shopping be handled? Will the sharers cook and eat together or separately?

6. How much companionship (and privacy) does your father or mother expect? Are individual tastes in television or music likely to mesh with the sharer? Will they share a phone? Does either party object to smoking or drinking? What about pets?

7. Does either person drive or have a car? Is parking adequate? Is public transportation available?

8. Are both parties clear about rents, salaries, duties, and what rooms will be private? Will they sign a formal agreement?

9. Can the arrangement be tried for a trial period?

ACCESSORY APARTMENTS

Many older people living in a large house would not wish to share a living room, kitchen, or bathroom. But they may be able to create an accessory apartment—a second, entirely separate living unit—in the unneeded space of their single-family home.

"We put in our second-floor apartment after Charles retired, and we started spending our winters in Florida," said Pauline Graham. "The tenants agreed to shovel the walks and forward the mail. After Charles died, my relationship to them got a lot closer. I wasn't away as often, but I was alone, and just knowing they were nearby made me feel secure."

An accessory apartment typically has a private entry to the outside and includes at least a bedroom/living room, a kitchen, and a bathroom. It could be carved out of an existing wing of bedrooms, a basement area, or a garage and might or might not have a connecting door to the main part of the house.

No one knows exactly how many accessory apartments exist in American homes, but Census figures indicate that about 2.5 million were added to single-family houses between 1970 and 1980 alone. Not every house has an appropriate layout, of course, but if your parents can add an apartment, they can use the rent to supplement their incomes. This could enable them to remain in a home that might otherwise be too large and costly. (Of course, they will have to report the rent as taxable income.)

In some cases, an exchange of tenant services can be negotiated. Renters might agree to mow the lawn or rake leaves in return for a rent reduction. Expectations about tenant responsibilities should be stated clearly when the apartment is rented, however.

There may be obstacles to creating an accessory apartment, of course. The first is money. Setting up such an apartment usually requires a capital investment that may be substantial, depending on the design of your parents' home. In a split-level or one-story house with an exterior door already in place, installing a kitchen may be the main cost. Homes with outside doors to basement recreation rooms could be ideal.

But when an apartment is installed in a previously unheated garage or in an upstairs wing of bedrooms, new wiring, heating ducts, and a separate entry may be needed, as well as separate metering for electricity, water, and heat. These costs could outweigh the expected financial return.

Perhaps more crucial are local zoning ordinances setting forth standards for all accessory apartments built in a municipality. Many cities and towns now tightly restrict conversions because a flurry of poor-quality jobs transformed a neighborhood of single-family homes into a series of tacky duplexes virtually overnight.

Most such ordinances require homeowners to get a special permit before installing an apartment. The permit procedure nearly always involves a public hearing before a zoning board, where plans are reviewed by local fire, building, and sanitation inspectors as well as by neighbors. Apartments usually are required to have entrances at the side or rear of the house and off-street parking for tenants.

HOME EQUITY CONVERSION

At 71, Norman Rowser realized that his son, Dave, would never come back to live in the house where both of them had grown up, in a New Jersey suburb of Philadelphia. "It's the family homestead all right, but Dave has a wonderful job in Denver, and his wife comes from Colorado," Norman said. "If I left the house to him in my will, he'd just come back East and sell it."

A widower since his wife died three years earlier, Norman lived on his Social Security and a small railroad pension, so he was instantly interested when he heard about a home equity conversion program in his state. "They had the house assessed at $57,000 and promised me 'reverse mortgage' payments of $228 a month as long as I live here, which is really helping with expenses," Norman said.

When he dies or moves, the house will be sold, and the mortgage company will get its loan paid back plus interest and a share in the appreciated value. Dave agreed to the arrangement before Norman made the final decision. "I'm doing okay financially, so I don't really need the money from the house, but Dad does. What makes this perfect is that he can stay in our house as long as he wants."

Americans over 65 own about 13 million homes with an estimated total value of $700 billion. As we have seen, four out of five have paid their mortgages in full, meaning that they have substantial home equity—the value of the wholly owned real estate. This resource represents the largest single asset of most elderly people.

In most cases, home equity isn't liquid, however, so it can be of little help when retirement expenses or health-care bills mount. In fact, home ownership often entails heavy expenses. Even so, most people prefer to remain in their own homes as long as possible, rather than selling to live on the cash.

Home equity conversion is a financial arrangement designed to help older people draw on the value of their homes while continuing to live in them. Your parents may regard the idea as too good to be true, but several alternatives are available, with the specifics depending on the kind of plan involved. In general, a bank or another investor—perhaps a relative—agrees to lend or pay homeowners all or part of the value of their house in fixed monthly payments over a specified period of time during which they continue to live there. At the end of that time, they must move, repaying the loan by selling the house or surrendering it.

Before detailing the different financial arrangements that can be used, you and your parents need to understand certain general characteristics:

Value of the Home   The amount of money available under home equity conversion depends on the value of the house when the agreement is made. People with high home values generally stand to realize more from a program than those with low values. For this reason, residents of growth-oriented areas where property values have risen have an advantage over people from places with depressed housing values.

Amount of Equity   Benefits depend on the homeowner's equity when a conversion agreement is made. Homeowners with paid-off mortgages will profit most. Those with a substantial remaining mortgage debt are *not* good candidates. Renters cannot participate at all.

Equity Depletion   Every plan uses up home equity. The more equity converted into income, the less your parents (and you, as their likely heirs) will have in the future.

Costs   Conversion plans involve interest on the loan and other costs. Depending on the kind of plan, homeowners may also have to pay origination fees and a brokerage commission, and they may have to give up the gain on their house's value.

Risk   All home equity conversion plans involve risk. With some, the risk is that your parents' equity in their home will be depleted before they are ready to move out. With others, inflation may reduce the value of fixed monthly cash advances. Some plans minimize these risks, but that usually means higher costs or lower benefits.

Home equity conversion is not for everyone. First, few programs are available commercially. And those that exist are limited to certain parts of the country. What's more, not all older people would want to remortgage their homes for equity conversion after working a lifetime to get out of debt.

As with any housing debt, equity conversion shifts title back to the lender, preventing elderly parents from leaving it to their children.

"They're putting their property in some kind of position of jeopardy," noted AARP housing consultant Leo Baldwin. "That's what justifies the investment interest of other people. No one will send you money unless they have a solid grasp on a solid piece of property."

An additional blow to one of the most common forms of equity conversion, sale-leaseback arrangements, came with the Tax Reform Act of 1986. Under previous tax laws, you or another relative could have purchased your parents' house—or bought them a more suitable home—and leased it back to them, turning the family homestead into a business property. Interest on your mortgage loan and other management costs, less their rent payments, could be deducted as business expenses.

Today, tax experts say the tax advantages have been diminished, since the new rules limit deductions on rental properties. Consult your accountant to see whether you can take advantage of the remaining incentives.

The ultimate appeal of equity conversion is still unknown. So far, relatively few older people have expressed an interest, and few programs are available. But supporters note that about one-third of all elderly people have no children to whom they can leave a house. They also claim many adult children today place little value on their childhood homes, since many have already cut family ties and moved perhaps a continent away.

Before you or your parents can consider home equity conversion, it's important to know what kinds of programs exist. Each has advantages and disadvantages, so sound legal and financial advice should be key elements of any individual decision.

Reverse Mortgages

Reverse mortgages, sometimes called RAMs (for reverse annuity mortgages), enable older homeowners to borrow money from a bank or other lender, using their homes as collateral. In most cases, owners can borrow no more than 60 to 80% of the appraised value of the property because of the risk that values may decline by the time the loan is due.

Borrowers usually receive a steady stream of monthly checks, with the installments depending on loan size, the prevailing interest rate, and the length of the loan period—usually 10 or 12 years. In some programs, a partial lump-sum payment may also be arranged. As installments on a loan (from which interest is deducted in advance), the payments are not generally subject to income tax.

Homeowners retain the title to the house and the right of occupancy for the term of the loan, but, at the end of that time, the home must be surrendered or principal and interest repaid.

Reverse mortgages differ from other home loans since no repayment of any kind is due until the end of the term. In addition, a borrower's credit-worthiness is determined by the value of the home equity, not by his or her income.

RAMs are a promising idea for the elderly, but there is an accompanying threat. After collecting monthly payments for the term of the RAM, your parents could lose their home in order to repay the debt and then be without a place to live. Banks find the situation distasteful, since they could end up evicting people who are frail and vulnerable in order to recover their money.

Only a few RAM plans exist in the United States, and none operates nationwide. Among the viable ones are the following:

Fixed term reverse mortgages offered through a program designed by the non-profit San Francisco Development Fund. The RAM program has closed on about 200 mortgages since 1981, most in Marin County, and has expanded into 10 different California locations. The program funnels loans of up to $150,000 from area banks to low- and moderate-income Californians over 62 who own and live in single-family homes or condominiums. As a typical example, the program arranged a 10-year RAM loan of $120,000 that netted the homeowner monthly payments of $463 after interest and other charges were deducted.

Since 1984, Don Ralya of the San Francisco fund has helped set up similar RAM projects in four other areas of the country—Boston, through Action for Boston Community Development; Tucson, through Catholic Social Services; Milwaukee, through the West Side Conservation Corp.; and in Hempstead, New York, through the Nassau County Family Services Association.

Program officials stress that fixed-term reverse mortgages are not appropriate for older people who wish to remain in their homes indefinitely. To be sure that borrowers understand they may have to move when the loan term is up, the San Francisco Development Fund hires housing counselors, some with social work backgrounds, to inform prospective borrowers both about home equity conversion and about other programs that may suit them better.

Older clients are told that RAMs may be useful as an interim device to raise money or if they feel they will be selling their homes soon anyway. The RAM payments also could be used to cover living expenses until a pension starts or the older person finds another place to live.

For further information, contact local RAM programs or

San Francisco Development Fund
   1107 Oak St.
   San Francisco, CA 94117
   (415) 863-7800

Shared appreciation reverse mortgages marketed as Individual Reverse Mortgage Accounts (IRMAs) by American Homestead Mortgage Corporation. The Mount Laurel, New Jersey, company guarantees fixed monthly payments for as long as elderly people live in their houses. "This plan allows elderly people to liquidate their savings in their own lifetime," said James J. Burke, American Homestead's president. "The agreements are made for as long as they live in the home."

When homeowners die or move, the loan must be repaid, usually through the sale of the house. At that point, homeowners (or their heirs) owe American Homestead the following three amounts: the total of all the installments received, the interest on that amount, and an agreed-on share of the appreciation. The terms of the loan specify, however, that the company can claim only the sales price (less a 6% realtor's commission) even if the instalments and interest total more than the home's value. "Heirs will never be assessed," Burke said.

Under the program, homeowners can decide how large a share the company gets in the house's gain in value from 20% to 100%—between the time the agreement is made and when the house is sold. The larger the company's share, the larger the homeowner's monthly check.

Other factors determining payment size are the appraised value of the house, the interest rate (which remains fixed for the life of the loan), and the age and marital status of the homeowners. Older people would get a higher monthly check, all things being equal, since a 65-year-old couple would be expected to collect checks longer than an 80-year-old widower, for example.

To participate, a homeowner must be 62, though the average age is 75. The average home in the program is worth $90,000, and the average monthly payment totals somewhat more than $400.

In running the program, the company hopes to make money on the property's rising value. To secure its position, American Homestead makes deals only with homeowners whose houses and life expectancies yield monthly payouts of $100 or more.

Backed by Prudential-Bache Mortgage Services, American Homestead had closed on 500 homes in New Jersey, Pennsylvania, Massachusetts, Connecticut, Ohio, and Maryland by May 1986, two years after the IRMA program started. An expansion into New York State was planned.

For more information about this program, contact

American Homestead
Executive Offices
305 Fellowship Rd. Suite 111
Mount Laurel, NJ 08054
(609) 866-0800
(800) 222-4762 (toll-free in New Jersey)
(800) 233-4762 (toll-free, except in New Jersey)

Special Purpose Loans

These publicly sponsored plans make it possible for needy homeowners, most of them elderly, to use home equity to pay for regular, periodic expenses like property taxes. The taxes and other expenses are paid by the public agency and then charged to the homeowner's account, which may be paid at any time. When the homeowner dies or sells the house, the charges in the account plus interest come due.

Tax-deferral programs exist in Alaska, California, Colorado, Florida, Georgia, Illinois, Iowa, Massachusetts, New Hampshire, Oregon, Tennessee, Texas, Utah, Virginia, Washington, and Wisconsin. The programs vary, but most place limits on income and require a minimum age of 65. Some are not available statewide.

In addition, some states make low-interest home improvement loans or life grants to older homeowners in designated neighborhoods, with no repayment needed until the title is transferred.

Legal Advice a Must

In any home equity conversion, sound financial and legal counseling is crucial to insure that your parents get enough income to justify participation and that the organization they're dealing with is reliable.

"The major element for protection of homeowners is that of disclosure," according to *Turning Home Equity Into Income for Older Homeowners*, a report by the U.S. Senate Select Committee on Aging. "The elderly homeowner should be provided with information which explains the program clearly and simply and which provides a basis for comparison with alternative plans."

In general, equity conversion is not practical if your parents are still paying on a large mortgage or if they live in a neighborhood where property values are declining. It is *most* appropriate for older people over 75, because annuities are less expensive and pay higher monthly incomes the older your parents are.

If your parents get benefits from SSI or Medicaid, home equity conversion could interfere with eligibility. Only one state—South Dakota—specifically exempts reverse mortgage proceeds from consideration in determining eligibilty for medical and public assistance.

For Further Information

For further information about home equity conversion, contact

National Center for Home Equity Conversion
110 East Main
Madison, WI 53703
(608) 256-2111

Fern and Floyd Bryant dated each other in high school in Columbus, Kansas, but each married other people and moved to other towns. Fern was married 40 years and Floyd was married 54, but they remained friends. After their spouses died, they decided to get married. That marriage has lasted six years, and now they live in Sun City, California. (PHOTO BY JEAN CRICHTON)

MAKING A MOVE

In a career that ended as executive vice president of a Fortune 500 company, Raymond Channing and his wife, Martha, had moved once every eight or nine years. When Raymond retired, the couple lived in a large, two-story home in a New Jersey bedroom community. "It was a beautiful house, but it was so large," said their daughter, Jessica, who lived nearby. "We all worried about break-ins when they went away in the winter."

A month after putting their home on the market, the Channings found a buyer and prepared to move to a condominium housing complex built around a golf course in a neighboring town. "The new house has two bedrooms and plenty of space," said Jessica, "but the best part is that there's a 24-hour security force and a regular snow-shoveling and leaf-raking crew."

Jessica's best friend, Carol, had a less happy experience after urging her mother to move out of a deteriorating neighborhood of Trenton and into her suburban hometown. "Just as Mrs. Krieger got settled in a nearby apartment, Carol's husband was transferred to Dallas," Jessica said. "Carol felt so guilty, but there was nothing for her to do but go." At first, the older woman stayed in New Jersey, but she later moved to a small apartment near Carol's family in Texas.

Because of today's longer life expectancies, older people who retire and sell their houses at 62 or 65 must consider their needs for the next 10 or 20 years before deciding where to move. Your parents may be facing some of the following issues:

To Buy or to Rent   As we have seen, most older Americans live in homes they own. Some who decide to sell may expect to remain homeowners. Others may look forward to renting a retirement house or buying a condominium or a co-op so a landlord or a housing corporation will be responsible for maintenance, yard care, and snow removal. But if your parents have rented housing for most of their lives, they may not want to face the unknowns of home ownership at retirement age.

Moving to Another Area of the Country   Most retirees remain near familiar neighborhoods even after selling the family home. But others want to move to a warmer climate, especially in the traditional retirement areas of Florida, Arizona, and California. In recent years, other Sunbelt states like Texas and North Carolina have become popular.

There are many advantages to such a move. Arthritis or asthma may improve in a warmer climate. Heating and clothing costs should drop. Outdoor hobbies—like playing golf or swimming—may be more accessible. And the perils of walking and driving through snow will be eliminated.

Such a move does not always have the desired effect, however. Some older people learn to their dismay that the new climate doesn't improve their health at all. And, when they fall sick, they may find themselves missing children or other relatives they could count on in case of emergency. As a result, many Sunbelt retirees have returned North when their health fails.

To Live Near You or Another Relative   Children of older people sometimes encourage their parents to move to a separate house, condominium, or retirement community in *their* hometown. If this works, the two generations can stay in close contact while maintaining their own individuality.

This solution may be a good one if the older people are able to make friends and find social activities. It may be necessary when a parent's health is failing. But gerontologists warn that the tactic may also backfire. If parents and children have never gotten along, their relationship is not likely to improve with age. Transplanted older people are sometimes so lonely that they expect more support than their children and grandchildren are able to provide.

Living in an Age-Segregated Setting Many older Americans look forward to a retired life among their peers, where all residents are near each others' age. Nearly all retirement communities insist on some degree of age segregation to preserve an atmosphere of calm. But not all older people want this kind of life. "I would never want to live in a place where there were no kids around and no one going to work every morning," said Marian DiSilvestro of the Bronx, New York. She and her retired husband continue to live in the home they have shared for many years, doing volunteer work at a nearby nursing home.

In discussing retirement housing for healthy and independent older people, all four of these factors come into play. Each retirement choice must be made individually, however, whether your parents choose a condo or a rental, Fort Lauderdale or Fort Wayne, an age-segregated or generationally mixed area, your hometown or someplace else.

ECHO HOUSING

Older people in good physical and financial health usually fear that they will jeopardize their independence if they live in the same house with their children. But your parents may see advantages to moving into an apartment or house near you or into an accessory apartment in your home.

They may also have heard of ECHO (Elder Cottage Housing Opportunity) housing. ECHO houses are small, self-contained cottages specifically designed and manufactured for placement in a backyard or sideyard. AARP housing consultant Leo Baldwin praised the idea since the small houses allow the elderly to be "in control of their own turf while being in close proximity to their families. With a separate house, they don't have to share the noise, clatter, and disruption that young people otherwise might impose on them."

In practice, however, few elder cottages have been built in the decade since the AARP and other retirement associations began promoting them. Why not? Second units are discouraged by zoning rules in most communities. What's more, few backyards are really large enough for them.

Some families may wish to consider the option, however, if they have adequate land and live in a receptive community. The idea is not new. Two houses on single property were something of an American tradition a century ago, especially on family farms. In Pennsylvania's Amish country, older widows often moved into *Grossmutter* houses, actually additions to the family homestead, when a son or daughter's family needed more living space.

Government funding has never been available for backyard cottages, however. Several possible prototypes exist, but none has really caught on. One option is a mobile home, but as AARP housing expert Leo Baldwin has observed, "the unfortunate part is that trailers are not designed for people who need orthopedic devices; they're difficult to maintain, and they don't have a long life expectancy." A custom-built cottage, designed individually by homeowners for their own properties and their parents' special needs, may well be prohibitively expensive, but it is undoubtedly more appropriate.

Advocates like Baldwin favor inexpensive houses manufactured to order for the ECHO concept. The ideal elder cottage would be designed to be convenient for both the healthy and the disabled; would be cheap to heat; would be easy to install and remove when no longer needed; and would be attractive inside and out, so as to blend in with the neighborhood.

One of the only companies to build such houses is Coastal Colony Corporation of Manheim, Pennsylvania, which markets three free-standing ECHO models—a 12-by-24-foot efficiency, a 22-by-24-foot one-bedroom, and a 24-by-30-foot two-bedroom house. Coastal Colony owner Edward Guion designed the houses for installation in the backyards of larger homes but now feels the cottages could also be clustered in small, low-cost housing developments or on the grounds of a nursing home.

If you and your parents are considering elder cottage housing, the following factors should be considered seriously:

Zoning Restrictions   Most zoning ordinances forbid backyard houses altogether or require homeowners to apply for special permits for a limited time period.

The state of California and several other local municipalities have adapted policies easing the way for ECHO housing plans. California's law directs local governments to permit elder cottages, accessory apartments and other kinds of second housing units, unless public health and safety are threatened.

ECHO units also may be allowed by individual variance under special-use permits, which would expire when the unit was removed. Whatever the regulations, it's essential to check with local zoning officials.

Backyard Space   Elder cottages appear to be most appropriate for people with a surplus of vacant land, usually in rural areas where there are few or no zoning restrictions. Lot sizes in many other communities may not accommodate even an efficiency unit, and a lack of alleys or adequate space between houses could make installation difficult or even impossible. In affluent suburban areas, neighbors may not want to glance next door and see a temporary cottage on a wood foundation, no matter how big the lot.

Be sure to ask yourself whether there really is enough space for a second house on your property. Does the family mind losing backyard space now enjoyed for recreation or gardening? Would your neighbors object?

Cost Available elder cottages are lower-priced than many homes on the market today, but the units still involve a substantial investment. In 1985, Coastal Colony cottages listed from $11,980 for the efficiency, $19,600 for the one-bedroom, and $23,575 for the two-bedroom model, with installation ranging from $1,100 to $2,200. Shipping and extending utility lines are extra. In addition, skeptics question whether there will be a resale market when units are removed, so homeowners can recover the purchase price.

Before proceeding, assure yourself that you (or your parents) can afford to build a second unit. Will utilities be metered separately? Who will pay for them or for any increase in property taxes? Will they pay rent?

Interior Space Does the elder cottage give your parents enough space to be comfortable? Does the design allow for wheelchair and walker access?

Housing Permanence Are you likely to remain in your current house long enough to justify installing an elder cottage? Do your job and your spouse's job involve unexpected moves?

Moving to Your Area Are your parents likely to adjust well to moving to your town or neighborhood? Are they flexible enough to be able to make new friends and find new doctors and churches or synagogues? Do they feel comfortable with your lifestyle?

For Further Information

For further information about construction and zoning issues for ECHO housing, contact

American Association of Retired Persons
1909 K St., N.W.
Washington, D.C. 20049
(202) 872-4700
Coastal Colony Corp.
Box 452-A, R.D. 4
Manheim, PA 17545
(717) 665-6761

CONDOMINIUMS AND COOPERATIVES

Independent older people may want to buy a condominium or cooperative unit in an apartment house or townhouse complex, either in a retirement community or in another neighborhood. Condominiums are common in most parts of the country, more so in most places than co-ops, but the two kinds of ownership are similar, except for some legal and financial details.

Condos and co-ops are both jointly held housing organizations, in which owners of individual apartments elect boards of directors to be in charge. In both, the directors set monthly fees for individual owners to cover staff wages, upkeep of areas open to all residents, street and hall lighting, and other utilities used in common. They may pass bylaws covering pets, overnight guests, and landscaping. Depending on the size of the complex, board members may hire a management firm or they may take care of day-to-day details themselves.

What distinguishes condos and co-ops is their different legal and organizational structures. The basic difference is in the way property is held. In a condominium, separate dwelling units are owned by individual investors, with the condo corporation controlling the walls, floors, ceilings, lobby, grounds, and other common areas. In a co-op, the co-op corporation owns the entire complex; an individual investor owns no property, only the right to an apartment or townhouse that stems from ownership of the corporation's stock.

As a result, the condominium owners are billed directly for real estate taxes on their units, while a co-op corporation's board receives a tax bill for the whole complex, prorates each stockholder's share, and adds the amount to monthly maintenance fees.

Owners of condominiums may feel they have more rights than co-op owners, since they are free to put their units on the market individually. A condo sale is transacted between a seller and buyer (and their real estate agents, if any) with simple notification to the condo board. By contrast, co-op boards usually have the power of approving or disapproving a buyer when a unit is sold.

The communal nature of condominiums and especially co-ops may upset some older people accustomed to exercising their property rights without scrutiny. On the other hand, board of director meetings and elections are open to all owners. Your father and mother may feel less constricted if they participate actively in community decisions and perhaps even run for a board position.

Conversion Plans

Regardless of the good points of group ownership, all but the most courageous elderly people may be fearful if the apartment house where they live is being converted to a condo or co-op. Older people on fixed incomes may be unwilling to draw on savings or incur debt to buy the apartment, even if they have been offered a discount as an "insider," or current tenant. If they feel pressure to move out, they may suspect that those handling the conversion

are unscrupulous developers greedy for the profits possible from more affluent buyers.

When considering whether to buy into a condo or co-op conversion
project, the following points are important:

Information   Be sure the developer provides tenants with all documents
having to do with the conversion, including the Enabling Declaration, the
bylaws, and the previous year's annual statement. Urge them to hire a lawyer
to review the documents if they're not familiar with condo or co-op law.

Communication   Before deciding whether or not to buy, your parents
should get a sense of how many other tenants plan to do so and how many
apartments are being sold to outside, non-resident investors. These owners
may not plan to live in the building and may not care about the stability or
quality of tenants.

Tenant Solidarity   In some buildings, tenants may organize an association
to fight the plan or ensure that condo conversions are handled equitably.
Talking to the tenant leaders may help your parents decide what to do.

Engineering Studies   To present a conversion proposal, developers must
pay for engineering reports on the condition of the roof, furnace, wiring,
plumbing, and other common facilities. If these studies reveal problems, the
landlord should set up a reserve fund to finance rehabilitation. Otherwise,
the new owners could be liable for large special assessments to pay for the
remodeling.

Help for the Elderly   Some cities, including New York City, have laws
guaranteeing elderly tenants the right to continue renting if their apartment
house converts to a condo or co-op. Urge your parents to find out what rights
they have as older people, and encourage them to act on those rights.

For Further Information

For further information about condominiums and cooperatives, contact local
housing advocacy organizations. Among the other resources are two free
pamphlets *Questions About Condominiums* and *Let's Consider Cooperatives* available from

Program Information Center
Department of Housing and Urban Development
451 Seventh St., S.W., Room 1104
Washington, D.C. 20410
(202) 755-6420

RETIREMENT COMMUNITIES

Once their working days are over, your parents may look forward to life in a retirement community—a housing development designed especially for older people. Thousands of these special developments now exist across the country, providing homes for about 3 million retired Americans.

Most of the best known are private developments of single-family houses, but many are garden apartment complexes, mobile home parks, or high-rise buildings. In addition, the nation's 3,400 federally subsidized senior citizen housing complexes count as retirement communities for low-income elderly.

About half of all retirement communities are located in the Sunbelt, but every state has some. Most of the larger complexes got their start on large tracts of land in semi-rural or suburban areas that could accommodate new, self-contained towns, but some can be found in the heart of big cities.

Before deciding to move into any retirement community, your parents should visit the area and talk at length with community leaders, management, and residents, as well as the sales force whose job it is to sell them on the place. Urge them to take their time in making a decision. In addition, the following factors should be considered:

The Adult Lifestyle   Most, if not all, retirement communities are based on the philosophy that older people enjoy living among others their own age. At Arizona's Sun City and Sun City West, advertising materials celebrate this age segregation as a "fun-filled lifestyle for active adults."

Just who qualifies as an adult varies community by community. Federally subsidized housing requires that residents be 62 or more. Most privately developed complexes try to attract early retirees. In Sun City, the average age of residents is 68, but entering households must include at least one person who is 50 or older. Other communities set the required age at 52 or 55.

Many retirement complexes do not allow children, except as visitors. In Sun City, no resident may be younger than 18. Nearby Youngtown, Arizona, permits children "only in unusual circumstances," said Civic Association president Jane Sutton, such as "where a grandparent *must* care for a grandchild."

What Does It Cost?   Except for low-income people who qualify for government-subsidized housing, many older Americans find retirement communities too expensive for their Social Security-based budgets. Some complexes have moderately priced rental units but, in many, houses and apartments must be purchased.

For this reason, the initial investment in a retirement community takes the worst bite, though many older people do have cash to pay for a retirement home after selling a mortgage-free family homestead. Purchase prices may range from around $35,000 to more than $200,000, plus attorney's fees, taxes, other closing costs, and moving expenses.

Many retirement communities charge additional monthly fees to cover maintenance of buildings and grounds, recreation, utilities for public areas, and other amenities. Personal utility bills and local real estate taxes may be added to the monthly fee or may be paid separately, depending on how the community is set up. If these expenses rise significantly over the years, they could strap residents on fixed monthly incomes.

In addition, your parents' expenses could be affected by the financial underpinnings of the community itself. A resident council or board of directors may levy taxes or occasional special fees. If the community is run by a development or management corporation, problems could arise in case the company has financial problems, fails to build all the promised amenities, or changes hands.

Services In most cases, the developer of a retirement community decides what public amenities are provided, usually on the basis of how much money is available for start-up and operation. All retirement complexes should have an activities or recreation program and a safe, crime-free environment. But some communities also provide other public facilities—a transportation network, restaurants or other dining areas, shops, banks, doctor's offices, and more intensive services.

Residents who are healthy and independent may be well satisfied with a relatively low level of services within the bounds of their retirement complex. But the process of aging involves changing needs. In advertising the "adult lifestyle," retirement communities often conveniently forget about the frail, older person who can no longer manage a daily round of golf and now needs home nursing or a sheltered living situation.

Importance of Driving In many retirement communities, independence requires driving. As long as they can drive, residents may enjoy a ten-mile trip to a nearby locality once or twice a week for shopping, cashing a check, or visiting the doctor.

The situation may change significantly, however, if gradually failing eyesight brings an end to driving. Older drivers sometimes lose their licenses after failing an eye test or having even a minor accident. Poor eyesight isn't the only stumbling block in a car-based community. Former city dwellers who never learned to drive may also feel helpless, and so may a new widow who depended on her husband and let her own driver's license expire.

Most communities provide transportation by van or minibus, but these transit systems sometimes don't prove satisfactory. Schedules rarely meet all

Residents of Sun City, Arizona, enjoying a game of golf on one of the community's 11 golf courses, eight of which are open to the public. (PHOTO COURTESY OF DEL E. WEBB COMMUNITIES INC.)

needs, leaving older women and men stranded in malls or supermarkets for hours rather than the minutes needed for an individual errand.

Your parents may think they know which kind of retirement complex suits them, but their needs may change in the future. To make a wise choice, it's important to have information about how the different kinds of communities operate.

RESORT RETIREMENT COMMUNITIES

Two gray-haired men carrying golf clubs emerge from neat, one-story bungalows next door to one another, cross a curving, tree-lined street, and walk across the grass to tee off.

Beside the golf course in the lobby of the Willow Hall clubhouse, a man and woman sit quietly in easy chairs watching morning television and glancing curiously at passers-by. Another woman, wearing a white shirt and slacks, sits at a card table, selling tickets to a choral concert.

Down the hall, a class of women bends and stretches to an aerobics tape of rock music, while next door, the Hadassah group looks at a fashion show by Israeli design students. Continuing door to door, a visitor sees an instructor dealing a hand in "Bridge for Beginners," five women and two men touching up oil paintings and, at the end of the corridor in a smoke-filled pool hall, a dozen men gossiping, chomping cigars, and lining up their cues with numbered balls.

Leisure Village West in Manchester, New Jersey, where all this activity takes place, is a resort retirement community, a housing complex designed for older people able to live independently. Sun City, Arizona, which had its 25th birthday in 1985, is the oldest, largest, and perhaps best known of this kind of retirement community, but many others exist in virtually every state.

Retirement resorts typically begin as real estate developments, where older people live in houses or apartments, usually of no more than two bedrooms, that they rent, buy outright, or purchase as condos or co-ops. As an attraction to buyers, the complexes generally offer a variety of recreational facilities and shops, as well as a crime-free atmosphere, where security may be provided through a uniformed guard force.

Each retirement resort is organized differently and has its own combination of housing, activities, services, and residents. In evaluating the benefits touted by the often aggressive sales people, prospective buyers get little outside help. Few states regulate these communities specifically, except under general anti-fraud rules that apply to all businesses.

For many people, the decision of whether to buy begins as a matter of real estate, climate, and activities—concerns of retired people who are fully independent and able to live on their own. If your parents consider the move as the last major one of their life, however, they will probably be interested in services to meet their needs as changes occur in their health and ability to care for themselves.

Among the issues you and your parents may want to consider are the following:

What Kind of Development Is It?

Sales Approach   Resort-style retirement communities often are marketed through sales offices that try to attract buyers by advertising in print and on the air. In some cases, gifts or free trips may be offered to lure prospective purchasers.

Many such real estate agencies operate ethically, but individual salespeople may use high-pressure tactics or make excessive claims for the development. In other cases, land may be offered for sale before roads or public utilities are installed. Other developments routinely sell unbuilt houses from blueprints.

Urge your parents to assure themselves that the house they buy will be ready for occupancy by the time they want to move. Visit the area and spend at least a few days. Check to see that the real estate agency is licensed and that the offering plans have won full state approval. Check into the financial standing of the developer and ask about prior projects. Hire a lawyer to review deeds and sales contracts. If you or your parents are suspicious of sales claims, check with the local Better Business Bureau.

Trial Periods Some retirement communities encourage prospective buyers to visit for a few days or weeks before buying. In other complexes, houses or apartments may be leased for an entire winter season, so that older people will be sure they like the community before investing in a home.

Suggest that your parents visit for a trial period to meet other residents, sample the amenities, and assess the community in terms of their own needs. If no such arrangement is available through the sales office, check local newspapers or outside real estate agents for individual rentals.

Future Development Plans Many older people are attracted by the small-town atmosphere of a retirement community, only to discover that hundreds more houses and apartments are to be built in a few years' time.

If the main attraction of a retirement complex is its intimate scale, you and your parents should ask specifically about future development. Examine housing plans, and check to see that enough community facilities are being added to accommodate new residents.

Sales vs. Resales Real estate offices run by developers are generally in the business of selling new houses and apartments only. In most cases, the new units are more expensive than homes built several years earlier that have come up for resale. Resales are usually handled by real estate agencies in the surrounding area, or homeowners may advertise them individually.

Before purchasing or renting a new home or apartment, you and your parents should explore the resale market.

What Kind of Retirement Home?

House Size Homes and apartments in retirement communities tend to be relatively small—with no more than one or two bedrooms. Only the most expensive models are likely to include a full dining room, family room, or enclosed garage.

Will your parents be satisfied with a small home and a carport? Will their furniture and hobby equipment fit? If not, are they prepared to sell what they use now and buy something more appropriate?

Type of Ownership Homes in retirement communities may be rented, owned privately, or owned through condo or co-op associations. In fact, the type of ownership may make little difference except in terms of an individual resident's responsibility for grounds maintenance. Generally, yardwork in condos and co-ops is handled at no additional cost by the housing associations, while private homeowners are responsible for their own work. Of course, they may choose to pay a management firm to handle lawn care.

Get your parents to query salespeople closely about any differences in ownership styles of various new and resale models. Find out what maintenance responsibilities belong to them.

Access for Disabled Most retirement homes are built on one floor, to spare older people the risks of climbing stairs. Unaccountably, however, many are built without special features for the disabled and handicapped. Ramps, emergency call buttons, and doors wide enough for wheelchairs may not be needed when a 55-year-old retiree moves in, but these aids may be crucial to staying in the home if a resident suffers a stroke or broken hip. Public buildings in a retirement community should also be wheelchair accessible, and parking spaces for the handicapped should be reserved.

Suggest that your parents check whether homes and public facilities are barrier free and have amenities for the disabled.

What Services Are Included?

Recreation Nearly all retirement communities offer an array of recreational opportunities as an incentive for buyers. The scope of the program depends on the size and style of the complex. As the nation's largest retirement community, Sun City provides its 46,000 residents with 11 golf courses, eight of them public, and seven recreation centers, including the $14-million R. H. Johnson complex. This center features, among other things, one outdoor and two indoor swimming pools, 24 bowling lanes, a 25-table billiard room, 15 tennis courts, a library, and a quarter-mile running track. There are 155 clubs, two newspapers, and 10 shopping centers.

Smaller communities tend to offer fewer amenities. At New Jersey's Leisure Village West, the 3,000 residents have one golf course, two outdoor pools, and a number of tennis courts. They can choose to participate in 46 clubs and can take frequent excursions to nearby shopping malls, the Atlantic City casinos, and New York City. Besides the warm but worn facilities of Willow Hall, there is a new pink and gray Art Deco recreation center called Club Encore.

More modest retirement complexes, often set up by churches, may not have extensive educational course offerings or elaborate sports clubs, but nearly all should have arts and crafts classes, recreational activities, and bus trips to local malls and nearby cultural events.

If salespeople emphasize recreational facilities, urge your parents to consider how active they expect to be. Perhaps they would be just as happy in a less expensive retirement community without a gym and golf course.

Transportation   Private cars are the primary form of transportation for residents of most retirement resorts, especially for shopping and other errands beyond walking distance from home. Some retirement complexes also permit the use of slower electric golf carts for errands near home. In Sun City, the golf carts are licensed, and one sits in nearly every driveway.

Most complexes also provide some system of community transportation, usually a van or minibus to carry residents to doctors and other activities within the community or beyond to nearby towns or malls. In some cases, the surrounding town may provide public bus service.

Among the many recreational opportunities available to Sun City residents is lawn bowling. (PHOTO COURTESY OF DEL E. WEBB COMMUNITIES INC.)

Encourage your parents to consider present and future transportation needs when selecting a community. Seek out non-driver residents for opinions on the minibus system. In a small retirement town with a range of shops, banks, and medical facilities, those unable to drive may be able to do all errands on foot.

Security   Most communities guarantee a crime-free environment for residents but opt for varied ways to accomplish the goal. Sun City West, for example, has a volunteer "posse" of 160 uniformed residents who serve as an auxiliary police squad for the Sheriff's Department of Maricopa County.

In other communities, private guard services are hired to supplement the local police forces from surrounding municipalities. These guards sometimes stand duty at the community's gates so that no one enters without permission of a resident. The cost of guard services is usually added to monthly maintenance fees.

When taking a sales tour, you and your parents should feel free to ask salespeople and residents about community safety and the security set-up. Do people really feel free to walk outside at night? How many criminal complaints are filed in a year? Ask how quickly municipal police respond and how far away their headquarters is.

Medical Facilities   Medical offices are located on the grounds of many communities, and physicians, podiatrists, dentists, and other health-care professionals may have regular office hours weekly or more frequently. Some communities also provide a nurse on duty to respond in case of emergencies. Only the largest complexes, like Sun City and nearby Youngtown, have their own hospitals. In most cases, doctors admit patients to local hospitals, using area ambulance squads if need be.

Encourage your parents to inquire about the community's health-care system. Sales offices may be able to provide a list of area doctors. If your mother or father is currently being treated for a medical problem, try to get a hometown doctor to make a referral or call a teaching hospital near the community for a recommendation.

What Does the Lifestyle Cost?

Housing Costs   The purchase price of a house or apartment depends on size, age, type of retirement community, and the style of ownership—private, condo, or co-op.

In deciding whether to buy, you and your parents should check to see whether their old home can be sold for enough money to cover the new one.

If a mortgage or co-op loan is needed, they should be sure their monthly income will be sufficient.

Monthly Fees   Condo and co-op associations nearly always charge monthly maintenance fees. In addition, most retirement communities assess all residents for the use of the clubhouse and other recreation facilities.

Salespeople should be asked to spell out all monthly charges and exactly what is covered. Is there an initiation fee for the use of clubhouses and other recreational facilities in addition to the monthly fee? Are renters charged a different fee from property owners?

Taxes   Property taxes are assessed by the municipality governing the retirement community. If your parents own their home or condo, they will get tax bills. If they have purchased a co-op unit, the tax will be included in monthly maintenance charges.

Ask salespeople what county, city, or town governs the community, and find out what the yearly tax bill will be. Are increases expected? Can your parents handle taxes in addition to other housing expenses on their retirement income?

Fixed Incomes   Elderly people who live on fixed retirement benefits from pensions and Social Security may be able to afford today's monthly charges but may find themselves strapped decades later when even modest inflation has reduced their spending power. Renters may be more adversely affected by inflation than purchasers.

You and your parents should ask whether any community agency provides financial counseling in case of an economic crisis. If your parents will be renting, urge them to find out whether the state or municipality provides any rent controls or other protection from spiraling rent increases or eviction? If the building changes hands, could rents or policies change?

Community Governance

Who's In Charge?   Only a few retirement communities are incorporated as cities or towns with their own elected officials, taxes, and public services. One is Youngtown, Arizona, incorporated in 1960, which elects its own town council and mayor. Most complexes, by contrast, are subdivisions of surrounding counties or cities.

Regardless of incorporation, nearly all retirement communities encourage resident participation, usually through elected councils. In some complexes, the councils are formal owners of all public spaces, hiring a management firm, setting standards for neighborhood appearance, and running the recreation facilities.

Your parents may feel that an association's insistence on conformity infringes on their property rights and self-determination. They should ask salespeople and long-time residents for a frank appraisal of how flexible the rules are, and they should ask themselves if they can live with these rules.

Participation by Developer   Developers continue to own land and community facilities in some retirement communities and, thus, play a continuing role in management and policy making. In some cases, developers willingly turn over clubhouse and office buildings to the governing council once the development phase is over.

Encourage your parents to ask about the development company's continuing role in community services and choosing occupants of homes, facilities and commercial space. Is resident input welcomed?

What about Changing Needs?

Scarcity of Services   In most retirement communities, residents must be able to live independently and must have the resources to shop and cook for themselves, visit the doctor, and get to religious services. Retirement resorts traditionally have assumed little or no responsibility for people in failing health. These people usually have to check into a nursing home or move to a community with long-term care.

You and your parents should ask salespeople what the community has to offer by way of doctors, hospitals, home health care, adult day care, home-delivered meals, and psychological counseling. Today, many communities or volunteer organizations within the communities provide directories of nearby services.

Nursing Homes   The first retirement communities generally excluded nursing homes or sheltered living arrangements. Today, age-related services like nursing homes and congregate care complexes are being built in clusters in and around retirement communities. Nearly a dozen nursing homes have been built in Sun City by private developers, and other facilities are in the planning stages.

Even if your parents are independent and in good health, encourage them to ask about long-term care facilities within the retirement complex or in the surrounding area.

CONTINUING CARE COMMUNITIES

Almost as soon as he retired, Dale Maust started to research retirement communities. The house in Brooklyn where he and his wife had lived for 30

In a continuing care community, elderly people can live securely in a non-institutionalized setting, knowing that if a health problem arises they will be cared for without burdening their children. Here, Dr. Margaret Hayes, a resident of Goodwin House, weaves in the arts and crafts center. (PHOTO COURTESY OF GOODWIN HOUSE, ALEXANDRIA, VA)

years had risen substantially in value, and Dale felt that he and Marlene could live comfortably outside the city with the proceeds of selling the house.

"Dad decided on a continuing care community in the Philadelphia area," said his son Dan, an oil salesman in Baltimore. "The entry fee was pretty steep—$85,000—but he and Mother got a nice two-bedroom apartment to live in, and they're entitled to live there all their days in whatever kind of accommodations they need, up to and including a nursing home."

The Mausts' community charges a fee for monthly upkeep that may rise depending on the kind of care residents need, "but it includes all their meals in the community dining room, which turns out to be a place to meet and socialize," said Dan.

What had worried Marlene most about old age was coping if Dale got sick, since she doesn't drive. "About a year after entering, my father had a gall bladder attack and needed surgery, and that experience proved the value of the place," Dan recalled. "The van picked Dad up with his suitcase for the trip to the hospital. Each day he was there, Mother took the van to visit him and to shop for groceries." If Dale had needed care after leaving the hospital, he could have stayed temporarily in the nursing home. As it was, he came home, and a visiting nurse from the community checked on him until he recovered fully.

"There were no worries," said Dan. "Older people want to feel secure, and I couldn't provide that to them by myself, though I did go up there when Dad was sick."

Over the past 20 years, a new kind of retirement community has been developed to provide continuing care for people as they age and need more intensive services. Like a retirement resort, a continuing care, or "life-care," community involves a substantial investment for housing, recreation, and other services. But instead of buying equity in a house or apartment, the older person purchases a contract guaranteeing lifetime use of a living unit, along with specified health-care coverage.

The first continuing care retirement communities (CCRCs) date back before the 1960s, and today an estimated 150,000 elderly Americans live in the 600 CCRCs across the country, according to a survey by the American Association of Homes for the Aging. By 1990, 2,000 of these communities are expected to be in operation.

Most of the existing complexes house about 250 to 300 residents, and many are built on wooded campuses with clustered cottages and a community center. To date, most have been built and operated by local, non-profit groups, many of them church-affiliated. But many future complexes will be built and run by large, for-profit corporations like the Marriott hotel chain and large nursing-home operators like Beverly Enterprises. Despite a lack of experience in health care, Marriott is banking on its hotel background to help it provide a range of appropriate services.

Common Characteristics

There's no one way of setting up or operating a continuing care community, but most share the following characteristics:

Minimum Health Standard and Age for Entry Most communities require newcomers to be at least 62 and able to live independently and get around on their own. Some accept one spouse directly for nursing-home care if the other is in good health.

Range of Living Units Cottages or apartments are generally reserved for those who can live independently, with a nursing home or infirmary in place for those needing long-term care. Some communities also provide an in-between level for people who need some help in dressing, bathing, or walking.

Life-Care Contract All residents sign contracts, which guarantee them housing in the most appropriate unit and various health-care services for at least one year and usually for life.

Prepayment Residents typically pay a sizable, one-time entry fee, designed to cover the contingencies of long-term care. Monthly fees are charged to cover ongoing costs of meals, medical expenses, or other services.

Requirement of Medicare Parts A and B Most communities require residents to be covered by both parts of the Medicare program as well as a Medicare-supplement policy.

With continuing care, elderly people are purchasing security in a non-institutionalized setting, contracting in advance for care so that if a health problem arises they will not have to worry about burdening their children. "The advantage of continuing care is that when something happens, they don't have to make a move," said Carroll A. Oliver, assistant administrator of Goodwin House West, a 350-resident continuing care complex in Alexandria, Virginia.

Continuing care communities do have disadvantages, however. First, there is the high price. Second, services sometimes do not live up to what was promised. In addition, some CCRCs have encountered serious financial problems, which have left elderly residents without resources. Continuing care communities have been subject to little federal regulation, and only 13 states have comprehensive guidelines.

Payment Methods

No two continuing care contracts are exactly the same, but most use a variation on one of the following payment methods:

Standard Entry-Fee Format The standard format is based on a lump-sum entrance, or founders', fee, covering future costs and a monthly charge to pay for current operating expenses. In 1985, CCRCs charged an entry fee averaging $50,000 or more and monthly fees averaging $700 or more, according to AARP housing consultant Leo Baldwin.

An example of a community with a standard entry fee is Twining Village, a privately-owned, for-profit community founded in 1978 in Holland, Pennsylvania. In 1986, Twining charged couples aged 76 and over $92,800 for a two-bedroom cottage, up from $83,000 in 1985. For a combined monthly fee of $2,130, the couple receives three meals a day (breakfast and lunch are optional), weekly housecleaning, and clean linens. Included in the fee are nursing and outpatient services provided in the Health Care Center, along with care from Twining doctors and physical therapists.

Some services—doctor's appointments, hospitalization, surgery, and physical therapy—are funded through Medicare, and residents must be covered by Medicare and a private Medicare supplemental policy. But as part of the same monthly fee, Twining provides prescription drugs and, if needed, an "assisted residential" level and nursing home care. The monthly fee rises about 7% every year and covers whatever kind of care a resident needs.

Pay-As-You-Go Format   With the standard format, healthy residents who require few medical and nursing services may be paying for more care than they need, in effect subsidizing their older and frailer counterparts. Besides being unfair, this tends to limit the appeal of such communities for younger people. As a result, pay-as-you-go contracts are becoming more popular. Communities that operate this way may or may not require a lump-sum entry payment, but they charge varying monthly fees that increase along with the level of care.

One community that uses this plan is Highland Farms in Black Mountain, North Carolina, where about 300 older people live in five different levels of accommodation, each with its own payment basis. Living arrangements include ranch-style "cluster homes" and apartments, both designed for those who can get their own meals and live independently; the hotel-style "lodge," which provides one meal a day and some personal care; Senior Care, a "rest home" with nursing aides on 24-hour duty; and the Health Care Center, a 60-bed skilled nursing and rehabilitation facility approved by Medicare.

Monthly fees vary by dwelling size, meal service, and care level. In 1986, cluster homes cost from $50,000 to $75,000, while entry fees for the apartment and lodge ranged from $8,000 to $52,000. There are no entry fees for Senior Care or the nursing home.

Turn-Over-Assets Format   At one time, what's now called continuing care was available only if residents turned over all their assets to the community in return for lifetime care. This format is rare today, and at least one state, Pennsylvania, prohibited the turn-over-assets formula in a 1975 nursing home regulation, since older people could be left without any resources if the community failed financially.

Pay-In-Full Contract   Another now-outmoded format, the pay-in-full contract, promised coverage of all future expenses in return for a large lump-sum payment and no monthly fee. This is now also considered unfair to potential residents.

Refundable Entry Fees   Traditionally, entry fees have been non-refundable, but in recent years communities have offered partial or even total refunds of the lump-sum fees, both to residents who wanted to leave and to the estates of residents who died. A Pennsylvania nursing home administrator familiar with the situation called it "only fair. It just wasn't right when someone would come in, put down all that money, and then die unexpectedly a week later."

Today, most communities will refund a predetermined proportion of an entry fee within the first few years of residency, but a substantial refund is unlikely if your parents stay more than a few years. At Twining Village, for example, full refunds are available for the first three-month "trial period" (minus an initial $2,500 deposit and the cost of medical care). Beginning with the fourth month, however, refunds of the entry fee are reduced by 2% for each month of occupancy, meaning that the entire amount would be drawn down by the end of the fourth year.

The $5-billion-a-year Marriott hotel chain plans to open three such communities in the next four years, with the first planned for retired Army officers at Fort Belvoir in northern Virginia. In its marketing brochures, Marriott assures buyers that the entry payment is 95% refundable at any time, without question a great selling point for the communities.

Critics have complained, however, that in most cases refundable fees are 50% or more above non-refundable entry charges. And the refundable fees came under Congressional fire in the Tax Reform Act of 1984, which defined them as no-interest loans that constitute tax-sheltered financing for Marriott and other for-profit developers. Language in the law exempted prior purchasers but said people entering continuing care communities in the future would have to pay federal income tax on the "inputed interest" earned by the refundable part of the fee.

The imputed interest issue is still up in the air. In the meantime, Congress exempted refundable entry fees of $90,000 or less from taxation.

Financial Risk

The history of the continuing care industry has been marked by financial problems that have led to more than one bankruptcy. In some cases, fraudulent operators were to blame. Most of the failures, however, were found to be the result of poor planning and management.

In addition, the increasing life expectancy of today's elderly is making continuing care more expensive. Young, healthy retirees of 62 and 65 may need only a few services, but, after 15 or 20 years of residency, their cumulative medical bills may be sizeable. What's more, long stays may mean a lower than expected turnover in housing units, and, in the words of one community's official, "there will be no continuing influx of capital if apartments don't turn over."

In response to this dilemma, some communities have begun to raise entry fees for younger retirees. Twining Village, for example, now charges residents who enter between 65 and 75 more than double the fees for those who sign contracts at 76 and older. To make the higher fees more palatable, these fees are totally refundable.

What to Look For

Good actuarial studies are needed on a continuing basis for each community, to track mortality rates, life expectancies, the likelihood of disabling illness, and the utilization rate of various facilities. Inaccurate forecasts can wreck community planning.

One of the worst problems is predicting the demand for the most expensive service, nursing care. In the first years of a community, few residents will enter the nursing home, and outside patients who pay privately are often admitted. In a decade or less, however, some residents will begin to need nursing care, meaning higher costs and fewer private pay beds.

Adequacy of Monthly Fees   Some continuing care communities have had problems because of guarantees that monthly rates would never change. Unfortunately, these fixed fees were doomed by periods of steep inflation and miscalculations in the rate structure. Residents on fixed incomes may be strapped by unexpected increases, but the entire community's financial health could be threatened if a community cannot raise monthly fees quickly enough.

Relationship of Sponsor   In some cases, residents bought into church-affiliated communities, believing that a particular denomination would bail the complex out in case of financial troubles. To the contrary, most continuing care communities are separate non-profit corporations with the religious group acting as a sponsor or supporter only.

Adequate Reserve Funds   To insure financial health, entry fees should be banked in reserve funds to protect against low turnover rates, costs, inflation, or failure by residents to meet payments. The potential for fraud is greatest through these funds, which may total millions of dollars in the early years of a community before nursing costs mount.

Regulation

Federal Regulation   Continuing care communities have been subject to virtually no federal regulation despite their complex network of financing. The main federal role is the certification of the communities' nursing homes for receiving Medicare and/or Medicaid funding.

In 1983, however, the Federal Trade Commission ordered full disclosure of financial risks and reserve-fund management by Christian Services Inc., which managed more than 50 continuing care facilities in 17 states. While the FTC order applies only to CSI, the commission regards it as "a statement of expectations" for all continuing care complexes.

State Regulation   Some states have adopted comprehensive regulations of the continuing care industry, while others have taken no action at all. One state—New York—has banned continuing care communities altogether under a 1969 regulation saying that no nursing home operator could accept prepayment for basic services more than three months in advance.

Thirteen states—Arizona, California, Colorado, Connecticut, Florida, Illinois, Indiana, Maryland, Michigan, Minnesota, Missouri, Oregon, and Pennsylvania—have adopted comprehensive laws regulating the continuing care industry. While the laws differ, most include definitions of continuing care and the proper relationships among operators, residents and the state. Most laws also set certain financial safeguards and require developers to be certified in order to sell contracts.

All the states require public disclosure of financial information, though the data asked for is not always the same. The laws also designate the agencies responsible for administering the program.

Considering Continuing Care

If your parents are considering a continuing care community, here are some specific suggestions about how to proceed:

Visiting and Research   Urge your parents to visit and do careful research on all continuing care communities in the area where they want to retire, talking to residents and staff.

Expect Full Disclosure   You should expect well-run communities to disclose all details about charges, management, use of entry fees, refund policies, tax liabilities, and the relationship of the sponsor in case of financial problems. Do not be shy about asking to see recent yearly statements and financial audits.

Suggest your parents question unrealistic promises about fixed monthly charges for life. If the community is not yet open, be sure entry fees are being put in escrow for future care and are not being used for current construction costs.

Clarify Costs   Can your parents afford continuing care? While communities can be expensive, the range of fees is "within the financial grasp of the majority of individuals over age 70," according to a study by the Wharton School at the University of Pennsylvania.

Most people fund their entry fee by selling their house, using the $125,000 one-time exemption from capital gains tax. In some communities, monthly fees cover most living expenses, including meals, utilities, and medical care, but in others residents may be responsible for all of these costs as well as for clothing, other personal needs, and outside doctors.

When to Enter   Most communities limit admission to people over 65, but the average entrance age is about 76, and the average continuing-care resident is between 80 and 82 years old. Continuing care is usually seen as a second stage of retirement housing, sometimes a move made after years in a resort retirement community, when additional services are needed.

But experts say more and more people are entering CCRCs in their 60s, especially widows and other newly single people worried about managing their own finances. Sharon Condon of Royal Oaks Continuing Care Community in Sun City, Arizona, says she has even helped manage residents' checking accounts, which makes them "feel comfortable here in a sheltered setting."

Trial Periods   Urge your parents to spend a trial period in the community before signing a contract. Most have guest rooms that can be rented temporarily.

CHECKLIST FOR CONTINUING CARE

HOUSING, LIFESTYLE

1. How many levels of care are there, and what kind of living units exist at each? What is included—draperies, carpets, full kitchen, furniture?
2. How many meals are included in the contract? Are there rebates for taking fewer?
3. Are pets allowed? Are overnight guests allowed? Is parking provided?
4. Does the nursing home offer private rooms? At extra cost? Can personal furniture be used there? What happens if one spouse needs nursing home care and the other doesn't?

5. What rights are guaranteed under the occupancy license? Can residents be removed from their homes against their will if they become severely confused? How long is the home maintained if the elderly person is hospitalized? Is there an extra cost?

COSTS

1. How much is the entry fee, and how will it be used? Request and study all financial statements and disclosure forms.
2. What are the monthly fees for different care levels? How are fees calculated? Do they go up each year?
3. What Medicare and other insurance coverage must residents buy?
4. What portion of the monthly fee is tax-deductible as a medical expense?
5. Is the entry fee fully or partly refundable?

HEALTH CARE

1. Is the health-care facility, or nursing home, in the same building? On the premises?
2. Is it approved for Medicare and/or Medicaid reimbursement? Is it state licensed?
3. How many beds are classified as skilled care? How many intermediate care? What is the ratio of nurses to patients? Are physical and speech therapy and other rehabilitative services available?
4. What health services are covered by the contract?

> routine checkups?   > psychological counseling?
> glasses?   > dental care?
> medical equipment?   > podiatry?
> care by specialists?   > prescription drugs?

5. Who chooses the community's doctors? Can residents use their own doctors?
6. What home health care is available? Delivered meals? Special diets?
7. Are nurses and/or doctors on call 24 hours a day?
8. What local hospital is used? What is the community's role in case of hospitalization? What is the family's role?
9. At the time of a couple's entrance, must both spouses be in good health?
10. What is the community's policy on accepting residents who are confused? People with Alzheimer's Disease and related disorders?

RECREATION, OTHER SERVICES

1. What recreational activities are provided? At extra cost?
2. Is there a hairdresser and/or barber shop?

3. Are religious services held? For what religions?

4. Is there a newsletter or newspaper?

5. Is there a resident council? What authority does it have? Do residents have a voice in menu planning?

OWNERSHIP AND GOVERNANCE

1. Who serves on the community 's board of directors? Who chooses them? What is the board's role? Do they have financial expertise?

2. What protection do residents have if the community's management changes?

3. Does the contract provide a grace period of several weeks or months for residents to change their minds?

CONGREGATE CARE FACILITIES

Large potted plants and colorful paintings adorn the lobby at King's Row, a congregate care residence in Middletown, New Jersey, which is home to 90 elderly men and women. Beneath the cathedral ceiling in the living room, about 20 people play bingo on a fall afternoon with an attractive, young social director calling out the numbers. A few other residents sit in easy chairs, reading or chatting.

"This is a second retirement for people in their 70s," said Elaine Serpico, King's Row administrator. "It's a new lifestyle. We have a dining room with three chefs, and there's maid and linen service, sort of like a luxury hotel. This is the right place when children worry that their parents aren't eating regular meals or can't keep their homes clean."

Not surprisingly, monthly rents are high—$1,365 for a studio and $1,580 for a one-bedroom in 1985—but the yearly lease includes three meals a day, transportation, 24-hour security, an emergency alert system, a recreational program, and a nurse's aide who helps with bathing and dressing, if needed.

The 128 apartments at the completely enclosed, two-story complex are grouped into four core areas on both levels of the north and south wings. Apartments are small, but residents may bring their own furniture, paintings, and plants. Carpeting and vertical blinds are provided. Heating and air conditioning are individually operated.

King's Row prides itself on its dining room menu, which might offer roast lamb, beef with mushroom gravy, roast chicken, and a cottage cheese fruit platter as dinner entrees on a single night along with a variety of potatoes, vegetables, desserts, and foods for those on special diets. Smiling uniformed waitresses take orders and deliver meals (and seconds). Residents can invite their children or other guests for meals by paying an additional fee.

Besides bingo and card games, the social schedule includes movies shown on a 40-inch television in the living room, crafts and exercise classes, trips, and special events, like the luau, where "we baked and served a suckling pig," Serpico recalled. "We asked everyone to dress in Hawaiian style, and a group of our ladies performed the hula."

Developed and operated by Basic American Medical, a nursing home chain based in Indianapolis, King's Row received part of its financing from a low-interest loan through the federal department of Housing and Urban Development. As a result, 26 of its apartments are federally subsidized for low-income elderly who pay 30% of their incomes in rent plus $200 a month for one meal a day, rather than the three offered in the private-pay plan. (They must provide the other meals themselves.)

The staff monitors the health of all residents, checking when they don't show up for meals or regular activities. Residents with pacemakers have their heart rates checked each week, so that irregularities can be treated. If hospitalization is needed, "we may call the ambulance before calling the children," said Serpico, "but we keep in close contact with families." If skilled nursing is required, however, residents have to move away and into a nursing home.

Congregate Care facilities enable people to live independently with the assurance that help is available. At King's Row, residents enjoy an active social life. (PHOTO COURTESY OF KING'S ROW, MIDDLETOWN, NJ. OPERATED BY BASIC AMERICAN RETIREMENT COMMUNITIES, INC.)

*   *   *

Congregate living facilities like King's Row are designed for older people too frail to live on their own but not so disabled that they need a nursing home. In a congregate facility, your parents can live in a private apartment as independently as possible but still get help with meals, shopping, and housekeeping.

Apartments are usually equipped with a small kitchen for making coffee or snacks. Meals are served in a group dining room. Housecleaning, fresh linens, recreation, and transportation are provided, along with help with dressing and bathing, if necessary.

Candidates for congregate living usually range in age from 75 to 90, though some people may enter in their early 60s depending on their health. Residents must be able to get to meals and activities on their own, but people with walkers or in wheelchairs usually would be accepted. In fact, confused persons and those with Alzheimer's Disease may also be admitted so long as they are cooperative and can meet schedules.

Congregate living can help keep frail elderly people out of nursing homes and, in fact, may help them leave institutions, according to a two-year study of 47 federally subsidized housing projects across the country, which was released in 1985. Some form of congregate housing is usually included as a middle stage in a continuing care community, but a number of congregate care facilities—including King's Row—operate on a free-standing basis.

Unlike continuing care communities, congregate living arrangements rarely include nursing units, in part because of the expense. "When life-care facilities are built with an attached nursing home, you have high operating expenses from day one," said Gregg Smith, who developed Gresham Manor, a congregate retirement residence near Portland, Oregon. "It's too costly."

The services offered in congregate housing are quite similar to those offered by two other housing options for seniors—the "residential living" units available in some nursing homes and the board-and-care homes, or personal-care boarding homes. These facilities typically charge far less than the luxury congregate residences, and they offer private or semi-private rooms rather than separate apartments.

For a monthly rental fee, personal-care homes usually offer room, board, utilities, housekeeping and laundry, and some contact with staff members. Some offer more extensive services like bathing, grooming, recreation, and transportation, but there is often an additional charge.

If your parents are considering a congregate care facility, the following points may be important to consider:

Visiting   Visit the facility with your parents and talk to both administrators and residents before signing a contract.

Meals   Arrange to eat lunch or dinner at the facility. Check to see whether residents enjoy their food. Is a staff member on hand to help with problems?

Security   Be sure that someone is on duty 24 hours a day in case of emergencies. Ask what happens if a resident gets sick at night. Find out whether residents are given keys to their apartment doors for internal security.

Medical Care   Does the facility have its own medical director, and are office hours ever held on the premises?

Independent Lifestyle   If both parents are interested, check to be sure that married couples can enter together. Check on whether there are any restrictions on leaving the facility for a late-night social event.

Trial Periods   Find out whether your mother or father can rent a room for a trial period to sample the food and lifestyle.

Contract Terms   Be sure the contract mentions all services to be provided and fees expected. Are residents charged for time spent away from the facility on vacation?

SUBSIDIZED HOUSING FOR SENIORS

Most cities and towns across the country have retirement housing for low-income elderly people, for whom the U.S. Department of Housing and Urban Development subsidizes the rent. The minimum entry age for most of these apartments is 62, but the handicapped or disabled may be able to qualify at a younger age. Older people occupy an estimated 1.5 million of these subsidized apartments.

You and your parents should be aware of the three main programs involved:

Section 8   The Section 8 program provides rent subsidies for low-income people in 2.2 million apartments developed either by private non-profit groups or by for-profit developers. Those who qualify pay only 30% of their income in rent with the government paying the rest. Elderly people occupy two out of five Section 8 units nationwide.

Housing Authorities   More than 514,000 apartments in the nation's public housing projects are occupied by older people, according to a 1985 HUD report. Some of these tenants live in specially designed senior citizen buildings, while others live in housing projects that serve all age groups. Rents in public housing are figured as a percentage of the fair market rent in the area.

Housing Vouchers   Housing vouchers issued by the U.S. Department of Housing and Urban Development go to 50,000 low-income people nationwide each year. The vouchers can be used to pay rent in the private sector. About half of the vouchers go to the elderly.

Who Qualifies?

Eligibility for most federal housing follows Section 8 guidelines. Under this program, low-income people qualify if their incomes are less than 50% of the median income in their area. Unfortunately, many elderly people with serious financial problems do not qualify for subsidized housing, since the guidelines are so low.

If your parents do qualify, other questions, including the following, may arise in their minds:

Space   Some older people may feel cramped in recently built public housing projects, if they have moved from a large, older home. Apartment styles range from one-room efficiencies to one- and two-bedroom units, all with small but complete kitchens. Two-bedroom models are usually reserved for married couples.

Services   Like many of the resort retirement communities, most senior citizen housing complexes offer residents few services, except for uniformed security guards on a 24-hour basis, if needed, to guarantee resident safety. In some complexes, however, units are equipped with bathroom grab bars and emergency call buttons. Wheelchair access and other features for the disabled depends on the individual building design.

Some complexes have large dining rooms, where a hot noonday meal may be provided by the Area Agency on Aging or an outside church or service group. In others, residents prepare and eat their own meals in their own apartments.

Congregate Housing   In 1980, HUD set up a demonstration program to investigate the value of congregate housing in keeping frail elderly people out of nursing homes. The program has since been phased out in a wave of government cost-cutting, but by 1985 it supported 69 projects nationwide.

Since HUD found the congregate program effective in preventing at least some nursing home placements, HUD has future plans to aid construction of a number of board-and-care homes nationwide to provide 24-hour care for the frail elderly.

Apartments Are Scarce

Even if your parents can qualify for a subsidized apartment, they may not be able to find one available. Most subsidized housing projects for senior citizens are filled, and there are long waiting lists for future vacancies.

To find out what subsidized senior citizen housing exists in your parents' hometown, call the local Housing Authority, the area HUD office, or the Area Agency on Aging for the names of specific complexes. Then call the building's management to ask about vacancies, the length of waiting lists, and eligibility.

CHAPTER IV

Community Services for the Elderly

Meal Programs and Senior Centers • Employment • Volunteer Programs • Education • Other General Resources

Many elderly people complain that they feel useless after they retire from the jobs and responsibilities that once gave meaning to their lives. Their fears may be exaggerated, however. So long as older people are in good health, there are many ways they can participate in community activities.

A number of state and federal programs funded under the 1965 Older Americans Act provide group activities and help for those over 60. Other older people may want to work part-time, either to supplement their retirement income or by volunteering for charitable organizations like the Red Cross, hospitals, churches, or nursing homes. In addition, there are government volunteer programs like the Peace Corps, VISTA, RSVP, and Foster Grandparents, which welcome the able elderly.

Education is another goal for seniors who want to learn more about a long-standing interest, delve into a new field, or get the education they didn't receive earlier.

MEAL PROGRAMS AND SENIOR CENTERS

One of the major services funded under the Older Americans Act is the nutrition program, offered either at central meal sites or delivered to homes. In 1984, nearly 212 million meals were provided to older people through the Older Americans Act.

Most meals are served through the nation's network of more than 14,000 senior centers, which are open to anyone 60 and older. During 1984, more than 3.2 million elderly received meals at the congregate sites, with the help of more than 25,000 paid staff and 230,000 volunteers, many of them elderly.

In addition, meals were delivered to more than 620,000 homebound elderly in 1984, with both paid staff and volunteers helping. Both the congregate meals and the Meals on Wheels are usually offered five days a week, though in a few areas, a sixth or seventh day is added. No charge is made for the meals, but participants are asked to make a contribution.

Senior centers also offer classes, films, cultural presentations, and group activities like dances, exercise programs, and trips. In addition, most centers

A growing number of colleges and universities encourage older people to take courses. These people are taking an Elderhostel class. Elderhostel is a network of more than 800 colleges and schools nationwide and abroad, offering hundreds of courses. (PHOTO COURTESY OF ELDERHOSTEL INC.)

provide help with filling out forms for Medicare, Medicaid, and taxes and refer people to legal assistance offices.

Congress specified that these programs be open to anyone 60 or older without a means test. Funds are limited, however, especially with recent budget-cutting initiatives, so some of these federal programs have been cut back.

Senior centers provide a focus for many, but your parents may balk at the thought of participating, because they associate federally funded programs with welfare. The choice is up to them, of course, but many centers do provide an excellent array of activities, and staff members are usually well-versed in the community's resources for the elderly.

EMPLOYMENT

Today, more than ever before in our nation's history, men and women are retiring from full-time jobs at 65 or younger. At the same time, the working public of all ages feels that part-time work after retirement would be desirable, according to a nationwide study done by the Louis Harris Organization in 1981. The poll found that three out of four workers age 55 and over felt they would benefit from a job that involves three or four days of work a week and a day or two at home.

Unfortunately, a job—even part-time—is not available for every retired person who wants one. Employers falsely associate youth with ability, even though discrimination against older people is illegal under the Age Discrimination Act of 1975. In fact, studies reported by the American Association of Retired People show that the elderly have better attendance records and fewer workplace injuries than their younger counterparts.

Federal Training Programs

Some federal programs are available to train and place older people for jobs. The Job Training Partnership Act of 1983 allocates at least 3% of its yearly funds for training and finding jobs for needy people age 55 and over in private, non-profit, and public organizations. Information about local programs is available from the local Area Agency on Aging.

In addition, job fairs for the elderly are sometimes sponsored by local area agencies. Each year, thousands of older men and women turn out for a job fair run by the New York City Department for the Aging, where private companies and public agencies come to talk about employment opportunities. No one is hired at the fair, but employers offer fact sheets and preliminary applications and make appointments for interviews.

Employment specialists often urge older people to downplay age when seeking a job, removing their date of birth from their resume. They say small and medium-sized companies that are growing are usually more open than large corporations to the assets of retired people.

"Older workers are very reliable," said Phyllis Worne, who runs a private employment agency for people over 50 in the Philadelphia suburb of Marlton, New Jersey. "They are always on time, always there. They were raised on a stronger work ethic than the one we have now."

VOLUNTEER PROGRAMS

Older people volunteer their time and abilities to a wide variety of organizations across the United States. In fact, people from 50 to 64 led the country in donating their time to charitable organizations and other service groups, according to a 1982 Gallup poll. Individuals 65 and over ranked second.

Most hospitals and nursing homes seek the assistance of volunteers for a variety of activities. So do the American Red Cross, public and private schools, day-care centers, political parties, and most religious groups. If your parents want to volunteer, urge them to call any non-profit organization they are interested in and offer their services.

Federal Volunteer Programs

More than 383,000 older people volunteered in 1984 for a variety of federally funded Older American Volunteer Programs that were operating under the umbrella organization of ACTION. Some of the volunteer programs are designed exclusively for older people, while in the Peace Corps and VISTA, individuals over 65 participate with people of other age groups.

These programs are as follows:

Foster Grandparent Program Low-income men and women 60 and over can earn a small hourly stipend for working up to 20 hours a week with disadvantaged, handicapped, or abused children. The services include counseling, help with reading and other basic skills, and providing emotional support. Foster Grandparent programs began in 1965, and more than 18,000 volunteers were working with 65,000 children in 240 projects in 1985. Besides the stipend, foster grandparents receive an annual physical, accident and liability insurance, transportation to and from their assignment, and a noon meal on the day they serve.

Senior Companion Program Begun in 1974 and modeled after Foster Grandparents, the nearly 100 Senior Companion programs currently offer part-time work to low-income people of 60 and over helping the frail elderly who are homebound or in a nursing home. Their work includes friendly visits, shopping, and emotional support. Senior companions are paid the same stipend and benefits as Foster Grandparents.

Retired Senior Volunteer Program (RSVP) ACTION's largest program, RSVP places retired people 60 and over with community-based organizations, like schools, courts, museums, libraries, hospices, and nursing homes. In 1984, 359,000 RSVP volunteers donated 64 million hours of service. They serve without pay but may be reimbursed for transportation and other out-of-pocket expenses. RSVP programs operate in more than one-fourth of the nation's counties, often through Area Agencies on Aging.

Service Corps of Retired Executives (SCORE) SCORE volunteers are retired business people who aid owners of small businesses or community groups in need of management expertise. Founded in 1965 and co-sponsored by the Small Business Administration, SCORE fielded about 9,000 volunteers in 1984 who counseled approximately 150,000 clients. Volunteers are reimbursed for out-of-pocket expenses.

Volunteers in Service to America (VISTA) VISTA workers help run programs to combat hunger, illiteracy, drug use, and child abuse in inner cities, rural areas, and on Indian reservations. Volunteers must be 18 years of age or older. There is no upper age limit. Recruited for one year from within the community where they will work, VISTA workers receive a basic subsistence allowance for food, housing, and incidentals.

Peace Corps Older Americans have served with younger people in the Peace Corps since it started in 1961. Volunteers are assigned to serve for two years in a developing country. They receive a monthly living allowance and a cumulative stipend at the end of their service.

For further information about any of the above volunteer programs, call or write

Older American Volunteer Programs
ACTION
806 Connecticut Ave., N.W., Room 1006
Washington, D.C. 20525
(202) 634-9355

EDUCATION

A growing number of colleges and universities encourage older people to take courses. Some seniors choose to enroll for credit, earning the college

Elderhostel courses aren't limited to the classroom. Here students enjoy a program at Johnson State College in Vermont.
(PHOTO COURTESY OF ELDERHOSTEL INC.)

degrees they never had time for as young people. Others want to learn just for the fun of it, so they audit courses, by making arrangements through the college's admission department.

Public colleges and universities often offer reduced or free tuition to the elderly. At the City University of New York, for example, students 65 and over pay nothing more than an initial $25 application fee to take any classes that have openings.

In addition, there are educational programs designed specifically for the elderly. One of the most outstanding is Elderhostel, a network of more than 850 colleges, universities, prep schools, and environmental education centers that offer week-long programs in literature, economics, and other fields.

Of the hundreds of courses Elderhostel offers each year, some are given overseas in countries ranging from Israel to Australia to Greenland. Courses operate year-round and are open to people 60 and over, though one member of a couple may be younger. More than 95,000 older people, some in their 80s and 90s, participated in the program in 1985.

Elderhostel programs in the U.S. and Canada cost about $200 a week. The fee covers tuition for three courses on a single theme, all extracurricular fees, and room and board—in adequate but not luxurious style—in the school's dormitory and cafeteria. Participants must provide their own transportation to get to North American schools. International courses, which may last up to three weeks, include airfare but may cost up to $1,900. Scholarships are available for those unable to pay.

For further information and a catalogue, call or write

Elderhostel
80 Boylston St., Suite 400
Boston, MA 02116
(617) 426-7788

OTHER GENERAL RESOURCES

The following membership organizations provide a wide array of general information and advice for the elderly and their children. Most concentrate on lobbying for legislation favorable to the elderly, but officers and staff members are usually excellent resources when you have a question about an especially difficult problem.

American Association of Retired Persons (AARP) The AARP, with its 20 million members age 50 and over, was founded in 1958 to improve the quality of life for older Americans. The group has more than 3,300 chapters from coast to coast with area offices in Boston; New York City; Atlanta; Dallas; Salt Lake City; Seattle; Kansas City, Missouri; Des Plaines, Illinois; Pinellas Park, Florida; and Washington, D.C.

The AARP acts as an advocate for the elderly on health care and second career opportunities and sponsors consumer programs, driver improvement classes, and counseling for widowed men and women. It also offers a mail-service pharmacy, sells insurance and travel services, and publishes a wide variety of informative books and pamphlets.

Membership dues of $5 a year include subscriptions to *AARP Newsletter* and *Modern Maturity*, a bimonthly magazine. For further information, contact

American Association of Retired Persons
1909 K St., N.W.
Washington, D.C. 20049
(202) 872-4700

National Council of Senior Citizens (NCSC) Another political advocate for older people, the National Council of Senior Citizens also provides insurance, health, and recreation benefits and some member's discounts on travel, lodging, and car rental. It operates a Nursing Home Information Service with a directory of long-term care options in and near Washington, D.C., and publishes several excellent pamphlets, including one on how to choose a nursing home.

With its 4.5 million members, the NCSC is about one-fourth the size of the AARP. It has about 400 local clubs. Dues are $8 a year per person, and there is no age requirement. For more information, contact

> National Council of Senior Citizens
> 925 15th St., N.W.
> Washington, D.C. 20005
> (202) 347-8800

Older Women's League (OWL)   The Older Women's League was founded in 1980 to serve the needs of women between the ages of 50 and 65, many of whom have become "displaced homemakers" in need of jobs and health-care services because of divorce or widowhood. Members also lobby for issues of special importance to this group, including pension reform, health insurance conversion rights for divorcees, and respite for care givers.

OWL's 14,000 members belong to 96 chapters in 36 states. Dues are $10 a year. For more information, contact

> Older Women's League
> 1325 G St., N.W., Lower Level B
> Washington, D.C. 20005
> (202) 783-6686

Gray Panthers   The Gray Panthers are a national intergenerational organization of 60,000 activists working for social change, particularly in the areas of health care, ageism, and peace. They lobby for reforms in Social Security, Medicare, housing, and nursing homes, testifying before Congress and mounting letter-writing and telephone campaigns. Their regional chapters are excellent sources of information about local legal and medical resources.

Dues are $12 a year. For information about the Gray Panther chapter nearest you or your parents contact

> Gray Panthers Project Fund
> 311 S. Juniper St., Suite 601
> Philadelphia, PA 19107
> (215) 545-6555

CHAPTER V

Paying for Health Care Through Medicare

Medicare Benefits • Cost Containment Policies • Making Medicare Work • Appealing a Medicare Decision

Younger retirees ordinarily are in good health but, unfortunately, your parents' strength and mobility can be expected to decline with age. Government studies confirm that older Americans are the heaviest users of health services. People 65 and over are hospitalized about twice as often as those under 65, their hospital stays are twice as long, and they use twice as many prescription drugs. The number and length of hospitalizations tend to increase with a person's age, peaking during the last year of life.

Medicare was enacted in 1965 specifically to help people over 65 carry this costly health-care burden, and it has gone far to improve the health of older Americans. Today, 93% have a regular source of medical care, and 83% visit a doctor at least once a year.

Yet, Medicare fails to meet many of the most pressing medical needs of America's elderly, largely because it is limited to paying bills for acute illnesses—heart attacks, pneumonia, and strokes, for example. At one time the most common health problems of the elderly, acute illnesses typically involve a relatively short crisis period, after which some patients may die, but others will recover with appropriate treatment.

With recent medical advances, however, today's elderly often survive acute illness, only to fall victim to chronic ailments like arthritis, Alzheimer's Disease, hypertension, or hearing loss. Chronic ailments are covered by Medicare only when they flare up into an acute phase. Medicare does not cover medications to control heart disease or high blood pressure, nor will it pay for hearing aids or for home attendants to help the family of an Alzheimer's victim.

In fact, Medicare regulations specifically rule out custodial care, which the 1985 Medicare handbook defines as "help in walking, getting in and out of bed, bathing, dressing, eating and taking medicine." The frail elderly often have chronic conditions that require exactly this kind of attention.

MEDICARE BENEFITS

Medicare is made up of two different programs—hospital insurance (Part A) and medical insurance (Part B). Each involves different kinds of treatment. To benefit under either part, your parents' care must be ordered by a doctor, and Medicare must agree that the treatments ordered are "reasonable and necessary."

Payments are made only when providers are certified by Medicare. This means the hospitals, skilled nursing facilities, and home health-care agencies must meet all state and local licensing requirements and certain other standards. Physicians and all health-care professionals must hold state licenses.

Who Qualifies?

Part A hospital insurance is provided without a premium to all Social Security beneficiaries 65 and over. Older people who don't qualify for Social Security may purchase Part A coverage, but the fee is steep ($226 a *month* in 1987).

No one gets Part B medical insurance free. For Part B coverage, older people must pay a premium ($17.90 a month in 1987), which is either automatically deducted from their Social Security checks or billed individually.

The government's explanation of Medicare is available in the pamphlet, *Your Medicare Handbook*, issued each year by the Health Care Financing Administration (HCFA) and available at all Social Security offices.

A Summary of Benefits

Here's a brief summary of what Medicare pays for and what your parents must contribute. The amounts are subject to change each year.

Part A—Hospital Care

Medicare provides hospital coverage in 90-day benefit periods, designed to cover spells of illness. Patients receive hospital care for as many spells of illness as they have, but they must remain out of a hospital or skilled nursing facility for at least 60 days before the next benefit period can begin. On a one-time-only basis, Medicare will also cover part of the cost of an additional 60 days of hospital care through non-renewable "lifetime reserve" days.

Period	Parent Pays	Medicare Pays
	(all 1987 figures)	
First 60 days	First $520	BALANCE
61st–90th day	$130 a day	BALANCE
91st–150th day (one-time-only, "lifetime reserve" days)	$260 a day	BALANCE
Beyond 150th day	ALL COSTS	NOTHING

Hospital care is covered when justified by a diagnosis and when a doctor orders it at a Medicare-participating hospital. Medicare pays for care in a psychiatric hospital for no more than 190 days in each individual's lifetime. In some cases, it can pay for foreign hospitals and Christian Science sanatoriums.

Part A provides a semi-private room (two to four beds), meals, intensive care beds, the operating room, general nursing care, lab tests, x-rays, in-hospital drugs, blood transfusions (except for replacement fees for the first three pints), medical supplies, and use of equipment. Inpatient rehab services by physical, speech, and occupational therapists are also covered.

Post-Hospital Skilled Nursing Facility (SNF)

Period	Parent Pays	Medicare Pays
First 20 Days	NOTHING	ALL COSTS
21st–100th day	$65 a day (1987)	BALANCE
Beyond 100th day	ALL COSTS	NOTHING

Part A coverage for skilled nursing facilities applies to a semi-private room (two to four beds) in a specially staffed and equipped nursing home, certified by Medicare. SNF care is covered only once each benefit period, after a hospital stay of at least three days and within 30 days of a hospital discharge. Medicare pays only if the doctor and the Medicare intermediary agree that your parent needs skilled nursing or rehab treatment on a *daily* basis, and if a bed can be found in a Medicare-certified home.

Medicare's skilled nursing home program is described more fully in the Nursing Home section of the book. See pages 205–230.

Hospice Care

Period	Parent Pays	Medicare Pays
Three periods totaling 210 days— 2 of 90 days each and 1 of 30 days	NOTHING except 5% of drugs and in-patient respite care	MOST COSTS

Medicare covers certified hospice programs when the doctor determines an illness as terminal. If services are still needed at the end of the coverage period, the hospice must continue care if the patient desires.

Part A applies to charges for hospice-affiliated nurses, doctors, home health aides, homemakers, physical and speech therapists, short-term inpatient care including respite care, counseling for patients and family, and drugs, including outpatient drugs for pain relief.

The hospice program is spelled out in detail in the Hospice section of the book. See pages 242–251.

Part B—Medical Insurance

Medicare's Part B, an optional program much like a privately purchased medical policy, can help pay for doctor bills both in and out of the hospital, outpatient hospital treatments, medical equipment, home health care, and a variety of other services.

In addition to the Part B premium ($17.90 a month in 1987), participants must pay for the first $75 in approved charges each calendar year.

In general, Medicare Part B pays up to 80% of "reasonable," or Medicare-assigned, charges. Your parents are responsible for the other 20% of the reasonable charge, as well as any additional amount on the bill.

Part B Benefits

Coverage	Parent Pays	Medicare Pays
Doctor bills, surgery charges, anaesthesia, needed diagnostic tests, ambulance if medically necessary, lab tests, emergency room, outpatient hospital treatment	First $75 a year; then 20% of Medicare's "reasonable charge," plus amount over the "reasonable charge"	80% of Medicare's "reasonable charge"

Medicare will pay bills for services provided by Medicare-certified hospitals, labs, and home health-care agencies. Outpatient treatment of mental illness is covered up to $250 a year.

If the doctor recommends surgery, Medicare advises a second opinion and will help pay for the consultation under Part B. Your parents may want to ask their own doctor for a referral to another physician to do the second opinion. Or they may want to call Medicare's Second Opinion Referral Center for the names and phone numbers of doctors in their area who provide second opinions. The center can be reached at

(800) 638-6833 (toll-free, except in Maryland)
(800) 492-6603 (toll-free in Maryland)

Durable Medical Equipment

Coverage	Parent Pays	Medicare Pays
Wheelchairs, other equipment ordered by doctor	20% of "reasonable charge"	80% of "reasonable charge"

Durable medical equipment (sometimes abbreviated as DME) includes wheelchairs, home dialysis systems for kidney patients, oxygen equipment, and other medically necessary gear. The Medicare carrier (the insurance company administering Part B in your area) decides how much Medicare will pay for each item that year.

Equipment may be either rented or purchased, depending on which costs less for the period your parents are likely to need it. The Medicare carrier may notify them of the preferred option.

Blood

Coverage	Parent Pays	Medicare Pays
Outpatient transfusions (Part B)	First 3 pints (or arranges replacement) each year, then 20% of "reasonable charge"	80% of "reasonable charge"

Coverage includes blood, blood components, and the cost of blood processing and administration. Sometimes there is no charge for the first three pints of blood, but when there is, patients must either pay replacement fees, replace the blood themselves before or after they use it, or arrange for someone else to donate it.

Home Health Care (Parts A and B)

Home Visits	Parent Pays	Medicare Pays
Unlimited, if condition warrants and Medicare approves	NOTHING (First $75 a year, if beneficiary has Part B only.)	ALL COSTS

Part A and Part B both pay for part-time skilled care in the home when it is provided by a Medicare-approved agency, a doctor sets up a home-health plan, and your parent is homebound. Medicare applies to periodic visits by nurses, home health aides, medical social workers, and physical, speech, and occupational therapists.

Medicare's Home Health Care benefit is described in detail in the section on Home Care. See page 186.

What Medicare Does Not Cover

What Medicare does not cover is just as important as what it pays for. Health-care services *not* provided include the following:

> Routine physical exams
> Routine eye exams
> Eyeglasses
> Most immunizations
> Dental care except for face and jaw surgery
> Acupuncture
> Full-time home nursing care
> Home-delivered meals
> Homemaker services, except for hospice patients
> Private hospital rooms
> Orthopedic shoes, except if part of a leg brace and on an orthopedist's bill
> Long-term nursing home care

> Routine lab tests
> Routine hearing exams
> Hearing aids
> Routine foot care
> Chiropracters except for certain spine manipulation
> Self-administered injections, like insulin
> Services provided by family members
> All drugs bought by patients and used at home, except for hospice patients
> Treatments covered by other insurance plans

Proposal to Cover Prolonged Hospital Stays

In February 1987, President Reagan proposed a plan to improve Medicare coverage for people stricken with illnesses so serious that they require long periods of hospitalization. If enacted by Congress, the new coverage would add $4.92 a month to the Part B premium ($17.90 a month in 1987).

Under the proposal, Medicare would provide 100% coverage of an unlimited number of days of acute-level hospital care after the deductible is paid (rather than the 60 full-paid days now offered). In addition, the plan would introduce a $2,000 annual limit on a beneficiary's out-of-pocket expenses for deductibles and copayments for Medicare-covered services. The limit would not apply to expenditures for services Medicare doesn't cover.

This "catastrophic illness" proposal was applauded by advocates for the elderly, and Congressional sources gave it a good chance of passage while noting that the plan does not change Medicare's focus on acute rather than custodial care. Long-term nursing home stays and home health care for the chronically ill would still not be covered.

COST CONTAINMENT POLICIES

Medicare has proved terribly costly. Nationally, in 1984, it paid out $53 billion in benefits, making it the federal government's second most expensive domestic program, surpassed only by Social Security. And like Social Security, the future of Medicare's Hospital Insurance Trust Fund has begun to look cloudy. (The Part B program has remained solvent because of the premiums paid by beneficiaries.)

In 1984, government financial analysts predicted that the trust fund, which pays for Part A hospitalization benefits, would be bankrupt within a decade. To prevent that disaster, payroll deductions for the fund were increased, and HCFA (nicknamed hick'-fah) adopted several controversial cost-containment strategies that have made newspaper headlines across the country—prospective payment and diagnostic-related groups.

Prospective Payment

Under prospective payment, Medicare reimburses hospitals a pre-set fee for each patient treated, with the amount of the fee depending on the diagnosis. This fee is supposed to cover the hospital's average costs for treating a particular illness plus provide the hospital with an appropriate profit.

If a patient can be treated for less than the pre-set amount allotted for the condition, the hospital keeps the balance. If the patient needs more time to recover, however, the hospital must absorb the loss.

Under the old payment system, hospitals billed Medicare for the number of days patients stayed, however many that might be, and for the services patients received. For the most part, doctors decided on length of stay according to the patient's need and their own professional standards, and hospitals set their own rates, based on local costs. HCFA argues that the old system erred in giving hospitals a financial incentive to hold onto patients longer than necessary.

Diagnosis-Related Groups

In organizing the prospective payment system, Medicare needed a way to figure the pre-set fees for each diagnosis. As a result, health planners established a framework of diagnosis-related groups, or DRGs, to which all illnesses and health problems are assigned.

On the list of 470 DRGs are such medical conditions as "angina pectoris" and "depressive neuroses" and such surgical procedures as "skin grafts" and "upper limb and toe amputations for circulatory system disorders." Every patient's ailment must be assigned to one of the categories.

Each DRG carries a specific reimbursement factor, or weight, which represents the average resources required to care for cases in that DRG. The weights reflect not just the number of days of a hospital stay but a total "menu of care," including lab tests, x-rays, drugs, and other services. But the number of inpatient days is one of the most important factors. And, in fact, HCFA includes an average length of stay for each ailment on the DRG list "for comparative purposes."

For example, DRG No. 1, "a craniotomy not caused by trauma," carries a weight of 3.5632 and an average length of stay of 21.4 days. DRG No. 89, "simple pneumonia and pleurisy" in those 70 and older, has a weight of 1.1768 and an average stay of 9.6 days.

To figure the hospital's reimbursement, the weight for the patient's assigned DRG is multiplied by the individual hospital's payment rate (based on local costs and wages). The resulting dollar figure is the amount Medicare pays the hospital.

The DRG list is a matter of public record and is printed in the *Federal Register* (on Sept. 3, 1985, among other dates). It is available in many public libraries, but for most people, interpreting it would be a bureaucrat's nightmare.

Prospective Payment and DRGs: Do They Work?

In the very first year of its existence, the DRG system had already helped cut hospital occupancy rates and Medicare costs. A 1985 HCFA study showed that the average length of a Medicare patient's hospital stay dropped from 9.5 days in fiscal 1983 (before DRGs began) to 7.5 days in fiscal 1984. By

1986, analysts predicted that the Hospital Insurance Trust Fund would survive at least through the turn of the century.

HCFA claims the shorter hospital stays have improved health care overall—by cutting down the exposure to hospital-based infections and by returning older people to their homes as soon as possible. They describe complaints about the system as start-up wrinkles that will soon be ironed out.

Advocates for the elderly disagree. They say the DRG system is unfair because it relies on a single diagnosis, rather than recognizing the multiple health problems common to the elderly, and because it makes no allowances for a patient's age or for severity of illness. What's more, they say, not enough Medicare-certified skilled nursing facilities (SNFs) are available to provide the degree of post-hospital care needed with the speedy discharges.

Arguing that hospitals are releasing elderly people "quicker and sicker into a no-care zone," Republican Senator John Heinz of Pennyslvania, the ranking member of the Senate Special Committee on Aging, has proposed changes to the DRG system that are still under consideration in Congress.

Some of these changes will undoubtedly be adopted as the cost-containment plan is refined. In the meantime, however, you and your parents will have to learn to work within the already labyrinthian Medicare maze to guarantee the best quality of care possible.

Assignment

So far, the DRG system applies only to hospital care under Medicare's Part A, though in the future, it may be extended to skilled nursing facilities and home health care. For Part B medical insurance, however, Medicare uses a different cost-cutting arrangement, based on "reasonable charges" and fee "assignment."

As you already know, the Part B program helps pay bills for physicians, other professionals, and the providers of supplies and equipment. Under the terms of Part B, the beneficiary pays 20% of the "reasonable charge," while Medicare pays the other 80%.

Medicare sets this "reasonable," or approved, charge individually for each medical condition treated by each of the nation's 300,000 doctors and by the nurses, therapists, and suppliers who provide home health and outpatient care. The fees are based on local costs and the individual professional's fee history.

The set-up sounds as reasonable as the charges are intended to be. Even so, beneficiaries may end up paying high bills out of their own pockets. Why? Because your parents' physician (or equipment supplier) may charge *more* than Medicare thinks is "reasonable." If so, your mother and father must pick up the balance—paying both 20% of the "reasonable charge" and the difference between that fee and the doctor's actual bill.

Depending on the physician, the extra can be substantial. In fact, the *average* physician's bill submitted to Medicare in 1983 was 23% higher than what the program would pay, according to a study by the House Select Committee on Aging. As a result, rather than paying 80% of the cost of physicians' services, Medicare ended up paying less than one-half the cost for the average patient that year.

Is there a way out? Yes, but it may require your parents to change doctors—or work out a different payment basis with their own physician. About one-third of the nation's doctors guarantee that they will always accept assignment of the "reasonable" fee. Others accept assignment case by case.

Besides charging less, doctors (and suppliers) who accept assignment also relieve patients of paperwork by handling their Part B claims for Medicare's 80% share of the reasonable charges. Patients of other doctors must pay bills in full and then file a claim for Medicare reimbursement, a time-consuming procedure.

One state, Massachusetts, requires all doctors who care for Medicare patients to accept assignment. Under a law that went into effect in 1986, physicians in the state may not bill older patients for Medicare-covered charges. Advocacy groups are pushing for similar legislation in other states.

PARL Lists

It's hard for many people—especially those of our parents' generation—to question doctors about their fees. But until the end of 1984, that was the only way to find out which ones accepted assignment. That year, responding to pressure by the Gray Panthers, Congress ordered the Department of Health and Human Services to print Physician-Supplier Assignment Rate Lists (PARLs) of all doctors and health-care suppliers that accept assignment routinely.

The PARLs are prepared yearly for each area of the country and are available for inspection at all Social Security offices and at some senior centers. A total of about 120,000 doctors, now known as "participating physicians," are listed nationwide, along with the pharmacies, equipment suppliers, and other medical groups that accept assignment.

Remember, though, that even with the lists, it may be difficult for your parents to find a doctor in their area who accepts assignment since the number of participating physicians varies state by state. About 40% of Maine's doctors, a total of 1,055, accept assignment, for example, while in South Dakota, only 63 physicians participate, just 5.6% of the total.

The choice of a doctor involves far more than fees, of course, and your parents may want to keep going to their own doctor, even if he or she is not one of Medicare's "participating physicians." Doctors can choose to accept assignment on a one-time-only basis, however, so if medical expenses are skyrocketing, your physician may be willing to accept Medicare's assigned charge in a specific situation.

MAKING MEDICARE WORK

Enrolling   To get coverage, your parents should file an application for a Medicare card and an individual claim number at least three months before turning 65. They can apply in person at the local Social Security office, bringing a birth certificate or another proof of age, or, if a visit is impossible, the contact can be made by phone. If the office is at a distance, the call can be collect.

Several months after filing, your mother or father should receive the Medicare card in the mail. The card should be presented on admission to the hospital or when receiving medical treatment.

It's not wise to delay enrolling, even if your parents do not retire at 65. True, Medicare Part A would cover any hospital stay retroactively for up to 12 months from the date your parents finally do apply. But medical insurance under Part B is not retroactive, and that means Medicare medical insurance will pay no doctors bills until the Part B application has been processed and the policy is in place.

In addition, a penalty may be imposed on those who don't sign up for Part B at the same time as Part A. The penalty adds 10% to the late enrollee's monthly premium for Part B, and the delayed enrollment can take place only between January and March of each year with a waiting period until July 1.

Filing Claims   Your parents will *not* be billed for Medicare-covered care received from hospitals, skilled nursing homes, home health agencies, or hospices, and they need not file claims for such services. Instead, Part A claims are filed by the facilities, and Medicare pays those institutions directly.

Even so, your mother or father may be mailed notices of these hospital charges on forms entitled Medicare Hospital, Extended Care, and Home Health Benefits Record. The forms will show what services and amounts Medicare paid for. In case of a lengthy hospitalization with numerous services, large amounts may appear, and the notices may arrive frequently in the mail.

The Benefits Record forms are clearly marked: "This is not a bill," but you may worry when they arrive, especially if you are thrust suddenly into the role of handling your parents' affairs. The anxiety may be especially keen if a parent has died.

Be patient. As a huge bureaucracy, Medicare often takes a long time to settle these hospital claims, so the forms may continue coming for months. If questions arise about the notices, call the agency doing the billing or the local Social Security office.

Part B Claims   Individual beneficiaries must file their own claims for services covered under Medicare Part B, except when they use a doctor or other provider who accepts assignment. Claims are sent to the insurance companies selected by Medicare as carriers for a state or part of a state. These companies are listed state by state at the back of *Your Medicare Handbook.*

Step 1: Paying the $75 Yearly Deductible and Proving It

Before your father or mother can get any Part B reimbursement, the individual involved must show Medicare that he or she paid $75 in applicable medical bills during the calendar year. (If qualifying medical bills total less than $75, Medicare pays nothing at all that year.) The $75 deductible may be paid to more than one doctor or supplier. Eligibility is determined separately for a husband and wife.

After the $75 deductible is paid, each parent must send proof to the state Medicare carrier, along with a completed and signed copy of Medicare's Form 1490S, A Patient's Request for Medicare Payment, available at Social Security offices, hospitals, and many doctor's offices. This form is used also to file claims for doctor bills and other covered medical charges.

Instructions for filling out the forms are listed on the back, but complicated claims sometimes present problems. Help is usually available from the Area Agency on Aging, senior citizen centers, or by contacting Social Security or the doctor's office.

Itemized Bills   Itemized bills must be attached whether the intention is to show that the first $75 was paid or to make a subsequent Part B claim. The bills must include the following information:

> — the service given (or product supplied)
> — the nature of the illness or diagnosis
> — when and where the service was provided
> — the charge for each service
> — the doctor or supplier's name
> — your parent's name
> — your parent's nine-digit hospital insurance claim number
>   (from his or her Medicare card)

In the case of medical equipment, the doctor's prescription for the equipment must be included along with the supplier's itemized bill.

Form Approved
OMB No. 0938-0008

PATIENT'S REQUEST FOR MEDICARE PAYMENT

IMPORTANT— SEE OTHER SIDE FOR INSTRUCTIONS

| PLEASE TYPE OR PRINT INFORMATION | MEDICAL INSURANCE BENEFITS SOCIAL SECURITY ACT |

NOTICE: Anyone who misrepresents or falsifies essential information requested by this form may upon conviction be subject to fine and imprisonment under Federal Law. No Part B Medicare benefits may be paid unless this form is received as required by existing law and regulations (20 CFR 422.510).

1 Name of Beneficiary From Health Insurance Card
(First) (Middle) (Last)

SEND COMPLETED FORM TO:

2 Claim Number From Health Insurance Card
☐ Male ☐ Female

3 Patient's Mailing Address (City, State, Zip Code)
Check here if this is a new address →☐
(Street or P.O. Box—Include Apartment number)
(City) (State) (Zip)

3b Telephone Number (Include Area Code)

4 Describe The Illness or Injury for Which Patient Received Treatment

4b Was illness or injury connected with employment?
☐ Yes ☐ No

If any medical expenses will be or could be paid by your private insurance organization, State Agency, (Medicaid), or the VA complete block 5 below.

5 Name and Address of other insurance, State Agency (Medicaid), or VA office
Policy or Medical Assistance Number

NOTE: If you DO NOT want payment information on this claim released put an (x) here →☐

I authorize Any Holder of Medical or Other Information About Me to Release to the Social Security Administration and Health Care Financing Administration or Its Intermediaries or Carriers any Information Needed for This or a Related Medicare Claim. I Permit a copy of this Authorization to be Used in Place of the Original, and Request Payment of Medical Insurance Benefits to Me.

6 Signature of Patient (If patient is unable to sign, see Block 6 on other side.)
6b Date Signed

IMPORTANT!
ATTACH ITEMIZED BILLS FROM YOUR DOCTOR(S)
OR SUPPLIER(S) TO THE BACK OF THIS FORM.

HCFA-1490S (6-80) Department of Health and Human Services—Health Care Financing Administration

HOW TO FILL OUT THIS MEDICARE FORM

Medicare will pay you directly when you complete this form and attach an itemized bill from your doctor or supplier. Your bill does not have to be paid before you submit this claim for payment, but you MUST attach an itemized bill in order for Medicare to process this claim.

FOLLOW THESE INSTRUCTIONS CAREFULLY:

A. Completion of this form.

Block 1.   Print your name **exactly** as it is shown on your Medicare Card.

Block 2.   Print your Health Insurance Claim Number including the letter at the end **exactly** as it is shown on your Medicare card.

Blocks 3 through 5.   Complete the information in these Blocks as Requested.

Block 6.   Be sure to sign your name. If you cannot write your name, make an (X) mark. Then have a witness sign his or her name and address in Block 6 too.

If you are completing this form for another Medicare patient you should write (By) and sign your name and address in Block 6.   You also should show your relationship to the patient and briefly explain why the patient cannot sign.

Block 6b. Print the date you completed this form.

B.   Each itemized bill MUST show all of the following information:

- Date of each service.

- Place of each service   —Doctor's Office   —Independent Laboratory
   —Outpatient Hospital   —Nursing Home
   —Patient's Home   —Inpatient Hospital

- Description of each surgical or medical service or supply furnished.

- Charge for EACH service.

- Doctor's or supplier's name and address. Many times a bill will show the name of Several doctors or suppliers. IT IS VERY IMPORTANT THE ONE WHO TREATED YOU BE IDENTIFIED. Simply circle his/her name on the bill.

- It is helpful if the diagnosis is also shown. If not, be sure you have completed block 4 of this form.

- Mark out any services for which you have already filed a Medicare claim.

- If the patient is deceased please contact your Social Security office for instructions on how to file a claim.

COLLECTION AND USE OF MEDICARE INFORMATION

We are authorized by the Health Care Financing Administration to ask you for information needed in the administration of the Medicare program. Authority to collect information is in section 205(a), 1872 and 1875 of the Social Security Act, as amended.

The information we obtain to complete your Medicare claim is used to identify you and to determine your eligibility. It is also used to decide if the services and supplies you received are covered by Medicare and to insure that proper payment is made.

The information may also be given to other providers of services, carriers, intermediaries, medical review boards, and other organizations as necessary to administer the Medicare program. For example, it may be necessary to disclose information about the Medicare benefits you have used to a hospital or doctor.

With one exception, which is discussed below, there are no penalties under social security law for refusing to supply information. However, failure to furnish information regarding the medical services rendered or the amount charged would prevent payment of the claim. Failure to furnish any other information, such as name or claim number, would delay payment of the claim.

It is mandatory that you tell us if you are being treated for a work related injury so we can determine whether worker's compensation will pay for the treatment. Section 1877 (a) (3) of the Social Security Act provides Criminal penalties for withholding this information.

✿ U.S. G.P.O.   1985-578-594

Step 2: Filing for Reimbursement

Once the deductible is paid each year, regular Part B claims can be filed for each qualifying medical bill.

When doctors or suppliers accept assignment "participating" doctors or agencies submit the claim directly to Medicare and then bill the patient only for the remaining 20% of the approved charge (after the year's $75 deductible is paid). The bill may exceed the 20% charge only if it includes regular medical check-ups or other services Medicare doesn't cover.

Most doctors or suppliers who "accept assignment" tell their patients. If your parents don't know, they should ask the doctor or the office secretary.

When doctors or suppliers do not accept assignment your parents will be billed for the entire service. They must pay the bill and then complete, sign, and send in the Medicare 1490S Patient's Request form, along with itemized bills, to recover 80% of the "reasonable charge." Claims should be mailed to the insurance carrier for their state or region.

Part B claims should be filed as soon as possible for prompt reimbursement and clarity in record keeping, but older people have a maximum of 15 months to do so. The legal time limits for each year's claims are listed in *Your Medicare Handbook.*

To facilitate the claims process, accurate records should be kept of all health-care expenses. All bills should be kept in the same place, along with records of all Medicare claims filed, the claim date, the date and charges for each service, and the person or agency who provided the service.

Step 3: Getting an Explanation of Benefits and the Check

After filing a claim, your parents should receive the Medicare reimbursement in about a month. Along with the check, they should receive a notice called Explanation of Medicare Benefits. This form shows what bills are covered and how much Medicare is paying for each.

Nothing about the Medicare program causes more confusion—especially for the children of the aging—than looking over the "Explanation" forms, which may arrive in a veritable blizzard after an episode of illness.

Coverage Decisions

As your parents begin to use Medicare, they may find that many needed—and seemingly legitimate—services are not covered. An individual stroke patient in a Skilled Nursing Facility may be refused benefits under Part A, for example, or Part B may reimburse a different amount for the same service on two separate occasions.

Payment decisions often seem to contradict the coverage promised in *Your Medicare Handbook,* and part of the reason can be found in a three-inch-thick book of interpretations by HCFA. These frequently updated interpretations are used by Part B insurance-company carriers, hospitals, and nursing homes.

The interpretations detail rules of thumb used to determine how much care will be provided under different Medicare programs. Advocates for the elderly criticize the interpretations as defining Medicare benefits far more stingily than Congress intended.

One such rule of thumb, for example, says stroke victims may receive physical therapy until they can walk 50 feet on their own. When that goal is reached, Medicare-aided therapy may be cut off on the premise that it is no longer needed. But physical therapists say this 50-foot accomplishment should not be used as a universal yardstick, since some patients stop walking altogether if therapy ends.

APPEALING A MEDICARE DECISION

Medicare's coverage decisions may be appealed, but there are several different ways to appeal, depending on what kind of complaint is involved. If you and your parents take issue with the amount of reimbursement, first carefully examine the Medicare Hospital, Extended Care, and Home Health Benefits Record form for a Part A claim or the Explanation of Medicare Benefits form for a Part B claim, and make a note of exactly what you object to.

To Appeal Part A Reimbursements

To challenge a Part A decision, call the local Social Security office, explain your complaint and request a review. If you aren't satisfied with the results and the disputed amount is $100 or more, your parents can ask for a formal hearing. If your parents disagree with the results of the hearing and the case involved $1,000 or more, the matter can be appealed to federal court.

To Appeal Part B Reimbursements

To start a Part B review, your parents should send a request in writing to the Medicare carrier, or insurance company, asking for a reconsideration of its decision. The insurer *must* review its original determination, no matter the amount of money in question.

If your parents still disagree on a bill or bills involving $100 or more, they can request that the insurance company's hearing officer conduct a more formal review called a "fair hearing," a legal proceeding that does not require the elderly person to have legal representation. The decision of the carrier's hearing officer is final. Congress is currently considering a change in the law, however, that would permit the case to go on to federal court, if the claim is over $500.

Protesting Premature Discharges

A different system exists for patients who feel they are being discharged from the hospital too soon. This process involves Peer Review Organizations (PROs), agencies under contract to Medicare in each state to monitor hospital services under the prospective payment program. The nation's PROs are listed state by state at the end of this book.

PROs are made up of physicians, nurses, and other health-care professionals charged with monitoring Medicare cases before, during, and after hospital admissions to be sure that treatment has been appropriate and sufficient but not excessive. All Medicare cases are subject to PRO review, but, because of time constraints, only about one in 20 can be reviewed except by special request.

As the prospective payment system geared up, most PROs concentrated their efforts on cost containment and making sure Medicare paid only for "medically necessary" hospital care. Very little information was available about the patient's right to protest early discharges or alleged shortcomings in care.

Appeals of a hospital discharge are particularly difficult, especially because elderly patients may be too sick and families too emotionally upset to mount a legal battle. But challenging a discharge date *is* possible with a knowledge of how the appeals process works.

Written Notice

Under HCFA's rules, hospitals must give *written* notice at least 48 hours in advance if a patient's Medicare coverage is ending. The "notice of noncoverage" should explain that a patient may stay in the hospital longer but, if so, families will have to begin paying the bill. The notice also must contain a brief explanation of why hospital care is no longer needed and a full description of the appeals process.

Here's a copy of HCFA's notice to patients on the subject:

AN IMPORTANT MESSAGE FROM MEDICARE

YOUR RIGHTS WHILE A MEDICARE HOSPITAL PATIENT
- You have a right to receive all of the hospital care that is necessary for the proper diagnosis and treatment of your illness or injury. *Your discharge date should be determined solely by your medical needs,* not by "DRGs" or by Medicare payments.

- You have the right to be fully informed about decisions affecting your Medicare coverage or payment for your hospital stay.

- You have a right to appeal any *written* notices you receive from the hospital or Medicare stating that Medicare will no longer pay for your care.

TALK TO YOUR DOCTOR
You and your doctor know more about your condition and your health care needs than anyone else. If you have questions about your medical treatment, your need for continued hospital care, or your discharge date, consult your doctor. These decisions should be made between you and your doctor. If you have questions or concerns about hospital services, you should talk to the hospital's patient representative or discharge planner. *Don't hesitate to ask questions*—you and your family should ask about your care, your stay in the hospital, and your planned discharge.

PEER REVIEW ORGANIZATIONS
Peer Review Organizations (PROs) are groups of doctors who are paid by the Federal Government to review medical necessity, appropriateness and quality of hospital treatment furnished to Medicare patients. Peer Review Organizations will respond to your request for review and appeal of written notices stating that Medicare will no longer pay for your hospital stay.

IF YOU THINK YOU ARE BEING ASKED TO LEAVE THE HOSPITAL TOO SOON
- Ask a hospital representative for a *written* notice of explanation *immediately,* if you have not already received one. The hospital's written notice is necessary if you decide to appeal to the PRO. The written notice must describe how you appeal.

- *If you decide to appeal, do so immediately—either call or write the PRO.* If you lose the appeal, you may be billed for all costs of stay beginning with the 3rd day after you receive the written notice. The appeals process can take up to three *working* days from the time your appeal request is received. Thus, if you appeal and lose, you may have to pay for at least one day of hospital cost.

- REMEMBER: WITHOUT A WRITTEN NOTICE, YOU HAVE NO RIGHT TO APPEAL.

The Peer Review Organization for this area is:

TELEPHONE: (   )

Regardless of the rules, a doctor or hospital administrator may mention casually that your mother or father's Medicare coverage will end soon or on a particular date. If you or your parents disagree with this, you should immediately discuss the foreseeable problems with the doctor. The decision may be final but, if so, you have the right to ask for a written notice. When you get it, make note of the date and time. Your parent is guaranteed an additional 48 hours of hospital care *after* the notice arrives.

You and your family may decide to pay the hospital charges yourselves, rather than see your mother or father come home without adequate care. If so, discuss this idea with the doctor. But if you decide to challenge the hospital's decision, contact the PRO as soon as possible, and request an expedited review.

Prompt action is essential, since PRO appeals must be made under a Catch-22 deadline situation: your mother or father has only 48 hours of Medicare coverage left, but the PRO has three working days to respond. If the PRO approves a continued stay, the charges will be covered by Medicare, retroactively if need be. But if the PRO upholds the hospital's discharge decision, you or your parent will have to pay for services beyond the 48 hours.

You can also request a reconsideration of the case. If the PRO reconsideration also results in a ruling against your family, and the Medicare reimbursement in question is $200 or more, you can take the further step of requesting a hearing by an Administrative Law Judge of the Social Security Administration.

Beyond the hearing level, you can take the case to court if the resulting medical bill is $1,000 or more. Legal assistance is recommended at this point.

You may find it frightening to take a stand against the hospital—and possibly the family doctor—when your parent's medical condition is perilous, especially knowing the staggering hospital bills the family will have to pay if the appeal fails. Nevertheless, a premature discharge may be costly in itself. Besides the possible strain on your ill parent, the home care required may be too much for the well one—or for you—and may lead to a quick rehospitalization anyway.

Medicare Fraud

A toll-free hotline has been installed by the U.S. Inspector General for use if you or your parents believe that a doctor, hospital, or other health-care provider is billing Medicare for unnecessary services or for services never rendered.

To report any evidence of Medicare fraud or abuse, dial the hotline at

(800) 368-5779 (toll-free, except in Maryland)
(800) 638-3986 (toll-free in Maryland)

Address complaints in writing to

Office of the Inspector General, Hot Line
Department of Health and Human Services
P.O. Box 17303
Baltimore, MD 21203-7303

Medicare Advocacy Programs

Fewer than 3% of Medicare patients exercise their rights to appeal payment decisions, even though half of the appeals result in higher reimbursements. Connecticut and a number of other states now fund Medicare advocacy projects to help elderly people file appeals.

These states' main motive in setting up the projects is to contain costs in their Medicaid programs, which are largely state financed, since older people denied Medicare reimbursement, especially for skilled nursing beds, often end up on Medicaid after depleting their resources to pay bills privately.

The first highly successful advocacy project was Legal Assistance to Medicare Patients (LAMP) in Connecticut. LAMP helps appeal reimbursement decisions and will represent patients in danger of premature hospital discharge through the PRO appeals process. If your parents live in Connecticut, contact LAMP for help with a Medicare appeal

Legal Assistance to Medicare Patients
872 Main St.
P.O. Box 258
Willimantic, CT 06226
(203) 423-2556

More and more Medicare advocacy projects are being set up across the country. Check with the local Area Agency on Aging to see if one has been started in your parents' area. Existing programs, which may cover only part of a state, include the following:

Massachusetts Medicare Advocacy Project
(covers eastern Massachusetts)
Greater Boston Elderly Legal Services
102 Norway St.
Boston, MA 02115
(617) 536-0400
(800) 323-3205 (toll-free in Massachusetts)

Minnesota Medicare Advocacy Project
906 Minnesota Bldg.
St. Paul, MN 55101
(612) 228-0771

California Health Insurance Counseling and Advocacy Program (HICAP)
c/o California Department of Aging
1020 19th St.
Sacramento, CA 95814
(916) 323-7315

For Further Information

For further information about a patients' right to appeal a Medicare decision, consult the government's publication *Your Medicare Handbook* and the booklet *Knowing Your Rights*, a publication by the American Association of Retired People.

CHAPTER VI

Augmenting Medicare Coverage

Group Insurance Plans • Medigap Policies • Private Long-Term Care
Insurance • Health Maintenance Organizations • Medicaid

Medicare paid only 56% of medical care for the elderly in 1980, according to a report by HCFA. There are five basic ways to supplement Medicare coverage—outside of your parents (or you) paying the bills yourself.

GROUP INSURANCE PLANS

About 8 out of 10 large corporations continue group health-insurance plans for retirees, according to the House Select Committee on Aging. In some cases, employers pay all or part of the cost for this coverage, which usually meshes with Medicare. But even if your parents have to pay the entire premium themselves, insurance experts say such a package will probably be worth it.

Group insurance usually pays a better ratio of benifits for each premium dollar than Medicare-supplement policies, both because the risk is spread among people of all ages and because the insurance firm can reduce marketing costs by working directly with employers and unions.

By federal law, people who continue working after 65 (for companies with 20 or more employees) must now be offered the same health insurance coverage as young workers. If an elderly person chooses the group plan but finds that only part of a medical bill is covered, Medicare acts as a secondary payer to pay an additional amount (up to its reasonable charge but no more) for that service. A group policy is often far more generous than Medicare, however.

To check on what the group insurance policy covers, your father and mother should consult their employer's benefits department or the insurance company—preferably well before retiring.

MEDIGAP POLICIES

More than two in three people over 65 pay premiums for private health insurance to supplement Medicare. This is in addition to the premiums paid for Medicare's Part B medical coverage.

Your parents probably have purchased this so-called Medigap insurance from Blue Cross–Blue Shield, the AARP, or some other major insurance company or retirement association. In 1985, yearly premiums ranged between $150 and $1,000 a year depending on coverage and the age and sex of the insured.

Medigap insurance coverage can be valuable in filling the holes in Medicare, but some of it is unnecessary. The House Select Committee on Aging estimates that up to $1 out of every $4 spent each year on Medigap insurance goes for unneeded policies.

Part of the reason is that the policies follow Medicare guidelines in covering acute, not chronic, conditions. Virtually none of them pay for long-term care in nursing homes. And with today's DRG system, your parents will probably be discharged from the hospital before the 61st day, when they would have to begin making Medicare copayments.

What's worse, the history of Medigap policies has been marred by the fraudulent practices of some unscrupulous salespeople who have misrepresented the scope of the insurance and used high-pressure sales tactics to frighten the elderly into buying. As a result, older Americans pay out hundreds of dollars a year on policies that either overlap or cover situations unlikely to materialize.

An article on Medigap insurance in the July 29, 1985, issue of *The Wall Street Journal* illustrated some of the pitfalls:

> Sadie Molyneaux's family was shocked to find that the elderly woman held almost 50 health insurance policies when she died in 1981 at age 83. The Newhope, Minnesota, widow had spent about $14,000 on insurance premiums over five years. "She didn't want to be a burden on anybody," says Karol Dooley, a relative. None of the policies covered the $1,000-a-month nursing home care Mrs. Molyneaux required for almost a year before her death . . .

To help correct this situation, Congress passed legislation known as the Baucus Amendment (for its sponsor, Democratic Senator Max Baucus of Montana) that requires clear disclosure of benefits offered by Medigap policies. In addition, insurance companies must specify the extent of supplementation to Medicare's Part A and Part B.

Advocates for the aging advise against buying more Medigap policies than are needed. In some cases, especially for low-income elderly, none may be needed: if your parents qualify, Medicaid may pick up Medicare deductibles and copayments.

When your parents are considering a Medigap policy, it's important to know what is available.

Types of Policies

In general, there are three types of policies: hospital indemnity, specific disease coverage, and comprehensive Medicare supplements. Indemnity policies pay specified lump-sum amounts for each day of a hospital stay; specific disease insurance covers cancer or some other serious disease; Medicare supplements fill Medicare gaps.

Indemnity policies are quite straightforward because of their fixed-dollar benefits. They don't depend on Medicare's rules or "reasonable" charges, so they can help with medical bills not covered by Medicare—private hospital rooms, for example, or the part of a doctor's bill over and above Medicare's reasonable charge. Rates tend to be predictable because they aren't linked to increases in Medicare copayments.

On the other hand, indemnity benefits are linked to length of stay in a hospital or skilled nursing home, and the policy may have a benefit-waiting (or elimination) period, meaning that benefits will begin only after a certain number of days. This could mean your father or mother won't get much from the policy, particularly if he or she is hospitalized for only a day or two but still runs up a high bill with an expensive specialist.

Specific Disease Coverage   Cancer insurance is the best known variety of this narrow kind of coverage, but policies are also available covering other major diseases. Cancer is one of the leading causes of death of older people, but only a small fraction of the elderly will suffer from it.

Medicare already covers many of the hospitalization costs for possibly terminal diseases. Consumer advocates say that the sale of cancer and other such disease policies often depends on scare tactics.

Medicare Supplement Policies Policies marketed under this name must meet the minimum standards set by the Baucus amendment. All such policies must now include:

1. Coverage of Part A hospital copayments for the 61st through 90th days ($130 a day in 1987) and for the 60 lifetime reserve days ($260 a day in 1987).
2. Coverage of 90% of Part A expenses for an additional 365 days of hospitalization. (None of those days would be covered by Medicare).
3. Coverage of 20% of Part B bills up to at least $5,000 a year, though the company could require a yearly deductible of up to $200 a calendar year. (These policies probably will not pay charges for doctors or medical suppliers over and above Medicare's "reasonable rate.")
4. Automatic increases in Medicare copayment amounts, if and when announced by Medicare.
5. A "free look" for 30 days at policies purchased through the mail and 10 days for policies bought from an agent. During that period, the policy may be returned and the premium must be refunded if the buyer isn't satisfied.

Check a policy's small type to be sure the above benefits are provided in any Medicare supplement policy. In addition, check on what the policy offers in each of the following areas:

First-Dollar Coverage This refers to policies that pay the deductible for Part A ($520 in 1987), the deductible for Part B ($75), or both. First-dollar coverage may be important for a person hospitalized for several different benefit periods each year, but premiums for it can be very expensive.

An alternative might be for older people to set up their own health-emergency fund to pay the deductibles, preferably in a joint account so someone else can get money out if need be. "It's better to determine how much you can afford to pay in deductibles without insurance, and then weigh the trade-offs," said John Mullen, national financial planning director for KMG Main Hurdman, a major accounting firm.

The emergency fund could also be used to cover the part of doctors' bills over and above "reasonable charges" and other expenses not covered by either Medicare or Medigap policies.

Underwritten Policies Some of the most comprehensive of the Medicare supplements may be "underwritten" and, as such, may require passing a physical exam or filling out a health questionnaire. Many older people have health conditions that can disqualify them. Since underwritten policies are so comprehensive, they also can be rather costly.

Pre-Existing Conditions Pre-existing health problems, whether or not your parents were treated for them or knew about them, may postpone coverage for a certain amount of time. Under the Baucus law, however, this waiting period may not exceed six months, and all limits on coverage for pre-existing conditions must be clearly stated in the policy.

Exclusions Some insurance policies exclude specified pre-existing conditions entirely. This is permitted under the Baucus language, but in most cases your parents would have to agree and sign an exclusion, which often appears on an attached page, or "rider." They should carefully examine everything they sign.

Waiting Periods Some Medigap policies have waiting periods—of three months to one year—before coverage begins for conditions like cancer or heart trouble. If one of these ailments turns up before the waiting period is over, that condition may not be covered at all. For other policies, there are waiting periods before any coverage takes effect.

Elimination Periods With some policies, benefits begin on the first day of hospitalization, while others start coverage only after a certain number of days. The longer this "elimination period," or benefit waiting period, the lower the premium will be. Long waiting periods may mean your parents never collect at all, now that hospital stays have been cut substantially through the use of DRGs.

Renewability Some insurance is "guaranteed renewable for life." If a policy is marked "optionally renewable," the company can end coverage at the end of the policy year or when the premium falls due (though not if the beneficiary has already begun a covered hospitalization). When the words "conditionally renewable" appear, the company can't drop you as an individual policyholder but may not renew that kind of insurance in a given area or state.

Medigap Hotlines

State insurance departments can be helpful in guiding older people through the Medigap maze. In addition, telephone hotlines exist in some parts of the country to counsel older people on health insurance to supplement Medicare. Such counseling programs do not recommend particular policies or companies, but they have extensive files of health insurance policies sold in a particular state and can give information about specifics of coverage.

Among these hotlines are

Medigap Hotline
  Wisconsin State Board of Aging and Long-Term Care
  125 South Webster, GEF 3, Room 17
  Madison, WI 53702
  (800) 242-1060 (toll-free, in Wisconsin)
  (608) 266-8944
  (Operates 5 days a week, 8 a.m.-4:30 p.m., with information about Medigap insurance and HMOs)
  Contact: Geralyn Hawkins
California Health Insurance Counseling and Advocacy Program (HICAP)
  California Department of Aging
  1020 19th St.
  Sacramento, CA 95814
  (916) 323-7315
National Consumers League
  600 Maryland Ave., S.W.
  Washington, D.C. 20024
  (202) 554-1600

Tips for Buying Medicare Supplement Insurance

1. Be sure the insurance company is licensed to sell insurance in your parents' state. If so, the state's Insurance Department will be able to help in case of a dispute.
2. Purchasing duplicative policies is usually not a good idea, so check on the specifics of coverage. In some cases, it could be useful to have two similar indemnity policies paying double benefits, but if both policies have long elimination periods, the additional coverage might never pay off.
3. When changing policies, be sure your parents do not cancel the old one until the new coverage takes effect. Waiting periods often delay the effective date by 30 to 45 days.
4. Read the policy carefully. Check for limitations or exclusions.
5. Pay premiums promptly, so the policy hasn't lapsed by the time it's needed.
6. Realize that total coverage is virtually impossible. Insurance experts say you may have too much insurance if its cost is out of line with the risk incurred.
7. Keep insurance policies in a safe, accessible place, probably in the same place your personal medical records are. Make a note of the date claims are filed, of all medical bills, and of decisions by Medicare and the insurance company as to what services are ordered.
8. Claims should be filed promptly, both to Medicare and your private in-

surance company. Insurance companies may ask that you send Medicare's Explanation of Benefits form with all claims payments. If so, don't send the originals. Make copies instead.

9. Before any policy is purchased, it should be examined carefully and compared with other similar policies to be sure its benefits serve your parents' needs. If you or your parents need help in doing this, a financial planner who specializes in insurance coverage can aid with the evaluation.

For Further Information

In addition, several booklets are available:

Medicare & Health Insurance for Older People, by the AARP

Guide to Health Insurance for People with Medicare, from the Social Security Administration.

How to Use Private Health Insurance With Medicare, by the Health Insurance Association of America.

Shoppers' Guide to Supplemental Medicare Insurance, by the National Senior Citizens Law Center, 1636 West 8 St., Los Angeles, CA 90017 (213) 388-1381

PRIVATE LONG-TERM CARE INSURANCE

About 1.5 million Americans occupy nursing home beds in the U.S., but only about 120,000 older Americans now have private long-term care insurance. With nursing home bills averaging $20,000 a year, long-term care insurance could be crucial in getting older people the care they need while allowing them to remain financially solvent.

Economists think the market for long-term care insurance could reach $3 billion or more within a few years, yet only a few insurance companies currently offer long-term care policies for at-home care or for nursing homes.

The leader in the field is the United Equitable Insurance Company, a small firm in Lincolnwood, Illinois, which had written more than 75,000 policies by the end of 1985. The company's nursing care policy covers two to four years of nursing home care, depending on whether the services needed are skilled or custodial. Other companies offering the insurance are Aetna, Amex Life Assurance (Fireman's Fund), and CNA Insurance of Chicago.

Most current policies pay daily fixed-dollar, or indemnity, benefits of between $30 and $100 for each day of nursing home or at-home care for a period of up to four years. Some policies also pay benefits for home care.

Insurance companies say they have been slow to introduce long-term care policies, because consumers aren't aware that they will need nursing home coverage—and don't like to think about it. An additional reason is expense.

Policies now offered carry premiums ranging upward from a few hundred dollars to more than $5,000 a year depending on age and sex.

Working-age people would be assigned lower premiums, but before retirement, few anticipate the eventual need for a nursing home. Afterwards when the need for nursing home coverage becomes more immediate, incomes fall and premiums rise.

The American Association of Retired Persons and other retirement organizations have been encouraging the development of long-term care insurance, and about two dozen insurance companies have begun demonstration projects. Some limit benefits to skilled nursing homes, while others include custodial and home care.

An example of one such experiment is the comprehensive, long-term care policy underwritten by the Prudential Insurance Co. of America that the AARP began test marketing in six states in late 1985. The offer was made to a random sample of 215,000 AARP members between 50 and 79.

The initial package carried premiums of $1,794 a year for people aged 50 to 59. The older the entry age, the higher the premiums with the maximum listed as $11,394 a year for the more vulnerable 75 to 79 age group.

Benefits of the AARP-Prudential plan included $40 a day for nursing homes, for a lifetime maximum of three years. Home care was covered at $25 a day for home visits by a nurse and/or physical and speech therapist and $20 a day per visit by a home health aide, for a lifetime maximum of 365 visits.

Buying a Long-Term Care Policy

Some older people may not be able to afford long-term care insurance, but if your parents are interested, you may want to help them financially as a way of protecting family resources. Economists predict that prices may fall in the future as more companies offer coverage.

Before buying, you and your parents should carefully examine the policy, watching out for exclusions that may be written in fine print. Among the important points are the following:

1. Read the policy carefully, making sure of benefits, level of care, and any time limit on coverage.
2. Be sure the policy covers custodial or convalescent care, not just skilled services.
3. Be sure the policy does not exclude Alzheimer's Disease or other mental illnesses. (A large percentage of nursing home patients are placed because of Alzheimer's Disease.)
4. Watch for exclusions of pre-existing conditions.

For Further Information

To find out which long-term care policies are offered in your parents' state, contact the state insurance department. Additional information is available from the American Health Care Association, the trade group for the commercial health insurance industry.

American Health Care Association
1200 15th St., N.W.
Washington, D.C. 20005
(202) 833-2050

HEALTH MAINTENANCE ORGANIZATIONS

Under recent legislation, Medicare now helps pay for the health care of people over 65 through Health Maintenance Organizations. Today, more than 19 million Americans get their health care through the nation's 480 HMOs.

Opting for HMO care means your parents may have to give up some of the benefits of regular Medicare, such as getting reimbursement for going to their own doctor. On the other hand, an HMO can provide more comprehensive medical services at a lower total cost.

What Is an HMO?

An HMO provides nearly all the health care a person needs through specially designated doctors, hospitals, skilled nursing facilities, labs, and other agencies. No matter how much service is needed, all costs are covered by a preset monthly premium paid in advance. Members must use HMO doctors, however, to receive coverage.

An HMO member typically chooses a primary-care physician from the HMO's team of participating doctors. The primary-care physician coordinates all medical care, either treating the patient directly or making referrals to a specialist affiliated with the HMO.

Quality of Care

In 1973, Congress passed a law setting special standards for federal qualifications of HMOs. About three-fourths of all HMOs now are federally qualified, meaning they must provide the following:

— physicians, including consultant and referrals
— hospital care, inpatient and outpatient

— medically necessary emergency service
— short-term mental health treatment and crisis intervention
— treatment for drug and alcohol abuse
— diagnostic lab and therapeutic x-rays
— home health services
— preventive services, including routine check-ups for children and adults, family planning, immunizations
— grievance procedure to settle complaints about service

Some good HMOs are not federally qualified, however, because they have sought qualification under strict state guidelines instead, especially in Minnesota which has its own regulation process.

Another indication of quality is membership in the Group Health Association of America, a trade group representing HMOs. To belong to the GHAA, an HMO must meet certain financial standards and have a quality assurance program and a grievance procedure in place.

Are HMOs Cheaper?

Because they provide both health care and health insurance, an HMO's financial set-up is quite different from both the conventional U.S. medical system and from Medicare, which operate on a fee-for-service basis. Monthly fees paid by the individual HMO member may exceed those charged for traditional health insurance, but more services are covered. In addition, there are few out-of-pocket costs, though some HMOs charge small fees of $1 to $3 for doctor appointments to discourage frivolous use.

HMO members pay no more to visit the doctor once a month than once a year. For this reason, HMOs must be cost-effective, and they have proven to be so. A Rand Corporation study of a Seattle HMO found that members received about the same amount of service as did a group covered under a conventional health insurance plan but at about 25% less cost.

The main reason for the savings appears to be that HMO members are hospitalized less often than workers with other kinds of health plans.

The emphasis on preventive care tends to prevent excessive hospitalization, since routine check-ups are covered and diseases can be diagnosed before they become severe. HMOs also tend to offer many lab tests and special procedures on an outpatient basis. For some of these tests, conventional health insurance plans provide coverage only if a patient is hospitalized.

Critics claim that HMOs have cut hospital usage primarily because most members have been healthy people of working age who make relatively little demand on HMO services. In establishing the Medicare program, however,

Congress took the position that HMOs could contain costs even for retired people with chronic medical problems.

Nevertheless, some HMOs have run into financial problems over the years, leaving members without medical coverage and even, in some cases, saddled with uncovered medical and hospital bills. The best-managed HMOs carry insolvency insurance and hold individuals harmless for medical bills if the HMO fails.

Three Kinds of HMOs: Group Practice, Individual Practice, and Social HMOs

The group practice style, as exemplified by the first and largest HMO, Kaiser Permanente Medical Program, based in Oakland, California, is the best-known kind of HMO. Founded in 1945, Kaiser Permanente now serves more than 4.8 million members, 7% of them elderly, in 14 states and the District of Columbia.

In a group practice HMO, doctors, nurses, and other health professionals are on duty at a central HMO headquarters, where patients visit primary-care physicians and where medical records are on file. Specialists may be on staff or may work by referral. Some group practice HMOs own their own hospitals (Kaiser Permanente owns 28 in California, Oregon, Hawaii, and Ohio). Others contract with local hospitals to provide inpatient care, when needed.

The individual practice association (IPA), a more recent kind of HMO, is actually an alliance of individual doctors practicing from their own offices, who band together and contract for hospital care and other additional services for their HMO patients. In cities that have IPAs, many doctors take part, so your parents' doctor may be able to continue caring for them if they become HMO members.

In some cases, doctors have formed IPAs to compete with powerful group practice HMOs that move into their area. Some of these newer organizations may not provide as wide a range of services as the longer-established group practices, though the IPAs may provide a more personal and traditional kind of care with physicians seeing patients in private offices.

The Social HMO, or S/HMO, is a third style that extends the basic group HMO concept to include long-term home care, home-delivered meals, counseling, and other services designed to keep frail elderly people out of hospitals and nursing homes. Four social HMOs were set up as demonstration projects under a 1980 federal grant: Elderplan, Inc., sponsored by Metropolitan Jewish Geriatric Center in Brooklyn, New York; Senior Citizen Action Network in Long Beach, California; Ebenezer Society Group Health Plan in Minneapolis; and Kaiser Foundation Health Plan in Portland, Oregon. Older people who live in the coverage areas of these projects can get a variety of valuable services for their HMO premium. Unfortunately, the projects may be short-lived unless Congress expands the demonstration.

Medicare's HMO Program

In part because of their history of containing costs, HMO coverage was added to the Medicare program in 1982. By May 1986, Medicare had contracts with 126 HMOs with more than 700,000 older members.

Eligibility

For coverage under Medicare, HMOs must be Medicare-approved but not necessarily federally qualified. You and your parents should check with the local Social Security office to find out whether Medicare approval has been granted to the HMO they're considering.

Older people are eligible if they:

1. Are covered by both Part A and Part B of Medicare. This means paying the monthly Part B premium ($17.90 a month in 1987).
2. Do not have end-stage kidney (renal) disease, which is covered by regular Medicare but not under current Medicare-HMO contracts.
3. Live in the HMO service area.
4. Apply for HMO membership. (Participating HMOs must accept Medicare applicants during at least a 30-day period each year. They may not have an opening for your parents, however, since federal regulations dictate that HMOs have one member under 65 for each one who is older.
5. Pay a special HMO premium (which averaged $26 a month in 1986) to cover Medicare deductibles and copayments.

Advantages

Many positive aspects of HMOs have been spelled out above, but there are several specific advantages Medicare beneficiaries may be unfamiliar with:

1) The monthly HMO fee makes budgeting for health care easier. As HMO members, the monthly premium (plus the Part B premium) is the only medical bill your parents have to worry about, except for the nominal fees some HMOs charge for doctor visits.

2) Older people do not need to file claim forms to be reimbursed for HMO doctor bills as they would under the regular Medicare Part B program. In addition, they have no worries about finding a doctor who accepts assignment.

3) With an HMO, your parents do not need Medigap insurance to supplement their Medicare. (Of course, they will have to pay Part B and HMO premiums).

4) HMO members get care from a team of doctors and other medical personnel. If they don't get along with their first choice for primary-care physician, they may switch doctors until they are satisfied.

5) As Medicare members, your parents may get additional HMO benefits at low cost, such as ambulance service, dental care, extended psychiatric benefits, and discounts on eyeglasses and prescription drugs. The combination of services depends on the HMO.

6) Your parents have the right to stay enrolled in the HMO, even if they develop complex health problems that require an intensive level of care. While Medicare will not accept victims of end-stage kidney disease as entering HMO members, older people who develop severe kidney problems after joining will not be ejected.

7) If your parents have complaints about HMO coverage, they have access to the organization's grievance procedure. Each HMO handles grievances differently, but many have staff members assigned specifically to take complaints. If the disagreement is unresolved, your parents would be able to appeal their complaint to the medical director, a review board, or to the board of directors. In addition, older members can appeal coverage disputes through the regular Medicare appeals process.

Disadvantages

Transferring from regular Medicare coverage to an HMO has one main disadvantage: elderly people lose the right to choose their own doctor. Instead, members must use the HMO's doctors, hospitals, and other service providers, except in case of emergency. If they don't, they will have to pay for the service from their own money. Some elderly people are unwilling to leave doctors they have established long-term relationships with, even to achieve cost savings.

Other disadvantages include the following:

1) Older people who travel often outside their home area may encounter problems with HMO coverage. Emergency care is always covered, of course. In that case, your parents pay out-of-pocket for the emergency services and then file for reimbursement from the HMO.

If your parents travel a lot or spend part of each year in a warmer climate, however, they may not be covered for routine check-ups or care for a chronic condition in their vacation area. Before joining, they should ask whether the HMO they are considering will pay for care in the area they will be visiting, either from another HMO or from private doctors.

2) Moving outside the HMO area can also pose problems. Some but not all HMOs accept transfer members. Some but not all offer reciprocal care while the transfer process is under way. If your parents plan to make a retirement move, they should inquire about HMO coverage both near their current home and in the retirement area they're considering. They may decide to wait until they have moved to switch from the regular Medicare program.

3) Switching back to regular Medicare coverage can take time. Your parents have the right to end HMO membership at any time by notifying the HMO in writing. In most cases, however, the HMO has at least a month to make the change. If your parents are dissatisfied with HMO coverage, urge them to find out about the HMO's transfer procedures and how long they take.

4) Resuming Medigap supplementary insurance coverage may be difficult if HMO members switch back to regular Medicare. Before joining an HMO, your parents should call their supplementary insurance carrier and ask whether there would be a problem or a lengthy waiting period for getting their coverage back if they change their minds. If so, it could be a good idea for them to keep their Medicare supplementary policy temporarily while trying out the HMO.

5) Some HMO members complain about long waits in making doctor appointments.

Consumer Checklist

Not all HMO programs are alike, so research is essential to determine what coverage is offered by the HMOs you and your parents are considering. Both for-profit and not-for-profit HMOs exist; neither type of organization guarantees quality of care.

Read brochures carefully. Don't be afraid to question the salespeople marketing the program. In addition, pay visits to each HMO, taking time to talk about the program with staff members as well as members.

The following checklist may help

THE BASIC PROGRAM

1) What is the name of the HMO?
2) Is it Medicare approved?
3) Is the central office convenient to your parents' home?

4) What services are offered and where? Are they convenient?

Physicians and specialists _____

Hospital care _____

Emergency room _____

Skilled Nursing Facility _____

Test laboratory _____

Other _____

THE BASIC COSTS

1) What is the monthly premium?
2) Does the HMO charge for doctor's appointments?
3) Are there other copayments?
4) How does the total compare with health-care expenses and benefits under the regular Medicare program?
5) Are Medicare members offered a "high option" plan above Medicare's standard benefit package at an additional premium? If so, what is covered and what is the fee?

MEDICAL STAFF

1) Ask for a list of doctors associated with the HMO. Does the list include doctors with the major specialities:

Gynecology? _____

Surgery? _____

Eye care (ophthalmology)? _____

Orthopedics? _____

Mental health? _____

Foot care (podiatry)? _____

Geriatrics? _____

2) Ask for the list of physicians with the HMO a year ago, and compare the lists. This will give an idea of physician turnover.
3) Can your parents choose any doctor from the list as a primary care physician? If they have a medical problem, may they select a specialist as their primary-care doctor?
4) How do they go about changing the primary-care doctor if they aren't satisfied?
5) Do nurse practitioners or doctor's assistants sometimes handle routine office visits? Can the patient choose to see a doctor instead?
6) How long is the usual waiting time for non-emergency appointments with the primary-care doctor? For a specialist?
7) If specialists are not on staff, where must members go to see one? What happens if the specialist your parents need is not HMO-affiliated?
8) If surgery is recommended, does the HMO pay for a second opinion, even from a doctor not affiliated with the HMO?
9) If the HMO is an individual practice association (IPA), can your parents

continue going to their current physician? Does the IPA physician give preferential treatment to private patients over HMO members?

USING THE HMO

1) What are the hours for regular health services and doctor appointments?
2) Where do members go for off-hour emergency care?
3) Are each patient's medical records kept in a centralized location? Where? If the HMO is an individual practice association, where are records kept?
4) Are supplementary services offered? Is there a fee?
Eyeglasses? _____
Prescription drugs? _____
Health education? _____
Ambulance service? _____
Dental care? _____

5) Are there any conditions the HMO will not treat?
6) Does the HMO offer any help if your parents need long-term care?
7) Is there reciprocity with HMOs in other parts of the country?

SATISFACTION WITH THE HMO

1) Ask for names of Medicare members you and your parents can call to find out how they like HMO services.
2) How does the grievance procedure work?
3) How does a member drop membership in the HMO? How much notice is necessary?

HMO'S HISTORY AND FINANCIAL STANDING

1) When was the HMO founded? How many members does it have? How many Medicare members?
2) How long has the HMO been in the Medicare program?
3) Is the HMO a for-profit organization or not-for-profit? Is it financially sound?
4) Does the HMO have insolvency insurance? Does it have a hold-harmless clause in its member contracts?
5) Are Medicare members or Medicare officials represented on the board of directors or the community advisory board?

For Further Information

For further information about Medicare's HMO benefit, get a copy of the pamphlet *Medicare and Prepayment Plans* from the local Social Security office.

In addition, consult the AARP's booklet *More Health for Your Dollar: An Older Person's Guide to HMOs.*

For a list of HMOs in your parents' area, write

Group Health Association of America
   1129 20th St., N.W.
   Washington, D.C. 20036
   (202) 778-3200

MEDICAID

Medicaid, the nation's health insurance program for low-income people of all ages, provides a generous array of services in some states and less complete coverage in others. It is financed jointly by federal and state money. Your parents may qualify if their monthly income and assets are very low.

Each state administers its Medicaid program individually, so in effect, the United States (with the District of Columbia) has 51 Medicaid programs, all providing a different combination of services. Not even the names are the same. Some states use the term "Medical Assistance." In California, the program is known as "MediCal." In Arizona, the Arizona Health Care Cost Containment System (AHCCCS, pronounced "access") provides Medicaid through about 20 HMOs.

Some services are mandated nationwide. Under federal law, all states receiving Medicaid funding must pay for doctors, inpatient and outpatient hospital care, rural health clinics, lab tests, x-rays, home health care, and skilled nursing homes. Depending on which additional options the state legislature votes to provide, states also may cover dental bills, medical equipment, prescription drugs, and other services.

One of the options, long-term nursing home care, is covered by Medicaid in the District of Columbia and all states except Arizona. This means that people who qualify for Medicaid are covered for custodial care (not just skilled care) in nursing homes. When older people in Arizona need but can't afford nursing home care, their home county is responsible for providing the care by contracting with a local facility.

Medicaid Eligibility

State eligibility rules differ in a bewilderingly complex series of ways, but Medicaid recognizes two general kinds of eligibility: categorical need and medical need.

The Categorically Needy   In 35 states and the District of Columbia, Medicaid designates people as categorically needy if their income and assets do not exceed guidelines for the SSI supplementary income program, with some states allowing more income and assets, and some less. A listing of 1986 poverty-level guidelines for SSI illustrates how low income and assets must be for Medicaid eligibility:

	Individual	Couple
Monthly income	$ 336	$ 504
Assets	$1,700	$2,550
Family Home	Any value	
Personal Effects	$2,000	$2,000
Funeral Expenses	$1,500	$1,500
Burial Space	Any value	

In most states, the family home, no matter its market value, does not affect Medicaid eligibility as long as one elderly spouse lives there or the nursing home resident intends to return. Medicaid may place a lien on the house, however, and may claim some of the proceeds to pay nursing home costs at the owner's death or when the house is sold.

In the other 15 states, Medicaid guidelines are set individually and are generally, but not always, more restrictive than the SSI standards.*

For nursing home patients, some states make an exception to the "categorical need" standard for patients in a "special income" group. Under this provision, people with incomes up to three times the state's regular income ceiling can qualify for Medicaid. Home care and other noninstitutional services are not covered under the exception, however.

Medically Needy   High medical bills not covered by Medicaid can pose a dire threat to the living standards of older people. But in states where "categorical need" is the only avenue to Medicaid eligibility, older people with incomes even slightly above the state ceiling won't be able to get Medicaid, no matter how much of their money goes to pay for doctors' bills.

To remedy this, some states† have adopted a second definition of Medicaid eligibility: the "medically needy" standard. Under this formula, Medicaid is available for people with medical bills so high over a given period of time that their incomes are effectively reduced. In these "surplus income"

* These states are Arizona, Connecticut, Hawaii, Idaho, Illinois, Indiana, Minnesota, Missouri, Nebraska, New Hampshire, North Carolina, North Dakota, Ohio, Oklahoma, Utah, and Virginia.
† As of 1985, the "medically needy" states were Arkansas, California, Connecticut, the District of Columbia, Hawaii, Illinois, Kansas, Kentucky, Louisiana, Maine, Maryland, Massachusetts, Michigan, Minnesota, Montana, Nebraska, New Hampshire, New York, North Carolina, North Dakota, Oklahoma, Oregon, Pennsylvania, Rhode Island, Tennessee, Utah, Vermont, Virginia, Washington, West Virginia, and Wisconsin.

states, elderly people may qualify for Medicaid by "spending down" their monthly income by the amount of their medical bills. In some states, bills can be averaged for up to a year in order to qualify for the spend down.

Medicaid still imposes an income ceiling under the "medically needy" program, but that upper limit is somewhat higher than the income maximum for categorical need in most states. Assets, including bank accounts, stocks, and real estate, must meet regular Medicaid guidelines, however.

To illustrate the difference between categorical and medical need, consider the case of Arnold Alexander, a recovering stroke victim, who receives a total of $580 a month in income from Social Security and a pension. With monthly expenses of $300 in rent, $75 in utilities and $150 for prescription drugs and other medical expenses, he has a meager $55 left for food and clothing.

Mr. Alexander wouldn't qualify as "categorically needy" under Medicaid, because his income is well above his state's monthly limit of $336. But he *could* qualify in a "medically needy" state, with the income ceiling of $336 increased by one-third to $448. (The medical expenses of $150 would offset the $580 income, leaving only $430 for Medicaid consideration.)

No Medicaid Claims

Unlike Medicare, Medicaid does not require copayments or deductibles. Nor do Medicaid beneficiaries have to file reimbursement claims as they generally do under Medicare's Part B. Instead, all Medicaid claims are filed by health-care providers—doctors and hospitals—and the providers are reimbursed for Medicaid patients directly.

This freedom from filing claims is convenient for Medicaid beneficiaries, but it comes at the expense of a trade-off. Medicaid services can be provided only by doctors, drugstores, nursing homes, and other suppliers that participate in Medicaid, and far fewer participate in Medicaid than Medicare.

For Further Information

Information on Medicaid eligibility is available from local Social Security offices, city and county offices of Public Assistance, and social service departments of most hospitals. Additional information about Medicaid financing for long-term care is included in the nursing home section of this book on pages 205–230.

If you live in a different state from your parents, be sure to direct your questions on Medicaid to offices in their area. Each state's Medicaid guidelines (and benefits) are entirely different, and officials in one state will have little knowledge about another state's program.

CHAPTER VII

Long-Term Care

Disability • Diseases of Aging • Your Role as Caregiver • Case Management • Adult Day Care

Many older people remain in good health throughout their lives, managing on their own for all but a few months or years. Usually at some point, however, frailty or ill health begins to threaten an older person's independence. The loss of ability to function independently means your mother or father may need long-term care, often on a permanent basis.

Long-term care refers to a whole range of medical and supportive services for individuals who have become unable to fend for themselves. Many people think the term is synonymous with nursing home placement. In fact, only 5% of all Americans over 65 live in nursing homes, while nearly 19% have some form of disability.

Also, contrary to popular belief, an estimated 80% of all long-term care for the elderly is provided at home by family and friends, according to Ron Hagen, insurance coordinator of the American Association of Retired Persons. Most of it is personal care, help with activities of daily living that can be provided by family and friends or by hired home attendants. Registered nurses and hospital care are necessary only when older people are sick enough to need intravenous feedings, changes of dressings, injections, or other complicated procedures.

Thus, acting as a caregiver for older parents may mean various things, from stepping in personally to managing a team of helpers, made up of family, friends, and paid staff. It may also involve arranging short-term hospital stays or home visits by doctors, nurses, and physical therapists. In some cases, arranging for a nursing home bed may become necessary.

Whatever its form, long-term care is usually maddeningly complicated to arrange—both for emotional and other reasons. If no one from the family is available to provide this care in person, it can be shockingly expensive.

If you live far away from your parents' hometown, the challenge of seeing that they are cared for may pose especially difficult problems. No one solution will fit every situation. But facing up to the challenge can be easier when you have a realistic overview of how long-term care is provided in the United States and a clear grasp of what resources are available.

When Do Your Parents Need Long-term Care?

All of us—old and young—are different, so there is no one way to determine your parents' need for long-term care. In some cases, you will know it when you see it. In other cases, your parents may insist stubbornly that they are fine, yet you may not be so sure. The bottom line is their ability to live independently.

"We had no idea that Aunt Marie was so confused until Uncle George died and we went out to Phoenix for the funeral," said a Pennsylvania man whose aunt and uncle had no children. "There was no way she could live alone out there. My mother and I packed her up and brought her back East. Then we had to figure out how to take care of her."

For most people, independent living may become impossible either because of gradually worsening disabilities or because of a serious illness or medical condition. Many older people face both disability and disease.

DISABILITY

Disability is usually defined in terms of an individual's ability or lack of it to carry out the basic activities of daily living: bathing, dressing, eating, using the toilet, getting in and out of bed, walking, and so forth. People unable to carry out one or two of these tasks are generally regarded to be mildly disabled, while those unable to handle most of them are seen as severely disabled and in need of personal care. Besides the basic activities, independent living also depends on being able to go out, handle money, shop, cook, clean, and take medications without assistance.

Few people, whatever their age, live an entirely independent lifestyle. Couples routinely share many of the tasks of daily living: shopping, cooking, dishwashing, yardwork. People who live alone obviously have to manage more housekeeping duties unaided but may expect to get help with heavy cleaning, washing windows, a paint job, or home repairs.

For the disabled, however, being able to handle the most basic personal care tasks—or having someone else do so—is not a matter of choice. It spells survival. If you live far away, you may not be aware of how much your elderly mother relies on your father unless he is no longer there. If she doesn't drive, neighbors or relatives may volunteer to take her shopping or to the doctor. But if she is also unable to cook or get in and out of the bathtub safely, she may not be able to continue living in her own home.

"I'd call every couple days, and Mom insisted she was fine and was getting plenty to eat," said a New Jersey social worker, whose widowed mother lives in a small town in Indiana. "Then one day, a neighbor answered the phone and asked me to call her later at her home. That's how I found out Mom ate almost nothing but cereal, toast, and tea. Her eyesight was so bad she worried about setting a fire if she cooked."

If you aren't certain about your parents' ability to live independently, have an understanding talk with them about their abilities and needs. Use the following as guidelines:

	Functions Independently	Somewhat Impaired	Needs Help
Personal Hygiene			
Going to the toilet			
Washing and bathing			
Getting in and out of tub or shower			
Brushing teeth			
Shaving			
Basic Mobility			
Getting out of bed			
Getting up from chair			
Getting to bathroom			
Using stairs			
Nutrition			
Feeding self			
Planning healthy meals			
Cooking			
Shopping			
Washing dishes			

	Functions Independently	Somewhat Impaired	Needs Help
Getting Around			
Choosing clothes			
Dressing			
Walking in home			
Walking outside			
Arranging ride with friend			
Taking bus or taxi			
Driving			
Housework			
Changing bed sheets			
Laundry			
Cleaning house			
Taking out garbage			
Yardwork			
Medical Needs			
Taking prescribed medications			
Monitoring chronic conditions, if any			

DISEASES OF AGING

Older people without serious disabilities may live independently with great success until they are hospitalized with an acute illness like a stroke or heart attack or gradually fall prey to a chronic condition like arthritis or a dementing illness like Alzheimer's Disease.

Each condition calls for a different kind of long-term care. The illnesses most common to the elderly are listed briefly below with the names of self-help associations formed to assist victims and families. Recent books are listed in the bibliography.

Alzheimer's Disease

This neurological disease is one of several forms of senile dementia that cause progressive loss of mental and intellectual powers. An estimated 3 million Americans are victims of Alzheimer's, including nearly 50% of the nation's nursing home residents. The disease is the fourth leading cause of death after heart disease, cancer, and stroke. Researchers have begun to learn about its cause, but as yet there is no cure.

Alzheimer's usually begins with occasional forgetfulness, but as it progresses, memory loss worsens. Later, victims may become disoriented, irritable, or abusive; they may hallucinate or wander away from home, and they often have trouble talking, concentrating, and sleeping at night. In the final stages, they may be unable to control urination or bowels or to communicate and will need constant supervision or skilled care in a nursing home.

When the German physician Alois Alzheimer named the disease in 1906, he described it as a condition primarily affecting people as young as 45. Today, however, researchers believe Alzheimer's Disease accounts for up to 70% of severe memory loss among the elderly.

Anyone suspected of having Alzheimer's Disease needs a thorough medical evaluation to rule out similar conditions that respond to treatment. Among these are multi-infarct dementia (caused by a series of small strokes), depression, reactions to prescription drugs, thyroid imbalances, head injuries, and brain tumors or infections.

For further information, contact the Alzheimer's Disease and Related Disorders Association, which provides family support and funds research into the cause of dementia. The association has more than 140 local chapters and 500 family support groups:

> Alzheimer's Disease and Related Disorders Association
> National Headquarters
> 70 East Lake St.
> Chicago, IL 60601
> (312) 853-3060
> (800) 621-0379 (toll-free, except in Illinois)
> (800) 572-6037 (toll-free in Illinois)

New York City and other localities have set up special telephone hotlines for the families of Alzheimer's patients. In New York, contact

> Alzheimer's Resource Center
> 280 Broadway
> New York, NY 10007
> (212) 577-7564

Arthritis

Almost half of all Americans over 65 suffer from arthritis, or inflammation of the joints. The cause of arthritis is not known, and there are few cures, but symptoms like swelling, redness, stiffness, and pain should be checked with a doctor so as to avoid severe crippling.

Osteoarthritis, the most common form, results from normal wear and tear and is almost always present in older people. Also called degenerative joint disease, osteoarthritis most often affects the spine, knees, and hips, especially in overweight people.

A more severe form, rheumatoid arthritis, causes inflammation of joint membranes and is three times more likely to strike women than men. Rheumatoid arthritis can affect many parts of the body but most often attacks fingers, wrists, elbows, hips, knees, and ankles, causing persistent swelling and pain.

For further information and various pamphlets about arthritis treatment and research, check the phone book for one of the 72 local chapters of the Arthritis Foundation nationwide or contact

> Arthritis Foundation
> 1314 Spring St., N.W.
> Atlanta, GA 30309
> (404) 872-7100

Osteoporosis

Osteoporosis is a severe loss of bone mass that occurs after middle age, especially in women, making bones unusually brittle and likely to break. It is the most common cause of hip fracture and "dowager's hump," which more than one in four women past menopause develop.

Researchers believe that bone deterioration may be slowed or stopped through a diet rich in calcium. In addition, calcium-supplement tablets and weight-bearing exercise, like walking, may help. Some doctors also recommend estrogen replacement therapy, especially for women who have had an early menopause. For further information about this condition, contact the National Osteoporosis Foundation, 1625 Eye St., N.W., Suite 1011, Washington, D.C. 20006, (202) 223-2226.

Cancer

Cancer, an uncontrolled growth of abnormal cells, can occur in almost any organ or system in the body and can spread, or metastasize, to other areas. Years ago, a cancer diagnosis meant a death sentence, but today doctors and researchers have developed treatments that can destroy cancer cells and prevent them from spreading. The three major kinds of treatment are surgery, radiation, and chemotherapy, or a combination of the three.

Among the associations providing help to cancer victims and their families are the following:

American Cancer Society with volunteers in 3,000 local units supports research, lends medical equipment, provides transportation to medical appointments, and helps women who have had breast cancer through the Reach to Recovery Program. Check the local phone book or contact

American Cancer Society
  National Headquarters
  90 Park Ave.
  New York, NY 10016
  (212) 599–8200

Cancer Care provides professional counseling and guidance without charge to cancer patients and their families through 50 chapters in New York City, Long Island's Nassau and Suffolk counties, and New Jersey.

Cancer Care Inc.
  One Park Ave.
  New York, NY 10016
  (212) 221–3300

Cancer Connection, based in Kansas City, Missouri, operates as a support system to match cancer victims with volunteers who have experienced the same kind of cancer.

Cancer Connection
  4410 Mail St.
  Kansas City, MO 64111
  (816) 932-8453

Leukemia Society of America supports research to find the causes and cures of leukemia, Hodgkin's disease, multiple myeloma, and other lymphomas. Some of the 58 chapters provide family support groups. Check the local phone book or contact

Leukemia Society of America
  National Headquarters
  733 Third Ave.
  New York, NY 10017
  (212) 573-8484

National Cancer Institute, part of the National Institute of Health within the U.S. Department of Health and Human Services, supports research at important medical centers nationwide. Through the institute's Cancer Information Service, callers can receive brochures and confidential answers to their questions. The nationwide hotline number is

(800) 4-CANCER (800 422-6237)

Arteriosclerosis, Stroke, and Heart Problems

Arteriosclerosis is a chronic condition in which artery walls thicken and harden, interfering with blood circulation. Any artery of the body can be involved. A stroke, or blockage affecting the brain, cuts off oxygen, which can kill brain cells and cause temporary or permanent paralysis. While stroke is the third leading cause of death among American adults, most stroke victims survive and recover with rehabilitation.

A heart attack, or myocardial infarction, occurs when one of the arteries carrying blood to the heart becomes completely blocked. Damage may be limited to a small part of the heart or it may be extensive.

Angina pectoris is a chronic heart problem that occurs when coronary arteries become narrowed over the years, reducing blood flow and the supply of oxygen. The resulting chest pain and shortness of breath, which occurs especially in periods of stress or physical activity, can usually be controlled at home with a prescription drug.

Anyone with arteriosclerosis, chronic heart problems, or stroke should be under the care of a physician. For further information, check the local phone book or contact

American Heart Association
   (stroke clubs and Mended Heart programs)
   7320 Greenville Ave.
   Dallas, TX 75231
   (214) 750-5300
National Stroke Association
   National Stroke Information
      Service Referral Clearinghouse
   1420 Ogden St.
   Denver, CO 80218
   (303) 839-1992
National Easter Seal Society
   2023 West Ogden Ave.
   Chicago, IL 60612
   (312) 243-8400
National Institute of Communicative Disorders
      and Stroke
   National Institutes of Health
   Bldg. 31, Room 8A–06
   Bethesda, MD 20892
   (301) 496-5924

Diabetes

Diabetes is a chronic disease affecting the ability of the pancreas to produce enough insulin. Insulin controls the amount of glucose, or natural sugar, in the blood. Symptoms include frequent urination and excessive thirst.

The most common form of the disease is diabetes mellitus, or Type II diabetes, which hinders the body's ability to produce insulin and usually crops up later in life. The problem can be controlled in most people by diet, exercise, and oral medication.

In Type I diabetes, sometimes called juvenile diabetes, the pancreas cannot produce insulin at all, so victims are dependent on daily insulin injections for survival. Type I patients are rarely diagnosed after the age of 30.

Diabetes patients should see a physician to determine the appropriate treatment. In addition, several organizations provide information and support for diabetes victims:

The American Diabetes Association has about 700 chapters nationwide, some of which run patient support groups and day camps for children. Check the local phone book or contact

> American Diabetes Association
> National Service Center
> 1660 Duke St.
> Alexandria, VA 22314
> (703) 549-1500

The Juvenile Diabetes Foundation sponsors a few treatment and support programs.

> Juvenile Diabetes Foundation
> National Headquarters
> 432 Park Avenue South
> New York, NY 10016
> (212) 889-7575

The National Diabetes Information Clearinghouse provides publications and other information about the disease.

> National Diabetes Information Clearinghouse
> P.O. Box NDIC
> Bethesda, MD 20892
> (301) 468-2162

Hypertension

Hypertension, or high blood pressure, affects about 60 million Americans, including 40% of whites and 50% of blacks over the age of 65. Most hypertension runs in families, but obesity and diets high in salt also pose risks. Some people mistakenly believe hypertension is found only in tense, nervous people, but even calm, relaxed individuals suffer from it.

To control hypertension, doctors often advise losing weight, avoiding salt, and getting regular exercise. Medications can also help lower blood pressure. Victims of hypertension should see their physicians. For reference materials, referrals, and other information, contact

> High Blood Pressure Information Center
> 120/80 National Institutes of Health
> Bethesda, MD 20892
> (301) 496-1809

Respiratory Ailments

Respiratory ailments cause shortness of breath and are aggravated by smoking and exposure to toxic pollutants. Among the specific ailments are chronic bronchitis, asthma, and emphysema, also known as chronic obstructive pulmonary disease (COPD).

Chronic bronchitis inflames the bronchi, the two major tubes branching off from the trachea, or windpipe, and clogs them with thick mucus. In an asthma attack, victims can't breathe in enough air because of swelling and mucus in the bronchioles, smaller tubes that branch off from the bronchi.

Emphysema damages the air sacs, or alveoli, at the end of the bronchial network, interfering with the exchange of oxygen into blood and leaving victims short of breath.

People with respiratory problems should be under a doctor's care. Treatments include medications, inhalants, and moderate exercise. Other information is available from the following organizations:

Emphysema Anonymous, a voluntary organization of 17,000 members that publishes a newsletter and has a number of support groups.

> Emphysema Anonymous
> P.O. Box 3224
> Seminole, FL 33542
> (813) 391-9977

American Lung Association

> American Lung Association
> National Headquarters
> 1740 Broadway
> New York, NY 10019
> (212) 315-8700

Vision Problems

Vision problems plague many elderly people. The problems can range from nearsightedness, farsightedness, and astigmatism to diseases like cataract (the clouding of the lens), glaucoma (a build-up of fluid within the eyeball), and detached retina (a break in the membrane that lines the back of the eye). As people age, the lens and muscles of the lens may lose elasticity, requiring stronger glasses or bifocals.

Many older people also lose vision because of a disorder called macular degeneration, which affects the central part of the retina, called the macula. The Amsler grid test, which can detect this condition, is easy to administer and can be given at home. If the test reveals problems, patients should go to a doctor.

For further information about vision impairments or blindness, the following associations may be of help:

American Council of the Blind publishes a national magazine, *Braille Forum*, and various pamphlets in large-print and Braille. Check the local phone book or contact

> American Council of the Blind
> National Offices
> 1211 Connecticut Ave., N.W., Suite 506
> Washington, D.C. 20036
> (202) 393-3666
> (800) 424-8666 (toll-free)

Better Vision Institute promotes awareness of proper vision care. Among its pamphlets (single copies are free) is one on vision problems of the aging.

> Better Vision Institute
> 230 Park Ave.
> New York, NY 10169
> (212) 682-1731

National Association for Visually Handicapped distributes large-print books, publishes a large-print newsletter, and provides information about optical aids and other services for people with impaired sight.

National Association for Visually Handicapped
22 West 21st St.
New York, NY 10010
(212) 889-3141
      or
3201 Balboa St.
San Francisco, CA 94121
(415) 221-3201

National Library Service for the Blind and Physically Handicapped distributes Braille and talking books and magazines at no charge through 160 regional libraries. For an application form, contact

National Library Service for the Blind and Physically Handicapped
Library of Congress
1291 Taylor St., N.W.
Washington, D.C. 20542
(202) 287-5100

National Society to Prevent Blindness offers annual glaucoma screenings through 26 state affiliates. It also offers a home test kit for macular degeneration in adults.

National Society to Prevent Blindness
79 Madison Ave.
New York, NY 10016
(212) 684-3505
(800) 231-3004 (toll-free nationwide)

Vision Foundation, an organization run mainly by volunteers, serves visually impaired people and their families. It runs self-help groups throughout Massachusetts and distributes information nationwide on various subjects, including *Coping With Sight Loss: The Vision Resource Book.*

Vision Foundation
818 Mount Auburn St.
Watertown, MA 02172
(617) 926-4232
(800) 852-3029 (toll-free in Massachusetts)

Hearing Problems

Hearing loss is the third most common chronic condition for the elderly, affecting an estimated 40% of people over 65. Much hearing loss is irreversible, but medical treatments or surgery work in some cases. Anyone affected should see a family doctor or a specialist—an otologist (ear specialist) or an otolaryngologist (doctor specializing in ear, nose, and throat). Hearing aids may help but should not be fitted without a thorough medical examination.

American Hearing Research Foundation publishes several booklets on ear care and hearing aids.

> American Hearing Research Foundation
> 55 East Washington St.
> Chicago, IL 60602
> (312) 726-9670

Better Hearing Institute maintains a toll-free Hearing Hotline and distributes literature on hearing problems and hearing aids.

> Better Hearing Institute
> 1430 K St., N.W., Suite 700
> Washington, D.C. 20005
> (800) 424-8576 (toll-free, nationwide)

National Hearing Aid Society, a trade group for hearing aid dealers, runs a toll-free hotline to provide general information on hearing loss and hearing aids. A consumer kit includes a list of hearing aid specialists in each region of the country.

> National Hearing Aid Society
> 20361 Middlebelt
> Livonia, MI 48152
> (800) 521-5247 (toll-free Hearing Aid Hotline, nationwide)

Self Help for the Hard of Hearing targets the hard of hearing rather than the deaf. Many of its 15,000 members (in some 170 chapters nationwide) are elderly. For information about local chapters, contact

> Self Help for the Hard of Hearing
> 4848 Battery Lane, Suite 100
> Bethesda, MD 20814
> (301) 657-2248

YOUR ROLE AS CAREGIVER

When one or both of your parents begins to need long-term care, you will have to think realistically about how you can help. The specific duties depend on how close you live to your parents, your relationship with them, your skills, and how much time and resources you can afford to contribute. If you live hundreds of miles away, your main job may be to keep in touch by telephone and let someone else provide the direct care.

Regardless of the details, your goal will be to make sure your parents receive the best possible care in a safe, secure environment while retaining as much autonomy as they can.

Most caregivers turn out to be women, often the daughters and daughters-in-law of the elderly, who struggle with the demanding roles of wife, mother, jobholder, and even grandmother while caring for their parents. But today more men are becoming members of the "sandwich generation," the group that finds itself pressed by the needs of both children and parents with little time for themselves.

Many people who care for an elderly parent are senior citizens themselves. "One of our caregivers is a 70-year-old woman taking care of her 94-year-old father," said Susan Holmes, director of an adult day-care program in Pennsylvania. "Another woman in her 70s brings her 92-year-old mom in two afternoons a week so she can go to the Y and swim."

These "children" face a difficult task. After years of needing and heeding parental advice, they must switch roles and become their parents' protector. "It can be difficult," said Carol Freeman, a former caseworker for an Area Agency on Aging. "When a child becomes a caregiver, there's a tremendous role change. You have to accept the responsibility of caring for your parent, and you can't be afraid to say 'no' to them."

At the same time, professionals in the field say it's important that the elderly retain a sense of independence. "It's important not to make decisions *for* them," said Rhonda Soberman, chief social worker for the Long-Term Health Care Program at Metropolitan Jewish Geriatric Center in Brooklyn. "It's so easy to fall into the trap of treating an older person like a child."

You may be regarded as the logical caregiver for your parents, because of a nurturing personality, training as a nurse or social worker, living nearby, having a spare bedroom in a roomy house—or even because you aren't married and are presumed to have more time to devote. You may take on the extra duties gladly, but there's a good chance you'll have some doubts about whether you are willing—or able.

How to Begin

Before you decide on how much you can do, try to determine what kind of help your parents need. You probably already have a good idea of your parent's current disabilities, though these may change over time. The key issue in developing what social workers call "a good plan of care" will be in deciding whether your mother and dad can stay in their own home, whether they need to live with a companion or relative (possibly you and your family), or whether nursing home placement is necessary.

If you are an only child, you may feel alone and without resources in making such a decision. People with brothers and sisters may have a different problem—coping with differences of opinion and emotional struggles among the siblings.

You will probably find that just about everyone—your parents, your brothers and sisters, your own spouse and children, even your neighbors and friends—has a different idea of what should be done and what you should do. Try not to be hurried, so that you can consider all the options. Get as much information as you can from experienced, objective resources in the community:

Your parents' family doctor Call the doctor, describe your concern, and make an appointment for a full discussion of your mother or father's condition. Go without the older person, so you can get a comprehensive report on all medical problems and functional difficulties, the outlook, test results, and prescribed treatments. Get the physician's opinion on your parent's emotional health, whether your parent can live alone and what medical equipment may be needed.

Hospital social workers If your parent is in the hospital, he or she will probably be visited by a nurse or social worker from the social service department. Medicare calls these people discharge planners, since they are supposed to help families make arrangements for post-hospital care. They usually are very well-informed about the community's nursing homes, home health-care agencies, and other facilities for elderly people.

Area Agency on Aging The AAAs in every county or region are excellent resources for information about Meals on Wheels, telephone reassurance, home health care, and volunteer programs that can help the elderly. Some also provide direct services. AAA staffers are especially well-versed about programs for low-income people but will probably know about privately funded care too. In addition, every AAA has a Long-Term Care Ombudsman who handles complaints about nursing homes and other long-term care facilities.

Clergy Call your parents' minister, priest, or rabbi or ask the AAA to refer you to a clergy person from your faith for personal counseling or for help in finding a social service agency. Churches and synagogues also may know of service groups or individual volunteers willing and eager to visit or do errands for your parents.

Facing the Obstacles

No matter what kind of care you feel you can give, it's a good idea to think about the characteristics of your own family that could complicate the job:

Relationship With Your Parents You'll do best at giving long-term care if your relationship with your parents has usually been harmonious. If you've never gotten along well with your mother, the situation isn't likely to improve when she becomes sick or weak. "In fact, the parent may have changed some, may talk more sharply to the children," said Bernice Shepard, a New York professor of social work and head of a case management agency that works with elderly people. "People don't change with age, they just get more so."

Even when things have gone smoothly in the past, problems can arise now. For example, you may find it very hard to help an unusually modest elderly person with intimate tasks like bathing or dressing. And you may feel shy yourself. "Some people will tell us they've never seen their mom with her clothes off, and they're embarrassed," said caseworker Carol Freeman.

The situation can be most ticklish for a man caring for his mother or a woman for her father. In these cases, help with bathing and going to the toilet may be possible only through hiring a nurse or aide.

Good Will of Siblings Your brothers and sisters may say they feel relieved if you agree to take the major responsibility for your parent's care. But you may also sense resentment or competition, in many cases because your siblings feel guilty for not contributing more. In some families, these feelings erupt into accusations that the caregiver is playing the martyr or currying favor for a larger inheritance.

"It's unbelievable what people fight over," said Gene Myers, a hospital social worker. "If there's any sibling rivalry, it will come up in these situations. Sometimes it can become greed. For example, a mother may have told a daughter there was $600 in a book. When the daughter goes to look, she may find only $400 and worry that the rest was taken, perhaps by a brother or sister. It may turn out that the mother was confused in the first place."

Time for your own spouse and children Giving long-term care to a frail parent can cut severely into the time available for your family. If your husband or wife does not support your decision to help, you may have to fight an uphill battle.

No matter how cooperative your family, you will need respite—rest and relaxation—away from your mother or father from time to time. A family vacation, a weekend ski trip, or even a night out for a quiet dinner or a movie may give you a break from what is often a frustrating experience. But if you are providing direct care, your peace of mind during a vacation depends on your finding a substitute caregiver or "sitter" so you know things are under control at home.

Concrete Steps

As you and your family decide who can do what, strive to maintain open, positive lines of communication.

1. Call **a family meeting** of everyone concerned with the elderly person's welfare. Be sure to include your mother or father, if feasible, as well as your husband and wife, your children, your brothers and sisters, and other concerned relatives. Outline simply your parent's needs as you see them, and spell out what you think you can do. Ask your parent for his or her reaction. Don't be afraid to ask relatives for help, and be honest about what you need and expect.
2. Think seriously about drawing up a **written agreement** that spells out the division of labor you decide on. The plan can be as specific as desired, detailing responsibilities for your father or mother's housing, food, laundry, shopping, transportation, personal care, and medical treatment.
3. Remember that each sibling's **contributions will vary.** Some may offer services and goods while others may provide financial help. If one brother lives near your parents, he may volunteer to take them shopping once a week, provide transportation for medical and dental appointments, take care of home repairs, or be on call in case of emergency.

   As an out-of-town sister, you might offer financial help as your share, agreeing to pay any doctor bills or other expenses not covered by pensions, Social Security, and Medicare. In addition, you might agree to be responsible for filling out complicated Medicare and insurance claims or to visit your parents for several weeks a year while your brother goes on vacation.
4. Don't forget **your parents' role,** especially when one of them is providing most of the day-to-day care for the other. The healthier parent may interpret your questions as criticism or an intrusion and may be too proud to accept your offer of help. If you worry that more care is needed, try to talk to your parents separately to get information about how well they are managing. Consider asking the advice of their family doctor, clergy, or a trusted friend or neighbor.

Long-distance Caregiving

But what if your parents live thousands of miles away from you? Long-distance caregiving poses definite problems, the worst being the sense of helplessness at not knowing whether your mother or father is all right. Frequent phone calls can maintain close contact and assure you that they haven't gotten sick or fallen down the cellar stairs. But the calls cannot guarantee that a frail person will remain well.

Long-distance parent care means financial burdens, beginning with the phone calls themselves. In addition, you may find yourself making frequent expensive plane trips back and forth between your parents' city and your own, only to have problems arise the very day you get back home.

Create a network of helpers   Social workers advise long-distance caregivers to set up a local network of responsible people to act as surrogates, or stand-ins, to keep tabs on elderly parents. The local contacts need not be relatives or even close friends; a neighbor who spends a lot of time at home may be willing to look in every day on an older person.

It's vital, however, that your stand-ins be trustworthy enough to be given a key to your parents' house or apartment. You might ask them to make a daily phone call or simply to be available for emergency phone calls.

Expect "personnel" problems if outside nurses, home health aides, or homemakers have to be hired, especially when these workers must shop, cook, clean, do laundry, and handle money. Naturally, you will want to maintain regular telephone contact both with your parents and with the workers, checking for complaints or gripes on either side. Ask your stand-in caregiver to visit occasionally, so you can get an objective impression of your parent's condition and the employee's performance and attitude.

CASE MANAGEMENT

You may be better able to stay on top of things through case management workers. Case management is a coordinated approach to health care, aimed at finding solutions to the full range of a patient's problems, be they physical, social, or psychological. The case management approach also aims at keeping the patient, family, and health workers informed about the entire treatment process.

Case managers begin their work by assessing a patient's needs and targeting the resources available to help, depending on the person's financial situation. Workers may then arrange for the service directly, in some cases hiring the staff and monitoring the care.

Non-profit case management   Case management services have been available traditionally through a variety of social welfare organizations, including some non-profit social service agencies, nursing homes, home health-care services, and the Area Agencies on Aging. These agencies may charge for their services, but most have a sliding scale or free services for the older people of low income.

Private Case Managment Agencies   In recent years, a number of private case management agencies have been established by experienced social workers who offer their services for a fee. Most are in large metropolitan areas.

"What we do ranges from bringing a vast array of services into the home and visiting with tender loving care all the way through to finding the right nursing home," said Bernice Shepard, head of Shepard Personal Services in New York City. "But we set out with our service to help elderly people function to the maximum extent possible at home."

These agencies are usually very effective, but they may carry a high price tag. Most work on a part-time basis with rates averaging $50–75 an hour. The number of hours may total six or more for the first several months, including an initial assessment lasting perhaps three or four hours. Continued monitoring and supervision might amount to four to five hours a month.

In designing a plan of care for your parent, the agency would discuss the family situation with you or another family delegate and then visit your mother or father at home or just before discharge from the hospital. The social workers try to develop a close, friendly relationship with the older person. If plans call for hiring aides or nurses, the case managers might locate a range of good candidates and then leave the interviewing, screening, and selection process to your parents or you.

In cases where the older person is confused, the agency may handle all finances, write checks, pay bills, and initiate more complicated financial planning should nursing home placement become necessary. Most case management firms prefer that the elderly person or the family do the formal hiring and handle the payroll, however.

Not every older person needs full case management. A one-time-only consultation may provide all the guidance needed to find a particular service—a once-a-week companion for a badly depressed older man or a lunch and activities program for a nervous but still communicative Alzheimer's victim, for example. Some non-profit agencies will make in-home assessments free, so that you can determine exactly what services your parents need, possibly without entering into long-term case management.

For those who can afford it, for-profit social work agencies can be invaluable, especially for long-distance caregivers. It's important to remember, however, that the field is a new one and is so far unregulated. Ask for a schedule of fees in advance, and be sure the social workers running the agency are certified or licensed. Ask for references, and call to chat with several families that have used the service.

Should Your Parent Live in Your Family's Home?

Deciding whether your ailing parent should come to live with you and your family can be one of the most difficult decisions you will face. This traditional use of the extended family may seem like the only solution to your mother or father's health-care, housing, and financial problems, especially because there will be no massive outlay of cash such as a nursing home requires. And even more important, your parents will be living with the people they love most.

"A few years ago, Mom broke her leg and couldn't take care of herself alone, so we brought her to our house," said a 44-year-old Kentucky woman with three children. She and her husband decided to convert the family dining room into a bedroom, since it was the only place a hospital bed would fit.

"My sister criticized me the whole time. She said we were driving our teenage kids out of the house. That was unfair. The kids got to know her for the first time. And being downstairs, Mom was in the thick of things, which she enjoyed. After a few months, she was able to go back to her own apartment."

This option may work out well for you and your family. Then again, it may not. If your parents move in with you, both your life and theirs will change. No matter how good your past relationship has been, you may feel like a child in your own home.

Think seriously about the options and your own capabilities before making a decision. Take your time, and be realistic. Some people just do not have the physical or emotional resources to share their home with aging parents. In deciding what to do, consider these factors:

Design and Space Your home's design may not be appropriate for an older person. A two-story house could mean a daily struggle for an arthritis victim, and your father or mother could become virtually bedfast if your only bathroom is on the second floor.

Privacy is another key question when two families live in the same house. You'll probably get along best if there's a spare bedroom and/or bathroom for your parents' exclusive use. And the adjustment may be easiest if your mom and dad can come with their own bed and favorite easy chair and can decorate their room with treasured pictures and knick-knacks.

If space is short, older people may have to share a bedroom with a child or grandchild. This can be fine as long as both individuals respect each other and are healthy, but problems can arise if the older person's condition begins to deteriorate.

An elderly New York man with Alzheimer's Disease lived with his son's family and shared a bedroom with a grandson. Eventually the grandfather had to be placed in a nursing home, according to the supervising social worker, after "the child sharing the room began developing various symptoms of illness." Once the little boy had his room to himself again, the symptoms disappeared.

When older parents occupy a communal area, like the living or dining room, remember to take special pains to preserve the private life of the younger family. This can be done by setting aside a specific time or a substitute living area for activities you enjoy doing together.

Who Will Pay Expenses?   Be sure you can afford to have your mother or father live with you. Calculate your parents' living expenses as realistically as possible. How much can they contribute? How much help can your brothers and sisters provide? How much can you afford to spend on the home improvements or new furniture that may be needed? Who will pay doctor and medical bills not covered by Medicare?

Discuss the situation openly with your brothers and sisters—and your parents, if possible. Be realistic.

Can you reasonably provide the needed care?   Your parents may be self-sufficient when they arrive, except for minimal aid in dressing and walking up and down stairs, for example. You may have plenty of time and energy to help out.

In case of a serious illness, the degree of disability may increase sharply. You simply may not have the strength to lift an overweight mother in and out of bed or to bathe your father and get him to the toilet. If both you and your husband or wife hold jobs, you will have to figure out how to put lunch on the table and get your parents to doctors' appointments.

There's no way to predict your parents' future needs, of course, but remember that lay people can rarely provide round-the-clock care. If you feel your father or mother may need this level of attention within a year or two, take it into consideration as you decide what to do now. Consult a doctor for advice.

Period of Adjustment   Caregivers often expect a rocky period of adjustment for themselves and their families as they begin sharing their home with an older relative. But many forget that older people may also suffer from the change, especially when the parents have taken pride in not wanting to be a burden.

Moving out of a house or apartment of one's own may be the dramatic first step in the gradual erosion of an older parent's personal autonomy, so it's not surprising that this can cause irritability, homesickness, or depression.

Your Need for Respite   Any caregiver needs rest and relief from the responsibilities for a frail parent, but the son or daughter who shares a home with an elderly person must guard his or her privacy, if only to prevent burn-out.

Open Communication   Talking things through with your parents may smoothe some of the wrinkles in your intergenerational living situation, though a certain amount of discomfort is almost inevitable. If the stress becomes severe, you may want to consult your doctor, a therapist, or your minister, priest, or rabbi. If you feel from the outset that having your parents live in your home would invite disaster, don't let guilt or the thought of what others will think deter you from searching for another alternative.

ADULT DAY CARE

Within weeks after her husband's death, Adelaide Newman had a stroke that left her partly paralyzed on her right side. She was able to live alone and fix her own meals, but she gradually became isolated in her third-floor walk-up apartment in New York City. Her doctor recommended adult day care.

"This is my family now," said Mrs. Newman, as she sat and chatted with other clients at a day center in upper Manhattan. "I've been a member for six years. I started coming two days a week, but I'm up to five days now. The van picks me up each morning and takes me home. Without this, I'd be so lonely."

On a typical day at the center, Mrs. Newman and the other participants (an average of about a dozen daily) may work on a crafts project in the morning, eat the same lunch menu served at a nearby senior citizens' center, and watch a recent film on videocassette in the afternoon. Participants can also make appointments to have their hair done by a beauty-school student or to see a podiatrist for foot problems. Occasionally, they take field trips to the theater or a shopping mall in New Jersey.

"In a way, though, the best thing about the day center is the socializing," said Gerry Porter, Mrs. Newman's married daughter who lives in California. "After Father died, Ma really had no one to talk to, and that was terrible for her. After all, she'd been active and worked all her life. She's made friends at the center, and if she can't attend for a day or two, someone calls—either the director or one of the other participants. If a problem comes up, the director calls me."

Adult day-care centers provide daytime group programs for physically or mentally impaired elderly people who live in the community—alone or with their families. There are about 1,000 adult day-care programs nationwide, and virtually all supply door-to-door transportation for participants, a nutritious lunch, health screening, counseling, and leisure time activities.

The day programs can be a tremendous asset for your mother and father if they live alone but are isolated because of their health problems. If your parent requires a lot of care and lives with you (or with a healthier spouse), a day program can provide some needed hours of free time to go out to work or just relax. Perhaps most important, such a program can help your frail parent stay in the community and out of a nursing home.

"Some of the families report dramatic personality changes after their parents begin coming," said Susan Holmes, director of the Parkview Center Adult Day Care Program in Johnstown, Pennsylvania. "They say their mother or father is not as reclusive. For some of these frail elderly, just going out of the house is a big stride."

Each center has its own personality, depending on its history and the age and condition of the people it serves, but there are two general types—medically-oriented programs, usually based in a hospital or nursing home, and social-recreational community programs like the one attended by Mrs. Newman.

Medically-Based Day Care

Geriatric Day Care, a medically-based program, occupies a second-floor wing at the Jewish Home and Hospital for Aged, a New York nursing home. Each day, about 40 older people, many in wheelchairs, spend five hours at the center using one of the home's occupational therapy rooms as a main activity area.

"I never knew how to do any handwork before, but I've been coming here for 12 years now," said an older, gray-haired woman with arthritis who wore one of her own creations—a hand-knitted pink and blue vest—as she worked on her current project, a brown and gold hooked rug. Chatting with her at a table in the occupational therapy room were three other women engaged in knitting, crocheting, and needlepoint.

The daily routine begins with an early morning phone call from a van driver to arrange a specific pick-up time around 9 a.m. for each participant scheduled to attend that day. After arrival, activities depend on the participants' tastes and their individual care plans. Choices range from an appointment with a nurse to occupational and physical therapy, group discussions on poetry and current events, or classes in exercise, music, or dancing. Participants are not required to join in, however, and some prefer to spend an hour or more chatting over a cup of coffee or just sitting.

Lunch is served in a special, airy dining room with white tables and wicker chairs. The schedule continues after lunch until the vans leave at about 2 p.m. "We also have a Sunday program for about 12 to 15 of the more able people," said Susan Tye, day-care director. "We start with a group meeting, then have lunch, bingo, and sometimes a trip. These people feel they're sort of special."

As a medically oriented center, Jewish Home and Hospital's day care has two nurses on staff to see participants with health problems. The nurses also keep in touch with participants' own doctors, notifying them about any sudden health problems and, in some cases, recommending that the physician make a change in medication, if needed.

The three staff social workers lead activities and are available for counseling, but participants rarely request formal psychotherapy. "Most of the social work is done on an informal basis," said Tye. "Monday is typically the worst day, after they spend a weekend alone in their apartments. Often when the drivers call, people will say they don't feel well enough to attend. We call them back, and it's up to the staff to motivate them to come in here where they'll be taken care of."

Community-Based Day Care

Often sponsored by an Area Agency on Aging or some other social-service organization, the community day-care programs are usually held in an informal setting such as a church or senior center. Like the medically based centers, these programs generally have social workers, nurses, and aides on staff to present a full program of activities. But as free-standing centers, they may not be able to offer rehabilitation therapies or nursing attention on a daily basis.

The Parkview Center in Johnstown, Pennsylvania, is located in a single, bright room on the second floor of a downtown office building. Of the dozen elderly patients, about five attend each day for a maximum of 8½ hours, paying from $3 to $21 a day depending on their financial situation.

The center provides mini-bus transportation and lunches, which are prepared at the local senior citizens center. A staff nurse takes blood pressure daily and also tracks other health problems. "We gear the program individually," said director Susan Holmes. "We have arts and crafts, occasional films, and a discussion period for current events. We don't encourage watching TV, but we do watch the noon news."

Community day-care programs generally offer warm meals, arts and crafts, and lectures in addition to a staff that can monitor health.

In addition, the center arranges for manicures by beauty school students and "visiting-pet days" through the local Humane Society. It also sponsors field trips to museums and to restaurants for special lunches out. "There's a constant turnover of participants," said Holmes. "Some come every day, but others come Wednesdays and Fridays only or just one afternoon a week."

Cost

Probably the main reason that adult day programs aren't used more (and that there aren't more of them) is the high cost and the lack of insurance coverage. Day care is not covered by Medicare (except for whatever part of the program qualifies as outpatient physical, speech, or occupational therapy). Medicaid coverage is available only in New York State and only then for certified, medically based programs, like the one at the Jewish Home and Hospital. Virtually no Medigap or long-term care insurance policies cover day care.

Adult day-care programs cost an average of $21–25 a day, according to the National Institute on Adult Daycare, but some centers, like the one at the Jewish Home and Hospital, charge as much as $50 daily. Many families could not afford to pay so high a tab privately, especially when parents need to attend five days a week.

Many community-based programs charge on a sliding scale for those in financial need, however. And other centers find funding sources that permit them to set very modest fees. The ARC (Action for the Retired Community) day center, a community-based program in the Washington Heights area of New York City, for example, charges 50 cents a day for lunch and $1 for round-trip transportation.

Day Care and Confused Elderly

Most adult day-care programs accept elderly people with mental disabilities like Alzheimer's Disease, especially in the early stages of the ailment. "A large percentage of our people are Alzheimer's patients, though we take anyone with a disability," said Bob Pangburn, executive director of Sun City Area Interfaith Service, a volunteer-staffed social service agency in the Sun City area of Arizona that runs four adult day-care centers with a total of 200 participants.

In addition, day programs specifically for Alzheimer patients and other seriously disoriented people are run by the Alzheimer's Disease and Related Disorders Association. Such programs require enough staff to give individual attention and make sure patients don't harm themselves or wander away from the day-care area.

Day-care supervisors say their mentally alert participants sometimes offer special help to confused counterparts, though the two groups may have little in common. At the ARC Center, for example, the capable members may "chat with the Alzheimer's people, help them cut up their food, or pay for them if they didn't bring their money," said Ingrid Rosas, the former center director.

Federally funded programs may not discriminate against disabled people, including those with Alzheimer's Disease, but day-care administrators say their centers might not be able to take care of severely disoriented people.

"If someone were very violent, we might not be able to accept them, since it would be very upsetting to other participants who might be struggling to stay in control themselves," said Susan Tye of the Jewish Home and Hospital program. "But if we got a referral like that, we would probably ask the family to have the person's medications re-evaluated by the doctor. We don't want them to be over-medicated, but if the medication helped, we would reconsider."

What to Look For

Even for the confused elderly, day care should be more than a sitter service. If you are considering adult day care for your parent, visit the center or centers in your area, taking your mother or father along, if possible. Talk to the staff and discuss your parent's needs. Spend as much time as possible watching how the center operates and how participants respond. Consider the following areas:

Physical setting   Make sure the center is clean, cheerful, well lighted, and free of hazards. Is there an elevator or ramp for wheelchair access? Are bathrooms convenient and wheelchair-accessible? Are rest areas available?

Staffing   Be sure the center has enough staff to care for the clients. Most good centers have social workers, nurses, recreation aides, drivers, and volunteers. Do staff members interact with participants and encourage them to take part in activities? Are they enthusiastic and capable? Are aides or other workers available when participants need help with eating or getting to the bathroom.

Assessment and plan of care   Every program participant should have an individual plan of care, developed after an assessment that usually includes a home visit. Check to see that your parent will receive this kind of personal attention. How often is a participant's progress reviewed?

Program   Find out what activities the center offers. Ask to see a daily schedule, and, if possible, attend some of the programs. Are activities varied? Are they suited to your parent's abilities? Are staff members skilled at leading them? What happens if your mother or father doesn't want to participate? Are field trips open to everyone, regardless of disability?

Coordination with other community services   The day-care staff should give families help in finding other community services that could help them. In some but not all cases, the center's director may act as a case manager, arranging for visiting nurses, home-care workers, or Medicaid eligibility and keeping in touch with you if you live far away from your parents.

Emergency services   Centers should have written agreements with families on what to do in a health emergency. Does at least one person on staff know how to administer first aid and cardiopulmonary resuscitation (CPR)? Will the center phone you and the doctor in case your parent has to be taken to the hospital unexpectedly?

Termination   Families should expect to get no less than two weeks' notice that participants will no longer be cared for by the program for any reason except an unexpected health problem. Find out what circumstances could lead to termination or suspension.

Patient rights   The National Institute on Adult Daycare stresses the rights of day-care participants to be treated as adults, with respect and dignity. The NIAD Statement of Rights emphasize both the importance of activities that promote growth and awareness and the right to decide not to participate in a given activity.

For Further Information

To find a day-care program near you, call your local Area Agency on Aging, the state Adult Day Care Association, or contact

National Institute on Adult Daycare
600 Maryland Ave., S.W.
West Wing 100
Washington, D.C. 20024
(202) 479-1200

CHAPTER VIII

Home Health Care

Preparing the Home • Telephone Reassurance • Emergency Communications Systems • Medicare's Home Health Program • Personal Care at Home • Hiring Home-Care Workers • 24-Hour Care

The outlook wasn't so good when 72-year-old widow Thelma Chandler came home from the hospital after a slight stroke. Her movement was affected on the left side and even though she could talk, she seemed depressed. Miles Lambert, Thelma's doctor, recommended a nursing home in her Iowa hometown, at least until she could walk by herself. But her two daughters felt sure that being in the house she loved so much would lift Thelma's spirits.

"We rearranged her bedroom, bringing in the TV, moving her bed as close to the bathroom as possible, and getting rid of throw rugs she could trip over," said Linda Chandler, who had taken a leave from her job as a TV producer in Boston. "We wanted to get her out of bed and dressed every day, but we had no experience with nursing and weren't sure just what to do."

Dr. Lambert told Linda that he had scheduled a visit by a nurse and a physical therapist from a Medicare-certified home health agency, and the day after Mrs. Chandler got home, the nurse, Hannah Babcock, called to set up a convenient time. "I want to examine your mother to see how we can help her," the nurse said. In her assessment, she recommended that a Medicare-funded aide make visits three times a week, that a physical therapist visit regularly, and that a wheelchair (80% Medicare-covered) be rented for a few weeks. Dr. Lambert agreed, writing out a home health plan for Medicare that included those factors.

After the interview, therapist Joe Sybark got Mrs. Chandler on her feet and ran her through some simple exercises to keep her muscles flexible. The therapist gave Linda a list of the exercises and told her to keep her mother as active as possible.

"Nothing seemed to interest her at first, and we felt so incompetent," said Cheryl Ogilsby, Linda's married sister and a Chicago bank officer. "The home health aide was very helpful, though, and answered all our questions. After about a week—it seemed like a miracle at the time—Mother started waking up a little stronger each morning. She got her appetite back and seemed eager to get on her feet—mostly to please Joe Sybark, we thought."

In a few weeks, their mother was sleeping through the night. She was able to walk, and the physical therapy ended. Once her physical symptoms improved, the home health aide stopped coming as well, though Thelma still needed help with bathing and going downstairs. But she was clearly on the mend. She began watching her favorite TV shows again and got irritated if the evening paper wasn't delivered on time.

After a month, Linda's boss called and asked when she would be back to work. Cheryl's husband, Charlie, came to town that weekend so the family could decide what to do.

"Mother was much better, but she really couldn't take care of cooking and cleaning. She needed someone to come in every day, and amazingly enough, she admitted it," said Cheryl. "We heard about a nurse's aide who had taken care of one of Mother's friends, and Mother liked her as much as we did."

"We arranged for her to work from 9 to 5 each day at minimum wage. Of course, Medicare covered none of this, but Mother had an insurance policy that covered home care at $25 a day. The rest came from Mother's savings and from us."

Thelma's best friend, Roz Schwartz, said she would drop in and phone often. She also offered to get the groceries when she did her own weekly shopping. The aide had a friend who would work weekends, and Cheryl promised to visit twice a month to take care of details and pay bills, at least for a while.

The main worry was leaving Thelma alone at night. She had a bedside telephone, but what if she got sick and couldn't dial? The family finally accepted the suggestion of a trusted, next-door neighbor that a doorbell-style buzzer be installed right next to Thelma's bed to connect the two homes.

With the home-care arrangement in place, Thelma has made a remarkable recovery over the past two years. She can now walk up and down the stairs and cook on her own, so she let the aide go. She now relies on another woman, a homemaker, to come in three times a week for a few hours to help with bathing and shampoos, do the cleaning, and drive her to the doctor, the supermarket, and to Roz's house for an occasional bridge game.

The buzzer was only used once—when Thelma thought she heard a prowler. "But I like to know it's there," she mused recently, "since it represents the kindness people have shown me."

Not all home-care situations work out as well as this, but even so, most older people want to remain in their own homes as long as possible, especially when their health begins to deteriorate. Their preference makes sense. First of all, staying at home means maintaining the social ties with neighbors and friends that can enhance well-being. Being surrounded with familiar belongings can add to the sense of contentment.

Hospital care may be necessary in times of severe illness, but today's hospitals are not a realistic long-term care option with Medicare's emphasis on shorter stays. Thanks to recent advances, many high-tech medical procedures can be performed at home enabling the sick to get intravenous feedings, kidney dialysis, or oxygen therapy, for example, in their living room easy chairs.

The Cost of Home Care

Most home care for the elderly is provided by family and friends. If you or another relative has the time and ability to provide this care, it may involve little by way of a cash investment. But you may not have the time—or live close enough—to help.

Medicare covers very little of the expense, since it pays only for skilled nursing and therapy on an intermittent basis when a patient's condition is acute. Medicaid can provide a wider range of home services, including custodial care, but the extent of coverage is limited by your parents' eligibility and by what state they live in.

Hiring nurses and other home-care workers on your own can be extremely expensive. But you may be determined to find a way to make home-care work to avoid placing your parents in a nursing home.

Who Is Home Care For?

Not every older person is suited to long-term home care. First of all, your parents must have a disability or condition that can be handled at home. Second, they must have a home to go to where care can be given. As we have observed earlier, some homes—especially those with two floors—aren't easy to adapt for the disabled. And financial problems may force elderly people to give up their homes after a long stay in a hospital or nursing home.

In addition, you or some other responsible person must be available to oversee the situation, even if nurses and aides are hired to provide the care directly. Without a family caregiver on hand, a frail elderly person may be afraid to complain about inadequate service. In cases like these, long-distance caregivers are at a disadvantage unless they have local stand-ins.

PREPARING THE HOME

When the need for home care arises, or even before then, you can help your parents equip their home so they'll stay safe and active as long as possible. Surroundings become increasingly important with age. Disabilities may force your mother or father to give up outside activities and spend more time in one room and one favorite armchair. If that chair is uncomfortable or hard to get out of, your parents will probably become more inactive—and seem far older—than necessary.

Most of the following ideas are simple and inexpensive, but some—like ramps, wheelchairs, or an emergency response system—may require sizable investments. You and your parents will probably have to pay for any remodeling or costly gadgets yourselves, unless durable medical equipment covered by Medicare is involved. In that case, your parents' doctor and Medicare will have to agree. You may be surprised to find that physicians sometimes advise against a wheelchair and other convenience items, if they feel it will decrease activity.

Better Seating

Age often brings changes in posture and body alignment, so be sure your parents have chairs that match their own body contours. Older people are usually most comfortable in chairs just high enough to support their feet on the ground. A chair that's too low may be difficult to get out of. One that's too high may result in numbness, coldness, and fluid build-up in the feet. If this becomes a problem, an angled footstool can help.

Wing-backed easy chairs with good support are usually best for conversation, while straight-backed wooden chairs probably work best for sitting at a table or desk. Small pillows or pillow inserts (available from medical supply houses listed at the back of this section) can improve a chair's fit.

Recliner chairs and lazy boy rockers are not always recommended for older people because they are hard to reposition and may place pressure on a small area of the buttocks. Geriatric wheelchairs with small-diameter wheels and a tray table may also be inappropriate, though they are often used in nursing homes and hospitals. Seating specialists say "geri-chairs" are difficult to maneuver, too confining, and poorly supported. Conventional wheelchairs work better, if they fit the patient.

If your parents have trouble getting up from a sitting position, they may profit from a seat-lift chair with a built-in motor that pushes users to their feet at the flick of a switch. These chairs, which are expensive ($750–$1,500), may be financed 80% by Medicare. Check with the doctor.

Capitalizing on Physical Abilities

Your parents may have trouble moving around because of arthritis or some other physical problem. Some of the following home improvements may keep them as active as possible:

Grab bars and non-slip surfaces in the bathroom   Grab bars for the bathroom and bathtub can be bought for about $20 and are easily installed. Safety mats and non-skid decals for the tub can be purchased in most hardware stores. Special support bars are available for the toilet itself to help people with trouble getting up from a sitting position.

Adjust furniture heights   Rather than buying an expensive hospital bed, help your parents decide how high their own bed should be for ease in getting in and out. Adjust the height with bricks, wood blocks, or special leg extenders, and then provide extra pillows for support in sitting. The same can be done with easy chairs. Elevated toilet seats and safety benches for shower or tub can also be purchased.

Customize kitchen and bathroom cupboards   Suggest that your parents rearrange cupboards so that often-used foods, utensils, and cleaning supplies are at the front within easy reach. Help shift heavy dishes or pots to more-convenient lower shelves.

Maximize mobility   If your parents' hands are weakened by arthritis, help them to utilize all the manual dexterity they retain by replacing doorknobs and faucets with lever handles. Touch-on lamps can be helpful, and so can tools, cutlery, and pens designed to be easy to hold and grasp. Zipper pulls can help with hard-to-reach back zippers, and special hooks can be purchased inexpensively to make buttoning a shirt or coat easier.

A little red wagon   Be creative in thinking about what common household objects can be pressed into service. A child's wagon with rubber wheels can be used to move heavy objects around the house. An office chair on rollers can help your mother or father move from room to room on days of unusual stiffness. Some older people resist using a walker on the street because it makes them look "handicapped." If your parents say this, remind them that a walker can still be used for support in the more private environment of their home.

Ramps   Ramps are necessary for wheelchair access, but they can be hazardous for people with poor posture or walking problems. A handrail can allow an unsteady older person to go down a ramp sidewards or to hold on with both hands.

Better Vision

Vision experts say older people need about three times as much light as younger people do to see clearly and avoid falls. Ironically, you may find that your parents try to save money or conserve energy by turning on as few lights as possible. The following lighting tips may help:

Use high wattage bulbs   Urge your parents not to stint when their safety is at stake. Encourage them to buy high-wattage bulbs, especially for reading and for shadowy staircases and hallways.

Incandescent vs. fluorescent lights   The incandescent light produced by ordinary bulbs casts a directional beam with more contrast than a fluorescent tube. Incandescent bulbs can produce glare, however, especially when they are placed overhead or are uncovered. Fluorescent tubes are best for general room lighting while incandescent bulbs work well for reading or desk work.

Rheostat controls   If electric bills are a real concern, replace wall and lamp switches with rheostat controls so that lights can be turned on at whatever level is needed. That way, your parents will have to pay only for as much light as they need.

Light placement   Lights should be placed where they're needed most, especially above staircase landings to illuminate the tops of steps. The edges of steps and handrails can be marked with two-inch wide reflecting tape to prevent slips.

Avoid glare   Glare can come from sunlight, bare bulbs, or ill-positioned lamps. It can cause vision problems and decrease attention span. Overhead lights can cause glare indoors, if light bounces off shiny floors or work surfaces. To remedy this, move the light or cover shiny surfaces with a carpet or work mat. Be sure every lamp has a good shade.

Venetian blinds and window shades can help with glare from the sun. Sunglasses and hats may aid visibility outdoors. Some older people avoid driving at night because of glare.

Enlarge labels and signs Books and kitchen cannisters with big print can help older people remain independent. Large-print numbers can be fitted onto conventional telephones, and special, large-print phones can also be purchased.

Contrasts Lenses yellow as people age, and that makes it hard to distinguish objects of similar color placed side by side. To compensate, raise the lighting level and use contrast to advantage, placing light objects on dark backgrounds and vice versa. Urge your parents to store light-colored dishes in cupboards with a dark interior. Wrap dark tape around handles on a white cabinet door.

Suggest your father avoid socks of different but similar colors, so there's no need for matching. Toss out old dim typewriter ribbons. In the medicine cabinet, store pills of similar sizes and shapes in distinctly different containers and place them on different shelves.

Help with Hearing

Impaired hearing troubles about 25% of Americans between 65 and 74 and 39% of those 75 and over. Men seem to suffer more than women. The two main hearing problems of the elderly are in not being able to hear high-pitched tones and not being able to distinguish voices against background noise. These hints may help:

Hearing Aids Most people with hearing problems have tried hearing aids, which amplify the vibrations reaching the inner ear. Many have stopped wearing the aids, however, because the devices made all sounds too loud—including background noise. Over the last 10 years, hearing aids have been improved and have been made smaller and lighter, so older people who rejected them may wish to consult their doctors again. Special hearing aids and amplification devices for telephones have also been improved.

Keep conversational seating separate If your parents have hearing problems, urge them to turn off the television or radio when having a conversation. If space permits, move the TV away from the telephone bench. If your parents are hard of hearing, get as close as possible when talking to them.

Have noisy equipment repaired A noisy furnace or refrigerator can make a hearing problem worse by distracting an older person from an ongoing conversation. So can a buzzing light or a squeaky fan.

Use fabric to absorb background noise A room with many shiny surfaces, like those in institutional settings, may cause "acoustical glare." Drapes, carpeting, and other soft coverings can help muffle background noise.

Public address systems Encourage speakers who make presentations to older people to use well-maintained public address systems. Otherwise it's difficult for an older group to participate in a public meeting.

Equipment Suppliers

Your local drug store or medical equipment supplier may stock products that can help your parents cope at home. In addition, the following mail-order companies sell aids for daily living:

National Rehabilitation Information Center
Catholic University of America
4407 Eighth St., N.E.
Washington, D.C. 20017
(800) 346-2742 (toll-free, nationwide)

Comfortably Yours
Aids for Easier Living
53 W. Hunter Ave.
Maywood, NJ 07670
(201) 368-0400

Fashion-Able for Better Living
5 Crescent Ave., Box S
Rocky Hill, NJ 08553
(609) 921-2563

Ways & Means
28001 Citrin Drive
Romulus, MI 48174
(313) 946-5030

Vis-Aids Inc.
86–30 102nd St.
Richmond Hill, NY 11418
(718) 847-4734

Independent Living Aids
11 Commercial Court
Plainville, NY 11803
(516) 681-8288

Maddak Inc.
Pequannock, NH 07440
(201) 694-0500

TELEPHONE REASSURANCE

Unfortunately, you can't guarantee that your parents will get help immediately in case of emergency if they live alone. But their ability to remain in their home may depend on their being confident that help can be summoned promptly. The first—and most obvious—emergency aid is the telephone. See that a list of emergency numbers in large, legible figures is placed beside each telephone in the house. This can help both your parents and anyone else visiting the house.

The list should include the local police and fire departments, an ambulance service (if there is no central 911 number in your area), personal physicians, the hospital they prefer, and a responsible neighbor or nearby relative. Include your own number.

Telephone reassurance systems—either on a casual or formal basis—are another way of keeping in touch. If you don't live too far away, a daily phone call at a mutually arranged time may reassure both you and your parents of each other's well-being. Some older people establish informal reassurance networks with friends who promise to check in with them daily. Your parents may have already given these friends a house key and emergency numbers for relatives or doctors, for use in case there's no answer.

Some churches and senior citizen organizations have established formal telephone reassurance programs, in which volunteers, many of them elderly themselves, agree to check in with homebound people daily. In some towns, commercial telephone answering services also provide the service for a nominal monthly fee. If the older person does not answer, the service will notify the police, a neighbor, or relative to go to the home to check in person.

Some elderly people may object to the idea of "daily surveillance," but others may appreciate a call, even from a friendly outsider. A skillful volunteer with time to explore mutual interests can make such a conversation more relaxed.

EMERGENCY COMMUNICATIONS SYSTEMS

Your parents may be afraid they won't be able to get to the phone when they need help. If so, you may want to subscribe to an emergency response system. These sophisticated communications set-ups allow older people to push a button on a portable transmitter to trigger automatic dialing of one or more emergency numbers.

Most of these programs are expensive, and they are not covered by Medicare, Medicaid, or most private insurance. Even so, they may be invaluable aids for your parents, particularly after a hospital stay.

Lifeline   Based in Watertown, Massachusetts, Lifeline serves 80,000 subscribers across the country through the more than 1,700 local hospitals and nursing homes that serve as emergency response centers.

Subscribers wear a personal help button on their neck or wrist at all times while they are at home. If they need aid and are within several hundred feet of the home unit, they press the button, which signals a home console beside the telephone to dial the Lifeline emergency center.

When Lifeline gets the call, the staff phones the older person. If there is no answer, they call the friend or relative designated as the "responder," who has a key to the subscriber's home. When the responder arrives, he or she notifies the center as to what further help is needed. The center will call for an ambulance, if necessary. As an added precaution, the Lifeline home unit dials the emergency response center automatically if the telephone has not

Subscribers to Lifeline wear a personal help button around their neck or wrist at all times when they are home. (PHOTO COURTESY OF LIFELINE SYSTEMS INC., ONE ARSENAL MARKETPLACE, WATERTOWN, MA 02172)

been used within a 24-hour period, in case a subscriber collapses and can't press the button.

Lifeline charges vary from one local program to another, but a typical service charges $20–33 a month plus about $60 for installation. Equipment is usually leased. For further information, contact:

> Lifeline Systems Inc.
>   One Arsenal Marketplace
>   Watertown, MA 02172
>   (617) 923-4141
>   (800) 441-4014 (toll-free, within Massachusetts)
>   (800) 451-0525 (toll-free, outside Massachusetts)

Voice of Help, operated by American Medical Alert in Oceanside, New York, resembles Lifeline, except that it offers voice contact. The system served 2,000-plus subscribers nationwide in 1986 from a centralized switchboard.

With Voice of Help, clients get a water-resistant, three-ounce, portable activator the size of a quarter that is worn around the neck. To call in, they must push the two buttons on the activator, signaling a speaker console to dial the emergency number automatically.

Switchboard operators answer, addressing the client by name over the speaker phone. The company claims voices can be heard at a range of 75 feet or more, through at least two housing levels. If help is needed, operators consult a computerized file for the name of a relative or whatever emergency number the older person has listed. American Medical Alert then follows up, making sure help has arrived.

The system resets itself automatically after about three minutes, permitting speedy second calls. The set-up also connects to a smoke-alarm device. In case of power failures, the speaker console has a rechargable battery.

In 1986, Voice of Help cost about $99 for installation and $30 a month, including as many calls as necessary. For further information, contact:

American Medical Alert
3265 Lawson Blvd.
Oceanside, NY 11572
(516) 536-5850

The AT&T Emergency Call System can be purchased privately and programmed to dial any two emergency numbers—you, a neighbor, a doctor, or the police. It involves no central answering service.

The system includes a telephone console and a lightweight transmitter about two-by-five inches that can be carried in a pocket or around the neck. When the transmitter button is pushed within a range of about 200 feet of the console, the system will call the first emergency number and then the second if the first doesn't answer.

When the phone is answered, the console delivers the spoken message, "There is a medical emergency," gives the older person's address and phone number, and then adds, "Please respond." The person answering then signals the elderly individual that help is on the way by pushing a specific number on a touch tone phone. This activates the home console to say, "Message received."

The system costs $399. There is no charge for installation. It is available from a national network of AT&T dealers.

Other Emergency Programs

Two other programs supply information about your parents' medical history if emergency personnel arrive to find them unconscious or severely confused.

Medic Alert is an organization that supplies elderly or disabled people with a bracelet or necklace engraved with the wearer's medical condition. The medals also list Medic Alert's 24-hour telephone line and the user's identification number. Emergency squads can call collect and get access to computerized emergency medical records.

The emblems are available in stainless steel, silver, and gold plate for a one-time membership fee ($20–38 in 1986). Further information is available from:

> Medic Alert
> P.O. Box 1009
> Turlock, CA 95381-1009
> (209) 668-3333

In a few communities, another program, the Vial of Life, operates through local chapters of the American Red Cross or other service organizations. Information about an older person's medical condition, doctor, relative, and preferred hospital is written down and placed inside a small bottle, or "vial," available free through the program. On seeing a distinctive "Vial of Life" sticker on the front door, local emergency personnel would automatically look for the vial inside the refrigerator.

MEDICARE'S HOME HEALTH PROGRAM

Medicare pays for periodic visits by nurses, therapists, social workers, and home health aides and for medical equipment for acutely ill patients. The federal program is the largest public provider of home care for the elderly, but it cannot help your parents at all if they need personal or custodial care.

To qualify for Medicare's home health program, your mother and/or father must meet the following conditions:

1. They must be confined to their homes, though not necessarily bedridden. To be eligible, they must be so disabled that they need crutches, a cane, wheelchair, or another person to help them get around. They must be housebound, except for going for medical treatment, a dentist's appointment, or for a short drive.
2. A physician must judge your parents in need of home health care and must set up a home health plan for them.
3. Their condition must call for skilled nursing care, physical therapy, or speech therapy on a part-time, intermittent basis.
4. The personnel must be supplied through a Medicare-certified home health agency. Medicare will not pay for care by nurses, therapists, or aides who don't work for a certified agency, even if you know that they are fully qualified.

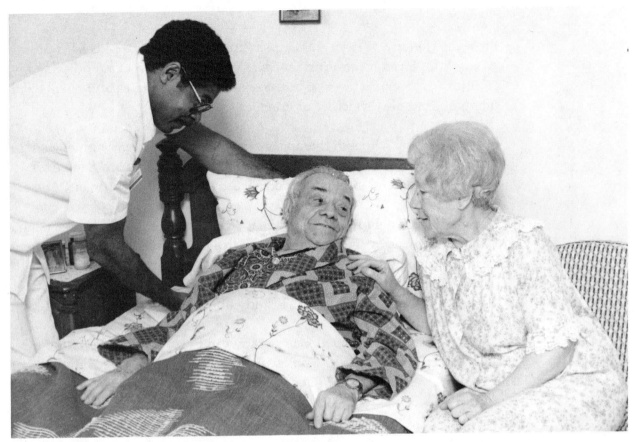

(PHOTO COURTESY OF QUALITY CARE INC.)

When all these conditions are met, either Part A hospital insurance or Part B medical insurance will cover 100% of the cost, except for the medical equipment which is covered 80%. This means your parents can get home care even if they aren't enrolled in both parts of the Medicare program.

Your parents do not need to file claims for any home health services they receive through Medicare. All claims are filed directly by the certified home health agency providing the nurses and therapists.

What Is Provided

If your parents qualify, the following services may be prescribed:

Part-Time Skilled Nursing Care Medicare's skilled nurses may be registered nurses (RNs), licensed practical nurses (LPNs), or licensed vocational nurses (LVNs). On their visits, they organize and supervise the home care program, administer drugs or injections, change dressings, and check to see that catheters, feeding tubes, and other medical equipment are functioning properly. Checking pulses or taking temperatures need not be performed by a skilled nurse.

Physical Therapy Physical therapists are trained and state-licensed professionals who focus on restoring physical movement to a person disabled by an injury or stroke. They use massage and exercise and also fit clients with the right kind of wheelchair or crutches.

Speech Therapy Speech therapists, speech pathologists, or audiologists are also state-licensed rehabilitation specialists. Their clients are people whose ability to speak and swallow is damaged by stroke, illness, or birth defect.

Occupational Therapy Occupational therapists focus on helping people with physical and/or mental disabilities live independently. OTs used to be associated mainly with art or music therapy, but today they concentrate more on suggesting practical activities that will help restore normal functioning. They also may do a quick study of a patient's home to find ways to circumvent disability.

Under Medicare, occupational therapy can begin only if one of the three qualifying treatment needs—skilled nursing, physical or speech therapy—is present as well. If OT is still needed after nursing or the other two therapies are discontinued, it can be extended and home health aides can also continue visiting.

Home Health Aides These aides can be the most important part of a home-care program, since they may visit your parents several days a week—but usually no more than one to three hours a day. They provide basic nursing tasks along with minimal personal care, and some agencies require them to have hospital or nursing home experience.

Basic nursing includes taking temperatures and pulse and respiration rates. Aides are not ordinarily allowed to give medications, though they may remind patients to take prescribed pills. Those with advanced training may take care of more complicated nursing tasks under the supervision of the skilled nurse.

As long as your parents need basic nursing care, aides may also help them with some personal activities, like getting out of bed or taking a bath. Homemaking duties, like cooking and light cleaning, are not covered, however. In any case, Medicare pays only for part-time care, so people who need daily help with activities of daily living will have to find assistance elsewhere.

Medical Social Services Social workers, trained to help families with financial or emotional problems, are covered only for "medical" social work under Medicare. As such, they usually make one visit to help fill out forms and try to direct families to other community resources that can help with the elderly person's medical problem.

Medical Supplies and Equipment   Medicare provides supplies prescribed by a doctor, including surgical dressings, splints, and casts (but not adhesive tape, antiseptics, or other common first-aid supplies). The program will reimburse 80% of the approved cost of durable medical equipment, including oxygen gear, wheelchairs, and home dialysis systems, when prescribed by the doctor.

The equipment may either be bought or rented from Medicare-certified equipment suppliers, depending on the cost and the judgment of the Medicare carrier.

What Isn't Covered

As mentioned earlier, Medicare never covers custodial care, either in a hospital or at home. That means, according to the 1986 Medicare handbook, that the home health program "does *not* cover general household services, meal preparation, shopping, assistance in bathing or dressing, or other home-care services furnished mainly to assist people in meeting personal, family, or domestic needs."

Medicare also does NOT cover:

full-time nursing care at home
drugs
home-delivered meals
homemaker services
blood transfusions at home

Medicare stops covering home health aides altogether when an elderly patient no longer needs skilled care for an acute condition. Administrators from the home health agency will probably notify you when coverage is ending, following guidelines supplied by Medicare.

Be Realistic About "Unlimited" Care

Over the past decade, Medicare has placed an increasing emphasis on home health care, at least in part because home visits are perceived as costing less than a hospital or nursing home. Some restrictions on the program have been eased. At one time, for example, no one could qualify for home care unless they had been hospitalized for at least three days beforehand. In 1981, Congress removed that condition.

As Medicare ushered in the prospective payment/DRG system and hospital stays were shortened, more home care was needed, and hundreds of home health agencies across the country set up shop and applied for certification in the hopes of meeting the need.

This may have given you and your parents unrealistic expectations about Medicare's home health program. No question about it, the coverage looks good, according to *Your Medicare Handbook.* For eligible patients, the handbook states, Medicare "can pay for an unlimited number of home health visits." While this claim is true in a way, it may come to seem misleading for several reasons.

First of all, Medicare offers its home health program in terms of *visits,* not hours of care, and these visits may not be sufficient to maintain a sick patient at home. "Even when nursing is ordered seven days a week, the nurse may only be there for a visit of an hour or an hour and a half," noted Martha Berman of the Visiting Nurse Service of New York City.

In addition, there are restrictions on the total number of home health visits, even for an acutely ill patient. Theoretically, the visits can be continued on an unlimited basis as long as a doctor determines home care is needed. In practice, the number of visits any one patient may receive and the number of hours per visit may be restricted by the government's interpretations of the Medicare law.

As consumers, your parents will not receive statements of these policy interpretations from Medicare. The home health agencies know the guidelines but may get caught in the middle, trying to provide adequate care but not knowing whether Medicare will agree with their appraisal of a case. If Medicare ultimately decides against reimbursement, the agency must absorb the loss.

"For example, we had a patient last year with breast cancer that had metasticized," said Kathy Rutkowsky, a supervisor for the Visiting Nurse Service's home-care program in Queens. "A bone was protruding; she couldn't turn over by herself; she wasn't getting proper nutrition, and she needed frequent blood work and urine tests."

The VNS provided nursing for 56 hours a week—at the time Medicare's theoretical home-care maximum—but Medicare okayed payment for only 20 hours. "We don't know beforehand what Medicare will pay for a specific case," Rutkowsky said.

This financial bind has led agencies to develop detailed assessment procedures to determine which patients they can afford to serve. "The agency might not want to provide nursing or a therapy to an individual patient, fearing the services wouldn't be covered," explained Robert Hoyer of the National Association for Home Care, which represents 3,000 home-care agencies nationwide.

If your parents need skilled nursing care and Medicare cuts off benefits to the home health agency, consider challenging the decision through the regular Medicare appeals process for either Part A or Part B.

Other Funding

Limited funding for skilled nursing care at home may also be available through Medicare-supplementary policies, long-term care insurance, or group health plans. Urge your parents to check the language in their policies.

PERSONAL CARE AT HOME

Seeing your parents on the road to recovery after a serious illness is good news. Unfortunately, your relief may be offset by the loss of Medicare coverage for home care. In many cases, this outcome is both tragic and ironic, since personal-care workers can be hired at less expense than skilled nurses and may be even more crucial to an older person's long-term survival.

"I was just getting back on my feet, feeling better about walking, when the nurse and the physical therapist stopped coming," said Ethel Wagner, 83, a Colorado widow with no children who had had a knee operation. "My neighbors have offered to help me with shopping, but my niece has to go back to Rochester now, and I really have to find someone to help me get in and out of the bathtub and do my laundry and cleaning at least for a while. I don't know how I can afford it."

Personal-Care Staffing

If you or another close relative live near your parents, you may be able to help them with personal care by inviting them to live at your home until they gain strength or by making frequent visits to help with bathing, cooking, or cleaning. Otherwise, you may have to find outside workers to step in.

You may feel that no one but a registered or licensed practical nurse can provide the quality of care you know your parents need. In fact, advanced nursing skills may not be required. The following kinds of workers specialize in personal care in the home:

Homemaker/home health aides Like Medicare-funded home health aides, these aides may do some basic nursing but they may spend as much time on personal care and homemaking as needed, since they don't have to follow Medicare guidelines. When you hire one, specify what your parents need—help with bathing, dressing, walking, shopping, or homemaking tasks like vacuuming, dusting, and cooking. Homemaker/home health aides don't usually do heavy housework, like scrubbing floors or washing down walls.

Chore Workers These workers do heavy cleaning, wash windows, and do other heavy household tasks. They may also be helpful when your parents need simple home repairs, like replacing a door lock or rewiring a lamp.

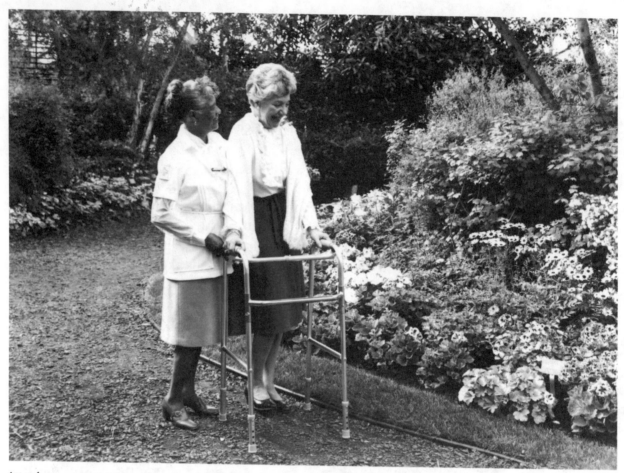

Attendants or companions act as friends to a lonely, older person, dropping by or phoning on a regular basis to chat or help with special problems. (PHOTOGRAPH PROVIDED BY UPJOHN HEALTHCARE SERVICES®, A WHOLLY-OWNED SUBSIDIARY OF THE UPJOHN COMPANY)

Attendants or companions Attendants or companions generally act as friends to a frail, lonely, older person, in some cases accompanying or driving them to doctor's appointments or for shopping. Churches and synagogues sometimes have volunteer programs that match older people with "friendly visitors" who can drop by or phone on a regular basis to chat or help with special problems.

Paying for Personal Care

Unfortunately, little financial help is available for elderly people in need of personal care at home, so you and your parents probably will have to pay for most services out of your own pockets. Benefits are sometimes available, however, under the following programs:

Private health insurance Home care has been added to many group and individual health insurance policies over the past few years. It is included in some of the new, long-term care, insurance policies as well.

Unfortunately, many of the same restrictions Medicare places on personal care exist in the private insurance industry. "There used to be a gap in home care in general," said Arlene Lilly of the Health Insurance Association of America, "but that's been closed. Now the gap is with custodial coverage."

Even so, check to see whether home care is covered on any group or individual health insurance policy your parents own.

Medigap policies   Few privately purchased Medicare-supplementary policies have covered home care since 1981 when Medicare eliminated yearly limits on the number of home visits permitted. Urge your parents to read their policies carefully to see what benefits may be allowed.

HMOs   Many HMO health insurance programs provide home care, but some do not offer personal or custodial care unless skilled care is also needed, as explained by Karen Hunt of the Group Health Association of America, which represents the nation's group HMO plans.

Social HMOs   Personal-care services that are purely custodial are usually provided through the still-experimental social HMOs, or S/HMOs. "The social HMOs are doing some very interesting things with home health care," said Hunt. "They're going beyond nursing care to homemaker services and the like to prevent institutionalization."

Medicaid   As the federal-state program that underwrites health care for the poor, Medicaid must provide some home health services to beneficiaries in all states. Personal care, not just skilled care, is covered and, in fact, about 75% or Medicaid's home health funds go for personal-care services.

As with other Medicaid programs, home-care benefits vary according to where your parents live. Only a few states have generous benefits, chief among them New York, where the Medicaid home-care program spent about $385 million in fiscal 1982. The next most ample, Massachusetts, New Jersey, and Georgia, together spent only 8% of New York's total.

In 1981, Congress decided to help the states beef up their home-care programs as a cheaper alternative to nursing homes and set up so-called "waiver programs" to help keep particular groups out of institutions. Most states participate, but the extent of benefits varies widely.

Your parents must be eligible for Medicaid, of course, in order to obtain home-care services under the program.

Older American Act Services   Keeping older people independent and out of institutions is a major goal of the Older Americans Act. As a result, each of the 660 Area Agencies on Aging offers such home-care services as home-delivered meals, personal care, homemaker and chore services, transportation programs, adult day care, and protective services. Other community-based programs, often coordinated through the AAAs, include friendly visitor services, telephone reassurance networks, and escort services.

No financial restrictions are imposed on these programs, though they are targeted at low-income people. Your parents may qualify for help even if they are not eligible for Medicaid. Unfortunately, services are limited in most parts of the country by a lack of funding.

For further information, call your parents' local Area Agency on Aging.

HIRING HOME-CARE WORKERS

Finding effective, reliable, home health aides and other workers to care for your parents is not always easy. What may be even harder is keeping them over the long-term. If you hire home workers through a Medicare-certified agency, you can have some assurance that workers have been screened for proper credentials and that they are adequately trained. Agencies have supervisors to oversee workers and handle a payroll.

If you hire independently, you will have to screen and supervise the workers yourself or find someone else to do so. You will be responsible for setting up a payroll procedure and for firing aides who don't work out. If you are willing to do this, however, you may find good care for your parents at a lower cost.

The Agencies

An estimated 12,000 agencies provide home health services in the United States today. Of that total, about 6,000 agencies are Medicare-certified. The field has grown rapidly over the past decade, both because of improved medical technology that can be used at home and because Medicare has been expanding the home-care program.

When your mother or father has been hospitalized and qualifies for Medicare-funded home care, the hospital social worker may suggest a specific agency and arrange for the first visit. You will probably be glad for the help, but you need not accept their recommendation, if you prefer another home-care company.

If you and your family decide on your own that your parents need home care, you should know what kinds of agencies there are.

Visiting Nurse Services (or Visiting Nurse Associations) were set up in many communities in the late 19th century so that people who could not afford to go to the hospital would get nursing care at home. Today, the nation's

About 12,000 agencies provide home health services today. Hiring home health aides and other workers is not always easy, but hiring through a Medicare-certified agency will ensure that workers have proper credentials. If you hire independently, you'll have to screen and supervise workers yourself, but you can find good care for your parents at a lower cost. (PHOTO COURTESY OF QUALITY CARE INC.)

500 Visiting Nurse agencies provide skilled nursing, social services, rehab, most therapies, and some chore services. Most are Medicare-certified.

Visiting Nurse Services are non-profit organizations sometimes affiliated with local United Way or Community Chest campaigns. If your parents don't qualify for government funding but can't pay the full price of home care, the Visiting Nurses sometimes offer a sliding scale of fees or, in emergency cases, foot the bill themselves.

If your community has a Visiting Nurse agency, it will be listed in the white pages of the phone book and probably also in the yellow pages, under Home Care or Nursing.

Non-Profit Social Service Agencies In some communities, home care is provided through non-profit social service agencies, like Catholic Charities, Lutheran Social Services, or the Jewish Association for Services for the Aged. Some of these agencies have home-care nurses and aides on staff, while others have staff supervisors but use personnel working for commercial agencies on a subcontract basis. Like the Visiting Nurses, many of these non-profit groups provide services on a sliding scale of charges.

Hospital-Based Home Health Agencies   Your parents' local hospital may operate its own home health agency. About 2,700 U.S. hospitals—more than one-third of the total—either offer home care now or plan to soon, according to the American Hospital Association. Of that number, more than half are Medicare-certified.

When your father or mother is discharged from a hospital, officials may suggest using that hospital's home health agency, but you have no obligation to choose it over another simply because your parent is a patient or the family physician has privileges there.

Hospital home-care agencies tend to specialize in the skilled care area—capitalizing on the institution's know-how in high-tech medicine and its experienced staff of nurses, therapists, and social workers.

One advantage of a hospital-based agency is that it usually has been surveyed by the Joint Commission on Accreditation of Hospitals if the hospital itself is JCAH-accredited (about four-fifths of the nation's 6,000 hospitals are).

For further information about hospital-based home-care agencies, contact

> American Hospital Association
>   Division of Ambulatory Care
>   840 N. Lake Shore Drive
>   Chicago, IL 60611
>   (312) 280-6216

Homemaker-Home Health Aide Services   About 5,000 homemaker-home health aide services exist nationwide, according to the National HomeCaring Council. Most are not Medicare-certified, because they provide mostly non-skilled, home support services, through home health aides, homemakers, and chore workers. Registered nurses are the supervisors.

Some homemaker-home health aide services are for-profit businesses, but many are attached to non-profit multiservice community organizations.

For information about these agencies, contact

> National HomeCaring Council
>   235 Park Avenue South
>   New York, NY 10003
>   (212) 674-4990

The Top National Home Health Chains   As home care has become big business, health-care companies and employment agencies have set up specialized home-care services with branches all over the country. Some but not all are Medicare-certified, so be sure to check on this if your parents qualify for Medicare-funded services.

Most large home-care corporations offer, at a minimum, skilled nursing, home health aide, homemaker, and companion services. Some also offer workers who will live in with your parents. Personnel policies vary, but most agencies require employees, including aides, to have experience and appropriate training. When considering an agency, ask what training is given newly hired aides and homemakers.

These commercial home health chains usually run credit checks on customers and send out bills weekly. Some accept payment by major credit card, delaying the need for you to pay for 30 days or more.

The five largest home health chains are the following:

Upjohn Health Care Services was founded in 1969 by Upjohn Company, the worldwide drug manufacturer. It now has about 300 offices and operates in most states.

> Upjohn Health Care Services
> 2605 East Kilgore Rd.
> Kalamazoo, MI 49002-1897
> (616) 342-7000

Medical Personnel Pool is owned by the tax-preparation firm H&R Block. Founded in 1966, MPP had 250 offices in 41 states in April 1986.

> Medical Personnel Pool
> 303 SE 17th St.
> Fort Lauderdale, FL 33316
> (305) 764-2200

Quality Care's 200 offices in 43 states concentrate on home-care patients who pay privately or have private insurance coverage. The firm also sponsors The National Resource Center, which helps consumers find home-care agencies nationwide. The center shares the agency's toll-free phone number.

> Quality Care Inc.
> 100 North Centre Ave.
> Rockville Centre, NY 11570
> (516) 678-3200
> (800) 645-3633 (toll-free, nationwide)

Beverly Enterprises, the nation's largest nursing home chain, started Beverly Home Health Services in 1982 and was operating in 30 states with about 50 offices by 1986.

> Beverly Home Health Services
> 23639 Hawthorne Blvd., Suite 202
> Torrance, CA 90505
> (213) 378-9263

Staff Builders Home Health Care was established in 1971 by the Staff Builders temporary-worker agency. It has about 80 offices in 28 states, the District of Columbia and Canada. The company has developed detailed manuals for every service it supplies and has a well-regarded continuing education program.

Staff Builders Home Health Care
122 West 42nd St.
New York, NY 10168
(212) 867-2345

Choosing an Agency

Choosing a professionally run agency can be difficult, since this relatively new field has developed quickly with few consumer watchdogs. Many consumers ask no questions, but industry observers say there's a big difference between agencies.

"It's very important to shop for an agency," said Steve Scheidt of Beverly Home Health Services. "Consumers need to be aware."

In screening agencies, it's helpful to know the following terms:

Certification In home health care (as in other health-care areas), certification refers to an agency's status in the Medicare program. As explained earlier, Medicare pays for home-care services *only* if they've been provided by a certified home health agency.

To become certified, agencies must offer skilled nursing and at least one of the therapies—physical, speech, or occupational. They must develop written and doctor-approved plans of care for each patient and must maintain records of each case. By law, an agency supervisor—usually a nurse—must visit Medicare patients at home every two weeks and file written progress reports on each one every 60 days.

Licensing Two-thirds of the states issued special licenses for home-care agencies, as of May 1986.* In states that do so, the special licenses are a requirement for certification. As with certification, licensing in and of itself does not guarantee quality, but it does imply regular scrutiny, usually by the state health department.

---

* The states issuing the special licenses for home care agencies are Arizona, California, Connecticut, Florida, Hawaii, Idaho, Illinois, Indiana, Kansas, Kentucky, Louisiana, Maine, Maryland, Mississippi, Missouri, Montana, Nevada, New Jersey, New Mexico, New York, North Carolina, North Dakota, Oregon, Pennsylvania, Rhode Island, South Carolina, Tennessee, Texas, Virginia, and Wisconsin.

All states require that physicians, registered nurses, practical and vocational nurses, and physical therapists be licensed. High-quality agencies will be sure that their employees' licenses are in order. If you are not sure, ask. Also ask about the agency's training and experience requirements for employees.

Accreditation   This is the process by which an agency arranges to have a non-profit review association examine its operations according to industry-wide standards of quality. Agencies pay for the studies, which usually involve both a written policy statement by the agency and a site visit by a survey team of industry experts.

Unfortunately, accreditation is relatively rare in home care. Only about 1,200 of the nation's 12,000 home-care agencies are currently accredited by one of the four accrediting organizations, and most of those are run by accredited hospitals. Look for the names of these four accreditation groups:

1. The Joint Commission on the Accreditation of Hospitals, a private, non-profit organization based in Chicago, currently accredits about 80% of the nation's hospitals and says that about 1,000 accredited hospitals now have home-care agencies. The Joint Commission plans to begin accrediting free-standing home health agencies (those not associated with hospitals) by 1988.
2. The National HomeCaring Council, based in New York City, is a membership organization for homemaker-home health aide agencies and also acts as an accrediting body. The NHC standards stress the need for adequate training and supervision of aides. By May 1986, the NHC had approved or accredited 141 agencies.
3. The National League for Nursing, also based in New York City, accredits non-profit community home health-care agencies not associated with hospitals. As of June 1986, about 90 home health agencies were NLN accredited.
4. The Council on Accreditation of Services for Families and Children, based in New York City, accredits social service agencies in 22 different health-oriented fields, including home care. As of April 1986, 40 home health agencies were COA-accredited. COA accreditation is *required* for organizations belonging to Family Services America, the Child Welfare League of America, Catholic Charities, Lutheran Social Services, and the Association of Jewish Family and Children's Agencies.

Bonding   This means that an agency or its staff are covered by insurance against claims filed by clients. Bonding would be a concern if an agency employee were charged with stealing something from your parents' home.

Agencies usually are bonded to protect themselves, but their individual employees may not be. Even if employees are covered, the mere fact of bonding does not guarantee automatic coverage of all losses. In general, your parents can collect damages only if the employee is convicted of theft or is sued for property damages and loses.

Insuring the Right Care

Federal and state requirements should insure that an agency's workers are properly supervised and trained. But there is no way to guarantee that a particular aide will work out for your parents. In some cases, assigned aides may not like your parents and thus may not go out of their way to be helpful. They may be chronically late for work, or they may not show up at all. In some cases, aides don't speak English well or don't cook the kind of meals your parents are used to.

On the other hand, you may suspect that at least part of the personality clash is the result of your parents' inflexibility, probably aggravated by their illness. If so, encourage them to try and make the arrangement work out. If this is impossible, urge them to phone the agency and discuss the situation with the supervisor or head nurse—or do so yourself. In most cases, another aide will be assigned to your parents' case.

Many older people hesitate to complain about poor care, fearing retribution by the worker or the agency as a whole. But agencies should be prepared to deal with complaints. In most cases, aides will be glad to be relieved of a situation that they can't deal with.

Hiring Home Workers on Your Own

You and your parents may want to hire home-care workers on your own, because you can't afford—or don't want to pay—the high prices that must be charged by an agency to cover rent, administration, and other office overhead.

If you decide to hire independently, you may choose someone found through a personal recommendation, a nurses registry, an employment agency, or a newspaper ad. Registries and employment agencies are usually listed in the Yellow Pages of the local phone book.

A personal recommendation may work best, since you will probably be able to get a feel for a candidate's working style. Families who have managed home care for a parent are usually knowledgeable about the skills and availability of a number of nurses and aides in their area. If you or your parents don't know someone with personal experience, ask friends, acquaintances, or local clergy if they do.

No matter how you go about your search, don't be shy about checking references. After all, the person you hire will have ready access to your parents' home, so trust is a major consideration. Whether you call hospitals or families, try to strike up a conversation with someone who actually knows the applicant.

Nurses registries generally provide some screening of the people they list, including being sure a nurse's license is current. But the registries may not have actually checked references. Registries run by hospitals or by nurses themselves are usually the most reliable.

When hiring independently, your responsibility will be substantial. Even with a personnel service, you must interview applicants with the double goal of finding an aide who can care for your parents *and* get along with them. In addition, you will have to negotiate wages, meet a payroll, provide supervision or find someone else to do it, have a back-up plan when the aide is late or sick, and be prepared to fire an employee who doesn't work out.

On top of all the above responsibilities, as an independent employer, you or your parent will be legally obligated to file forms and pay (or withhold) taxes for Social Security, unemployment assistance, and the Internal Revenue Service. Employer social security tax (FICA) must be paid on wages of $50 or more for each quarter. Federal unemployment tax is owed on wages of $1,000 or more a quarter.

The IRS requires that employers withhold federal income and social security taxes on employee earnings and mail the taxes to the proper authorities. In addition, employers must handle W-4 forms and file quarterly and year-end employee wage statements (W-2 forms).

24-HOUR CARE

At some point, your parents may need round-the-clock nursing care. Nursing homes are set up to provide such care, of course, but you and your family may be determined to keep your parents out of an institution. Some individuals have chosen virtually to sacrifice their personal lives to care for their parents.

"Dad had been failing for years, but when Mother died, I had to take over," said Iris Johnson, an unmarried high school teacher in Maryland whose father's advanced case of Parkinson's disease left him partly blind and deaf and nearly bedridden. Physically unable to handle all her father's needs singlehandedly while holding down a job, Iris hired a number of aides and homemakers, putting together a succession of care teams over the past six years.

"I've had some wonderful people here, but I can't pay them much, so it seems I'm always looking for somebody new," she explained. "It's not quite a 24-hour schedule. Sometimes I'm here alone with him, but I do manage to get to work and get out to see friends."

A married sister, who lives in Norfolk, several hundred miles away, visits occasionally to allow Iris to take short trips. "I never go away unless someone from the family can cover for me. But my brothers don't have much sympathy. They feel we should put Dad in a nursing home. I've thought about it a lot, but I worry that he wouldn't survive long without the attention we can give."

You may already be trying to cope alone with a situation like this. So may one of your parents, if the other is in poor health. In fact, one of the best books on the care of an Alzheimer's Disease victim is called *The 36-Hour Day*, in recognition of the intensive work needed to keep such a person out of a nursing home.

Providing 24-hour care is a difficult task, even on a temporary basis. Large, well-organized families may be able to divide the labor, but you—or whoever becomes the primary caregiver—will probably begin to face great stress.

If this happens to you, your team of helpers—from your family doctor to trusted friends—will probably become essential. Don't be too proud to consider suggestions and offers of assistance. If you can afford it, hire aides to help part-time and to give you regular periods of respite.

You probably will have no choice but to hire, if your parents live far away from you and need round-the-clock care. When skilled nursing care is needed, agencies and nurses registries can provide trained nurses on eight-hour shifts around the clock, but this is often a very expensive option. More likely, your parents are mainly in need of personal care, so individuals with fewer technical skills may be able to do the job more reasonably on a "sleep-in" basis. You may find them either through an agency or a personal recommendation.

These aides may take virtual charge of the household, handling basic nursing, cooking, light cleaning, and shopping. They are not technically on duty at night, but they usually sleep in a spare room or on the living-room couch so as to be close if they are needed. In some cases, these aides may be willing to work for a week or two at a time without a break, though they will obviously need some time off if they are to remain effective.

If you hire workers on a 24-hour a day basis and decide to supervise them long distance, remember the following points:

Local Supervision Someone you trust must be available to act as liaison—a friend, relative, or some other local stand-in. Introduce that person to the aide and make it clear that he or she will drop in from time to time. Call this person occasionally to see how things are going, and encourage your parents to call him or her in case of a problem.

Personal Communication   If you hire through an agency, get the phone number of the agency supervisor in charge of your parents' case, and call if you have questions. If possible, get the home phone number of aides so you can call in case of emergency or to find out how things are going from their point of view.

Turnover   Some live-in aides enjoy their jobs and understand what is involved. But problems may arise on a long-term basis, since demands on the helper are great and the pay may be low. (Live-ins are expected to be in a patient's home 24 hours a day, but agencies may pay them for less since the workers are guaranteed time off for meals, personal time, and sleeping.)

If you hire through an agency and one aide quits, the agency will find a replacement. If you hire on your own and interview several likely candidates for the job, keep a list of the names and addresses of those you don't hire in case your first choice doesn't work out or you need a substitute. Even if these people have other jobs by that time, they may know other workers whom they can recommend.

Need for Fallbacks   No hired support system can be fail safe. But when aides show up late or not at all for a person who needs 24-hour care, your parents may be without food and help for hours or days. Set up a procedure for your parents, in case this happens. Be sure your parents know who to phone, and together set a reasonable time limit after which the call should be made.

You may want them to call you, even long-distance, if you are in an office or some other place where you can be reached. If not, arrange with your local stand-in to be generally on call and give this person the phone number of the agency or the aide.

Drawbacks of 24-Hour Home Care

Home care may not work out if an older person is in need of round-the-clock attention but lives alone and far away from family members. Remember that an orderly move to a nursing home that has been selected with care and love may be a better living situation for your mother or father than a lonely house shared with hired aides.

"At a certain point, we have to ask how far we go to keep someone at home," said Rhonda Soberman, chief social worker for a Brooklyn long-term home health-care program.

In fact, a nursing home or some other kind of sheltered living situation sometimes can help isolated elderly people by bringing them in contact with others of their own age and experience.

"Here I have an active life," said Jennie B. Williams, a 94-year-old retired secretary, who has lived in a Pennsylvania nursing home for the 14 years since her husband died. Many of her friends have died also, she said, "so it's good that I've met some new people. Otherwise, I'd be all alone in my house."

Mrs. Williams has no children and decided for herself to enter the nursing home. At some point, you may find yourself having to make such a decision for your parents, however, and the process may be very painful.

CHAPTER IX

Nursing Homes

Making the Decision • What's Available • Financial Options • Consumer Watchdogs • Choosing a Home • Helping Your Parents Adjust • Monitoring Care

Evelyn McDonnell was known by family and friends as one of those remarkable people who seem to remain nearly unaffected by age. Trim and alert at 80, she seemed to enjoy life despite her modest income—baking cookies for her great-grandchildren, working in her garden, and driving to the local shopping center each week to get groceries and do her banking.

"Mom lived by herself after Dad died, and she always kept physically active, even walking a mile or two a day," said Dave McDonnell, Evelyn's son who runs a small factory in the same Pennsylvania town where his mother lives. "What a shock we had when her neighbor called terribly upset because he had found her collapsed on the lawn. Things have never been quite the same since."

As it turned out, Mrs. McDonnell had a stroke that left her partially paralyzed. "She was in the hospital for a week or two, but instead of bouncing back as she always has, she got less and less interested in life," recalled Dave's wife, Meg, a real estate agent. "The doctor suggested a nursing home. At first, Dave couldn't even discuss that, but I was sure we could never take care of her, and the hospital was talking about discharging her."

Dave's brother, Alan, took the initiative by calling two different homes he had heard of and arranging for visits to both. "I have to admit it was pretty upsetting to get there and see all these sick people," Alan said, "but we liked the administrator very well at one place." The home they liked did not have

Ninety-seven-year-old Lucy McIntyre lived in her own home until her daughter, a retired school teacher, could no longer care for her. Lucy now resides in a nursing home, where her daughter visits frequently to help Lucy adjust. (PHOTO BY JEAN CRICHTON)

an empty bed right away, but Mrs. McDonell's name was placed on the waiting list and, five days later, a bed became available in the skilled care wing.

"What upset us next was the price—$1,800 a month," said Dave. "Mother needed the skilled care, but the administrator told us Medicare would not pay the bill for longer than three weeks and maybe not that long. After that, we'd have to pay the full rate of $60 a day."

With Social Security of about $500 a month and an average of about $100 more a month from her savings and investments, his mother had to go onto Medicaid, after cashing in her stocks and using up most of the money to pay the nursing home. "She's not too aware of things—if she were she wouldn't like this," said Dave, "but neither Alan nor I can afford to split $1,200 a month."

In the months afterward, Mrs. McDonnell improved somewhat, at least in part because of physical therapy and the encouragement from nurses and aides, and she was moved into the intermediate care section. Regular visits from Dave, Alan, Meg, and younger members of the family seemed to cheer her up.

"I can't say we're pleased, because Mother just isn't herself," said Dave, "but she could never have gone home on her own, and we feel she's getting pretty good care."

Deciding whether your mother or father needs to be in a nursing home can be one of the most stressful aspects of long-term care. Many families of the elderly wear themselves out juggling the pressures of career and their personal lives along with concerns about parents before considering this step.

Even so, many older people do enter nursing homes. Virtually all the country's nursing home beds are occupied at all times, and more are needed—an estimated 600,000 more nationwide by 1990. Despite this, some states have placed moratoriums on the building of new nursing homes because of the high resulting cost to the Medicaid system.

Who Are the Residents?

Only 5% of all elderly Americans are in nursing homes at any one time, but these people tend to be the oldest, sickest, and most dependent of all the elderly. Nearly four-fifths of them are over 75. More than three-fourths are in poor physical health. About half are victims of Alzheimer's Disease. And 75% have no spouse to care for them at home—being widowed, divorced, or never married.

You may recognize your mother or father's problems in one or more of these characteristics, but you may despair of finding a high-quality nursing home to care for them, especially after reading newspaper stories and Congressional reports about patient neglect, indifferent staff, and cleanliness that's slipshod at best.

Nevertheless, there are also well-run homes in all parts of the country with experienced staff members who work hard to deliver good care with affection and humor. Such nursing homes are designed to provide frail elderly people with medical and nursing care round the clock. There, nurse's aides and orderlies help with dressing, eating, and walking. Meals are planned and prepared with the assistance of a dietitian, and a diverse schedule of activities includes everything from religious services and field trips to arts and crafts programs and visits from community groups.

MAKING THE DECISION

You may wonder whether your parents really need to be in a nursing home. Their physician probably has a good idea, and most homes insist on a medical examination before a person can be admitted.

In some states, a doctor or nurse must fill out a state-mandated form assessing what specific nursing services a patient needs, in terms of medical problems, functional disabilities, mental status, and physical impairments. The resulting "needs score" may indicate that your parents are not in need of nursing home care at all, though a doctor convinced that this is the right step may be able to override a score that presents only part of the picture.

If your parent is in the hospital, the family doctor or the hospital social worker probably will make a recommendation. If they have not approached you about what happens after hospital discharge, ask them.

More likely, with Medicare's current emphasis on short hospital stays, you may be told your mother is about to be discharged while she is still seriously sick and the entire family is still emotionally upset because of her illness. Given the short notice, you and your family may be pressured by the hospital to find a nursing home bed immediately or accept a bed found by hospital social workers. Otherwise, you may be told that the family must begin to pay the hospital bill.

First, remember that under Medicare rules, your parent must be given *written* notice 48 hours in advance of a hospital discharge. If you feel such a discharge is premature, you have a right to appeal to the Peer Review Organization (see page 120).

Without a written notice, you and your parents will not be responsible for Medicare-covered bills. Even so, it's important to respond as promptly as possible, since it may be difficult to find a bed in a well-run home in even a few weeks' time. Your input is essential in avoiding a home where you doubt the quality of care. In most cases, if you are actively searching for an acceptable home, you can insist that the hospital continue caring for your mother or father until one is found.

If your parent is not in the hospital, nursing home placement is up to the family. Try to discuss the idea with your elderly parent, your brothers and sisters, and other relatives long before the situation reaches crisis proportions. This is especially important, because high quality homes sometimes have waiting lists of years or more.

Phone each home you are considering, and have any required application forms sent to you. Get an estimate of the waiting period. Find out whether applications must be updated to keep them active.

If your parent has organic brain disorder Most nursing homes are equipped to caring for confused elderly people, but some do not accept residents with advanced Alzheimer's Disease or some other severe brain disorder. These patients do not generally need intensive nursing, but they do require more supervision than other patients.

Homes that do not accept people with severe senile dementia may not have enough staff or facilities to do so. If a home is not adequately staffed for an Alzheimer's patient, your parent is probably better off somewhere else.

On the other hand, it is illegal for adequately staffed facilities that receive federal funds (from Medicaid or Medicare) to discriminate against people on the basis of a given disability like Alzheimer's. If you suspect discrimination, you have a right to challenge the home's decision. Contact the Office for Civil Rights at the regional offices of the U.S. Department of Health and Human Services or contact

Office of Civil Rights
   Public Affairs Division
   Department of Health and Human Services
   300 Independence Ave., S.W.
   Washington, D.C. 20201
   (202) 245-6671

WHAT'S AVAILABLE

America has nearly 19,000 nursing homes—some of them brand new facilities and others dating back to the turn of the century. Most are modest in size, averaging 90 beds. But some have as many as 600 beds or more and are larger than many hospitals.

Nursing homes today offer three basic levels of care, sometimes on separate floors or wings of the same building, though some homes specialize in one level only. In general, the care levels are as follows:

Skilled Nursing Facilities (SNFs) provide the highest level of medical and nursing attention outside an acute care hospital. For skilled care, a skilled nurse—registered (RN), licensed practical (LPN), or licensed vocational (LVN)—must be on duty around the clock. Some skilled homes also provide rehabilitation in the form of physical, speech, or occupational therapy.

All states require SNFs to be licensed, but each state sets its own safety and staffing standards—the frequency of fire drills, for example, or the nurse-patient ratio. Both Medicare and Medicaid pay for skilled-level care, but not all skilled nursing facilities are Medicare- or Medicaid-certified.

Intermediate Care Facilities (ICFs), known as health-related facilities in some states, provide personal care, some nursing, lodging, and meals for patients who are ambulatory at least to some extent. In an intermediate-level home, patient care is directed by a licensed nurse and provided by nurse's aides and orderlies. Medical decisions are made by a consulting physician or medical board. Medicaid funds intermediate-level care in homes that participate in the Medicaid program. Medicare does not cover intermediate care at all. All states license intermediate care facilities, but state standards vary.

Personal-Care, or Board and Care, facilities resemble nursing homes in that they provide room, board, housekeeping, laundry, and some personal care, but no nursing is provided. Residents must be able to dress and get to the dining room by themselves for the most part. (These facilities may also be called rest homes or homes for the aged. Some nursing homes offer residential living sections that approximate this level of care.)

Many personal-care facilities are small mom-and-pop operations that offer residents a homelike atmosphere at a lower price than a nursing home. Not all states license or inspect personal-care homes, so careful research is necessary before signing a contract. Neither Medicare nor Medicaid pays for personal-care homes.

Who Owns the Homes?

More than three-quarters of all nursing homes are for-profit businesses, most of them owner-operated. The rest are either governmental facilities, operated by states, counties, and cities, or voluntary, non-profit homes run by religious, benevolent, or fraternal groups.

Increasingly, the nursing home in your community will be owned by a large corporation. The top five nursing home chains owned or ran more than 1,800 homes—one in ten—nationwide as of April 1986, and the number is growing as the chains buy up small, privately run facilities.

Beverly Enterprises of Pasadena, California, is the largest of the chains with 1,024 homes in 44 states, Canada, and Japan as of April 1986. The firm was founded in 1963. All Beverly homes have both skilled and intermediate care beds, and nearly all are certified for Medicaid.

Second in size is Hillhaven Corporation of Tacoma, Washington, with about 380 nursing homes in 38 states in 1986. A subsidiary of a large hospital corporation, Hillhaven is known as an innovator and was the first chain to set up a special unit for Alzheimer's Disease, though a number of homes now have these.

Other major chains are ARA Living Centers of Houston, which owned, leased, or managed more than 250 homes in 13 states in 1986; Manor Care Inc. of Silver Spring, Maryland, with 138 homes in 22 states; and Care Enterprises of Orange, California, with 124 facilities.

Homes run by national corporations may have some advantages over their locally based counterparts. For one thing, management policies are set nationally, so billing, insurance, and quality assurance can be handled in a standard way nationwide. If problems arise, patients and families generally have recourse to higher corporate officials.

Even so, a national "brand name" does not guarantee good care. "Not all corporate-owned homes are bad, and you can't assume that if a home is non-profit it will be good," said Joy Spalding of the National Citizens Coalition for Nursing Home Reform, "but corporations are there to make money and to be responsive to stockholders."

Non-Profit and Governmental Homes

Many homes run by non-profit groups, especially religious organizations, have developed a good reputation for quality care. Some, like Metropolitan Jewish Geriatric Center in Brooklyn, New York, have expanded their scope to serve older people in varied settings. Founded in 1907 as a 70-bed home for the aged, the center now provides a broad range of programs including rehabilitation, home care, a hospice, a social health maintenance organization (S/HMO), adult day care, and two nursing facilities with a total of 900 beds.

In addition, Metropolitan has set up an ambitious respite program, supplying homemakers to "sit" for a day or two with frail elderly people so families can take time off. In another part of the respite program, frail seniors who live at home can become "visiting residents" for up to six weeks so that caregivers can go on vacations or recuperate from an illness.

Religious-affiliated homes may not legally exclude members of other faiths if they participate in Medicaid and Medicare, but most provide worship services and special diets for their own adherents, if appropriate.

These homes often have no formal financial connection to the religious group, however. In entering, some people believe that if the home failed or patients ran out of funds, the religious denomination would assume financial responsibility. This is not always true, though many non-profit homes do keep long-term patients who encounter financial hardship.

Governmental nursing homes, operated by counties, cities, and states, are often on the other end of the economic scale from the non-profits. In fact, families often feel ashamed if they can find no nursing home bed for a parent other than one in the nearby "county home."

With the current scarcity of nursing home beds in some parts of the country, you may find yourself unable to avoid placing your mother or father in a governmental home. You may be surprised to find the care better than expected. No matter who owns a nursing home, you will have to do regular monitoring to insure that your mother or father gets good treatment.

FINANCIAL OPTIONS

As you probably already know, nursing home care is very expensive. Charges vary across the country, but the American Health Care Association, a trade group for nursing homes, says the national average is $60 a day, or nearly $22,000 a year. In large metropolitan areas like New York City, yearly bills as high as $65,000 are not uncommon.

Older people and their families pay nearly half (48%) of the nation's annual nursing home bill, which totaled $27 billion in 1982. Medicaid pays just about the same percentage (49%). With its coverage limited, Medicare funds only 2% of total nursing home expenditures, and private insurance pays the balance (less than 1%).

If your parents need nursing home care, it's important to check all their health insurance policies. They may be able to get benefits if they have nursing home or long-term care coverage, but, as we have seen, few people do. It's very unlikely that their Medicare-supplementary (Medigap) insurance will cover long-term care, but the policy may pick up Medicare copayments.

Medicare's Skilled Nursing Home Coverage

Medicare hospital insurance under Part A can pay for 100% of your parents' first 20 days in a skilled nursing facility and for any daily charges over $65 (in 1987) for the 21st through 100th days, if certain stringent qualifications are met.

1. Your parents must need and receive skilled nursing or rehabilitation on a daily basis, and a doctor must certify this. Medicare won't pay if they need custodial care or if they need skilled care only occasionally, for example once or twice a week. Funding may be *cut off* if the rehab could be done outside a nursing home and without trained physical therapists or if Medicare determines that the rehab is no longer helping improve the condition.
2. Your parents must have been hospitalized at least three days in a row before entering the home, not counting the day of discharge.
3. They must be transferred to the home within a short time (usually 30 days) after the hospital discharge.
4. They must need skilled nursing care for a condition treated in the hospital.
5. The Peer Review Organization (or the home's review committee) must agree with the doctor that a skilled care home is needed.
6. The nursing home must be certified by Medicare and must participate in the Medicare program. Unfortunately, most nursing homes are not certified by Medicare as skilled nursing facilities. All states have some certified and participating homes but, in some states, there are very few.

If your parents' situation meets these conditions, they may receive care in a semiprivate room (with two to four beds), meals, nursing care, rehabilitation, in-patient drugs and medical supplies, blood transfusions, and the use of wheelchairs and other equipment. Medicare will not cover private-duty nurses or a private room, unless it's determined to be medically necessary.

Medicaid's Program

Medicaid, the joint federal-state program that provides health care for the poor, is the only way to pay for custodial care in a nursing home when private resources are depleted. You may think your parents will never need Medicaid, but the program pays all or part of the bill for about half of the nation's nursing home residents.

As we have seen, Medicaid covers different services in each state, but skilled nursing facilities (SNFs) and intermediate care facilities (ICFs) are covered in the District of Columbia and all states except Arizona.

Since Medicaid covers the neediest Americans only, qualifying requires virtual impoverishment (except that the family home may be retained). Tragic as this is, nursing home residents themselves may not suffer, since the nursing home bill that Medicaid pays includes food and shelter along with whatever nursing care is needed. In addition, each nursing home resident on Medicaid gets a monthly allowance of $25 (or more in some states), hardly a generous sum but enough to cover at least some personal expenses for toiletries, newspapers, clothing, and so on. Families must supply extras.

Medicaid Discrimination

Many nursing homes willingly accept Medicaid patients, but others are not eager to do so, claiming that government reimbursements do not cover their costs. As a result, some homes set seemingly arbitrary ratios of public-pay to private-pay patients. If the public-pay quota has been reached, a Medicaid applicant may be placed on a waiting list—even if a bed is available.

Other homes demand that the families of Medicaid applicants pay cash contributions or several months' private-pay charges in advance as a condition of admission. Some states rule that these demands for advance payment constitute Medicaid discrimination and are illegal, but other states have not taken a position. The 1986 report by the Senate Committee on Aging notes that the federal Department of Health and Human Services has done little to fight such instances of discrimination.

If you feel that your parents are being discriminated against because they are on Medicaid, check with the long-term care Ombudsman program or the Medicaid office in their area. If your parents qualify for Medicaid, they have a right to all benefits and should not be treated with less consideration than a private-pay patient. With nursing home beds at a premium, however, you may not feel completely free to question a particular home's policies.

Spending Down for Medicaid

Far from fighting to stay off Medicaid, many elderly people who need nursing home care try to get benefits by transferring their assets to a son or daughter—in effect, impoverishing themselves voluntarily. (The same thing is done to get home care in states with generous home health programs under Medicaid.) The practice is common but controversial.

Older people can legally preserve their estates and qualify for Medicaid, if they transfer their assets well before they apply. Under federal regulations, Medicaid is denied for two years from the date of the transfer of assets until the date the Medicaid application is filed.

In most states, the two-year rule covers amounts of $12,000 or less. For larger amounts, Medicaid will be denied for two years plus an additional month from the date of the transfer for each $2,000 over and above the $12,000.

"An applicant who has transferred funds in this manner can qualify for Medicaid sooner only if he or she can prove that the transfer was exclusively for some purpose other than qualifying for Medicaid or if he or she incurs medical expenses equal to or greater than the amount transferred," wrote New York lawyers Ellice Fatoullah and David E. Frazer in their paper, *Money Management and the Cost of Health Care: Options for the Elderly and Disabled.*

As part of the application process, Medicaid officials probably will ask you or your parents if a transfer of assets has taken place and when. Your answer will be confirmed through bank statements and other financial sources, so it does no good to try to conceal a recent gift.

Obviously, the earlier any assets were transferred, the easier it is to qualify for Medicaid. On the other hand, few older people would want to make such a transfer as long as they remained in good health.

Family Responsibility

At one time, family members—including children and the healthy spouse—were legally responsible for all nursing home bills. Medicaid would pay nothing until all family funding sources were exhausted. In some cases, entire families were reduced to the poverty level.

To prevent this tragedy, lawyers specializing in the field sued on behalf of impoverished family members, and corrective legislation was proposed. Current federal and state regulations have shifted in the direction of aiding families, but the entire area is still in flux and is highly complex because of conflicting state laws.

The following is a summary of the current issues:

Children's Responsibility   Under current law, sons and daughters in every state have been relieved of responsibility for their parents' long-term care expenses. Medicaid will look only at the income and assets of the parents in determining eligibility, unless a substantial transfer was made to a child within the previous two years. In that case, Medicaid coverage may be delayed, but the state will not put a lien on the assets of the child.

Spousal Responsibility   In most states, spouses of nursing home residents under Medicaid may be legally required to contribute to the cost of care. As a result, the healthy spouse may be impoverished to such an extent that he or she may end up on Supplementary Security Income or as a ward of the state. No one wants such an outcome, but a nationwide solution to the problem of spousal impoverishment has yet to be found.

At one time, the only way the spouse outside the nursing home could legally preserve assets and income was to divorce—a sad fate for older couples whose long, happy marriages are already devastated by a debilitating medical problem.

Under recent rulings, healthy spouses in most of the states are now permitted to separate their assets and income one month after their mate goes into the nursing home, since the couples are no longer living together.

The only exception to this one-month limit on responsibility is if both husband and wife apply for Medicaid at the same time and are found eligible. In this case, the assets (but not the income) of the spouse outside the nursing home will be considered available to pay nursing home bills for six months.

Separation vs. Equal Division of Assets and Income   Separating a couple's assets and income does not always mean an equal division of the resources. Instead, it means parceling out the assets and income to whichever spouse has formal title. All stocks, bonds, and bank accounts in the name of the nursing home resident as well as pension and Social Security checks in that name go to pay the nursing home bill (with the monthly $25 or more personal needs allowance reserved). The other spouse (in Medicaid jargon, the "community" spouse) retains title to all property and income in his or her name.

What happens to jointly held property depends on state law. The eight "community property" states and some others order that all assets and income acquired during a marriage (except Social Security checks) be split 50-50 when a couple no longer lives together. Other states use different formulas.

Whatever way the division is made, the community spouse may not have enough money to live comfortably. Typically, the situation is worse for women whose husbands enter nursing homes than for men in a comparable situation, since a woman's own income may be limited to a Social Security check half that of her husband. The husband's entire pension and higher

Social Security benefits, meanwhile, would go directly to the nursing home.

If the woman's income is *very* low, the state may award, or "deem," some of the husband's income to her, but only enough to bring her monthly total up to the Medicaid ceiling, still a small amount. As a result of this, these women (or sometimes men) may be reduced to a pitifully small livelihood. Besides the personal tragedy of this, two people may be forced onto the public assistance rolls, not just one.

A different problem could result if a wife (or the person with the lower income) is in the nursing home and the income of her husband (or the spouse outside the home) *exceeds* the Medicaid ceiling. In that case, Medicaid could ask the community spouse for a specific "contribution" toward the nursing home bill. With incomes large enough, most spouses would be glad to contribute, but when their incomes are only slightly higher than the Medicaid limit, such "contributions" have caused financial despair.

In New York State, legal experts in estate planning and Medicaid law have sued the program on behalf of impoverished spouses. Generally, judges have ruled in favor of the community spouses, granting them extra income. The effect on the Medicaid programs of other states is still up in the air.

For Further Information

For information on spousal responsibility in your parents' state, contact legal assistance attorneys connected with the state Office on Aging or the local Area Agency on Aging. If you or your parents can afford private legal fees, ask for references to private attorneys with experience in estate planning or the legal issues of aging. Remember that each state's Medicaid program works differently.

CONSUMER WATCHDOGS

If your parents must go to a nursing home, you'll want to be sure they get the best possible care. Both state and federal governments regulate nursing homes, and the records of their inspections are supposed to be a matter of public record, though it may take some hard work to see them. In addition, some nursing homes participate in a process of self-regulation.

Licensing

Every state requires nursing homes to hold current state licenses. To get a license, homes must be inspected once a year or more by a team from the state Survey and Certification Agency (usually the state Department of Health). The survey is a lengthy process of a few days to a week, and homes are usually notified as to the date.

In the survey, the home is assessed according to state standards of safety, sanitation, financial management, medical care, and nutrition. All states require homes to have licensed administrators. In many, the guidelines include a patient bill of rights.

When violations are found, surveyors are supposed to visit more frequently to be sure problems are corrected. In addition, special inspections are to be made, often on an unscheduled basis, when formal complaints are made by patients, families, or members of the public.

In most states, the resulting reports are supposed to be made available to the public, but disclosure laws vary. In some states, copies of reports may be available in a state office in the same region as the nursing home. Unfortunately, in others, you must travel to the state capitol and track down the right office before you can get access.

Certification

Before a nursing home can receive federal funding—either through Medicare or Medicaid—it must be certified. To receive certification, homes must hold state and local licenses, meet state safety and sanitation standards, follow the federal Civil Rights Act prohibiting discrimination, and "substantially meet" Medicare's nationwide "conditions of participation" for skilled facilities or Medicaid's "standards" for skilled and intermediate-level care.

These guidelines cover administration, nursing, rehabilitation, patient activities, and medical and social services, among other areas. They also include a patient bill of rights.

To be sure homes comply, at least two inspections must be conducted yearly: the Inspection of Care and the Long-Term Care Survey Process, instituted in 1986. In most states, the Inspection of Care is conducted by the state Medicaid office, which checks up on all Medicaid-funded patients to be sure their care is appropriate.

Medicare has no inspectors of its own. Each home's Long-Term Care Survey is carried out by the same state Survey and Certification Agency responsible for licensing. An inspection team visits the home, possibly at the same time as the state licensing survey, looking to see whether homes substantially meet federal standards. The current survey process also requires that at least 10% of the nursing home's residents be interviewed and that residents' opinions be used in arriving at the survey conclusions.

Homes that pass the inspections receive certification. Any deficiencies noted under the Inspection of Care or the survey are supposed to be corrected within one year. If not, the homes could lose certification, and all federally financed patients would be moved out.

Lesser penalties are now under Congressional consideration, so nursing home operators with frequent violations can be penalized (and pressured to make improvements) *before* conditions get bad enough for decertification. These suggested penalties include the banning of new Medicare and Medicaid patients until deficiencies are corrected and the appointment of receivers, or masters, to take over the management and upgrading of such homes.

Patient Rights

Federal law requires the protection of specific patient rights in all nursing homes that participate in Medicare or Medicaid. The rights are listed in Medicare's Conditions of Participation for SNFs and in Medicaid's ICF Standards and can be found in the Code of Federal Regulations, volume 42, Section 405.1121 and Section 442.250.

Unfortunately, a home's respect for its patients' rights is not always easy for an inspection team to spot in an occasional visit. "Often patient rights are a minor issue to the surveyors, compared to something that's easier to verify, like roaches in the kitchen," noted David Schulke, a nursing home specialist with the Senate Special Committee on Aging.

The language differs somewhat for Medicare and Medicaid, but federal law requires that written policies on patient rights be given to residents, their families, and the public in both levels of care. The rights include the following:

Information   Patients have the right to be fully informed about the services provided by the home, the charges, and what fees are not covered by the federal program. In addition, patients must be notified of the home's rules on conduct and responsibilities.

Medical Condition and Treatment   Doctors must keep nursing home residents fully informed of their medical condition (unless the physicians write in a patient's record that discussing the information would not be wise). Patients must also be allowed to participate in planning their medical treatment and to refuse to take part in experimental research.

Exercising Rights   Residents must be encouraged to exercise their rights as patients and citizens. No interference, coercion, or reprisals are permitted if patients complain about the home to the staff or to outsiders.

Personal Belongings and Funds   Patients have the right to keep and use their own clothing and possessions as space permits, unless this infringes on the rights of other residents. They may manage their own personal financial affairs. They may delegate financial responsibility to the facility in writing, but, if so, they must be given a full accounting of financial transactions made on their behalf. Each patient's funds must be kept in a private account.

Freedom from Abuse and Restraints   Patients must not be abused mentally or physically. They must be free from chemical and physical restraints (i.e., drugs or restraining straps), except when a physician authorizes the restraints in writing for a specified period of time or in case of emergency to protect patients from injury to themselves or others. In such an emergency, the patient's physician must be notified promptly.

Privacy   Residents must be treated with consideration, respect, and full recognition of their dignity and individuality. They must be given privacy during treatments and for personal needs. Their records must be treated with confidentiality.

Married residents must be given privacy during visits by their spouses, and when a husband and wife are both patients, they must be permitted to share a room.

Freedom of Association and Correspondence   Residents must be allowed to communicate and meet privately with individuals of their choice, unless this infringes on the rights of others. They must be allowed to participate in social, religious, and community group activities of their choice.

They must be permitted to receive and send personal mail unopened, unless a doctor specifies in writing that this is not medically wise.

Work   No resident may be required to perform services for the nursing home.

Transfer and Discharge   Residents may be transferred or discharged only for medical reasons, their welfare, the welfare of the other residents, or for nonpayment of charges, except as specifically prohibited by the Medicare and Medicaid laws.

Access to Federal Reports

Under federal law, nursing home operators are given 50 days to comment on the survey reports. After 90 days, all federal surveys and reports resulting from complaints must be open for inspection by the public at the home. (Don't ask to see the complaints themselves; they are confidential.)

"It can take a lot of work to get these reports," said David Schulke, the Congressional nursing home specialist. "You might have to fight to get them, and then it's time-consuming to look at them. But if they're not available, people should protest."

Long-Term Care Ombudsman

The Long-Term Care Ombudsman program provides a person attached to every Area Agency on Aging who works full-time to investigate and resolve complaints on behalf of nursing home residents, while keeping names of the resident and the person making the complaint confidential. The program also collects data on complaints about specific nursing homes and gives it to the state survey and certification agency.

If you need information about a specific nursing home, contact the Ombudsman program by calling the local Area Agency on Aging or the state department on aging, listed in the back of this book. Ask the Ombudsman about the performance of the home you're considering. Also ask how to get information from the survey and certification agency in your parents' state.

Is the Home Accredited?

As in the rest of the health-care field, accreditation is a voluntary program of oversight intended to insure that nursing homes are run according to strict professional standards.

Only one agency accredits nursing homes, the Chicago-based Joint Commission on the Accreditation of Hospitals. As of 1986, JCAH's Long-Term Care Council had accredited 1,100 of the nation's 18,900 nursing homes, or about 6% of the total. In addition, the joint commission extends approval to all homes run by JCAH-accredited hospitals.

Unlike hospitals, nursing homes have not made accreditation a priority. Many homes claim the process is unnecessary what with the continuing round of inspections for licensing and certification.

Ask if the home you're considering is accredited. If so, it shows that administrators have been willing to subject their facility to a tough process of scrutiny and that it has passed.

Peer Reviews

Some state affiliates of the American Health Care Association operate peer review systems, in which nursing home owners periodically visit the homes of fellow association members to assess the quality of care. The AHCA set up the professional review format in 1971, and since then more than half the state associations have formed peer review committees.

In all but one state, peer review is voluntary, however, so an individual home may decide not to participate. Only in North Carolina does the state association require all member facilities to submit to peer review.

CHOOSING A HOME

Once you know something about your mother or father's needs and how you'll be paying the bill, it's time to begin doing research on the nursing homes themselves.

Preliminary Research

Your parents probably will be happiest in an area where their friends and family can visit as often as possible. But if you live far away from them, you will have to decide on the *location* of the nursing home, whether it should be near their hometown, yours, or someplace else altogether.

Your parents may say they want to stay near their own home, where they have friends and doctors they trust. This may not result in frequent visits, however, since older people sometimes forget that many of their old friends have moved away or died, and their doctors may be ready to retire. A move to your hometown or that of a brother or sister may result in more socializing for them—and more convenience for you.

Next, *draw up a list* of suitable nursing homes in the city or town of choice. Ask everyone you know with experience or knowledge on the subject, including doctors, social workers, and clergy. Be sure to ask for suggestions from friends and neighbors who know someone in a nursing home. Cull the list to two or three likely names.

Then, *call each home,* and ask about skill levels, Medicare and Medicaid participation, the number of beds, basic services, and admission requirements. Find out if a bed is available for your parent or, if not, the likely waiting period.

Get a written schedule of rates and extra charges. Find out specifically whether patients are charged extra for laundry, ironing, hand feeding, special diets, doctor's visits, wheelchairs, drugs, and other supplies. Is a deposit required for admission? Is this returned if a patient's private funds are depleted?

Next, *examine the record.* If you have questions about the quality of care, inquire about the home with the Long-Term Care Ombudsman program or the state survey and certification agency (usually the state Department of Health). Ask the home's administrator about any serious violations, and ask to see copies of the recent federal survey and certification reports, Inspection of Care reports, and reports resulting from complaints.

Rule out any nursing home if the home and/or the administrator are not licensed. If a nursing home's license is suspended because of violations, question the administrator on the problem areas, and do not settle for evasive responses. Find out what is being done to bring the home back into conformity with regulations.

Visiting the Homes

When you have located one or two appropriate homes, schedule an appointment with the administrator and a tour of the home. Take your mother or father along, if possible. Keep your mind open, don't be afraid to ask questions, and expect to be answered without impatience. The administrator's attitude will tell you a great deal about the tone of the nursing home as a whole.

Getting a feel for a nursing home depends on keeping all your senses alert. Gerontologists say the process is not easy. "It's like a sense of smell," said a New York City social worker. "You keep alert for odors, of course, but also for the total feel of a place. The trick is finding the right home for the right person."

A Nursing Home Checklist

The following checklist is very detailed. Review it before making the visit, and jot down questions you want to be sure to ask on the spot.

THE STAFF

Nursing   The director of nursing has the most impact of anyone on patient care in a nursing home. Ask to meet her (or him), and get the specifics of staffing in different wings of the home.
— How many skilled nurses and nurses' aides are on each floor or wing during each shift? What duties are each responsible for?
— Are nurses and aides dressed neatly and are they well-groomed?
— Does the home have a training program for new employees and continuing education for the entire staff?

Doctors   Every home should have a medical director or physician on staff, or on call, to supervise patient care and emergency services.
— Who are the staff physicians, and how often do they visit?
— May patients continue to be treated by their own private physicians, or must they rely on the home's doctor?
— How can family members keep in touch with the doctor?
— Are psychiatric or psychological services and other medical specialties available?

Rehabilitation   Many nursing homes have rehabilitation programs for people with movement and speech disabilities.

— Does the nursing home have a physical therapy program carried out by a licensed physical therapist?

— How do patients qualify?

— Is the therapist on staff full-time? If not, how often does he or she visit? Ask to see the therapy area and the equipment.

— Is there a speech therapy program?

— Does the home have occupational therapy to help patients adapt to disability?

Activities Staff   A schedule of activities should be planned and posted where all nursing home residents can see it and take part.

— Ask to see the program schedule. Would the activities be of interest to your parents?

— Are recreational events held both at night and during the day?

— What religious services are held and how often?

— What activities are available for patients unable to leave their rooms?

— Is the activities director a paid staff member or a volunteer? Is the activities staff on duty every day?

Dietitian and Kitchen Staff   The difficulties of adjusting to nursing home life often cause elderly people to lose weight—in some cases because not enough food is offered, but in other cases because frail patients lose their appetites when presented with institutional food. In most states, inspectors keep careful track of patient weight losses and rigorously enforce requirements that daily menus contain enough calories and nutrients. Try to schedule your visit for a mealtime, so you can see for yourself whether residents seem to enjoy their food.

— Does a dietitian (on staff or working as a consultant) plan the meals or check the menu?

— Are portions ample and are there hot substitutes for people who don't like the main dish? What about second helpings?

— Does the menu include fresh fruits and vegetables?

— Are aides available for people who need help eating?

— Are special diets available for health-related problems or for those who keep Kosher? Does this cost extra?

— Does the staff plan special meals for holidays and other special occasions?

— What happens if residents don't want to come to the dining room for some reason? Will a meal be delivered to them?

— What can be done if your parent has a history of eating problems?

— May food be brought in by visitors?

— Are snacks available (or encouraged) between meals?

PATIENT MORALE

The best nursing homes work hard to keep the atmosphere homelike and insure a patient's sense of dignity and personal worth. Even the most confused patient deserves respect.

Resident Care   Unless they are sick, nursing home residents should be out of bed and wearing street clothes during the day.

— Do patients appear alert and happy? Are they involved in activities or conversation?

— Does the staff mingle with patients or do they tend to gather at the nurses' station?

— Do nurses and aides seem responsive to patients' individual needs to go to the bathroom or get out of a chair?

— What's done in case of bladder problems, incontinence, and bedsores?

— Ask the administrator to introduce you to one or two residents. Take some time, possibly after the formal tour, to talk to them about the home and their care.

Personal Belongings   Having some of their own possessions around them can help incoming residents adjust.

— Can newcomers bring furniture, televisions, and radios to furnish their rooms?

— Are rooms equipped with telephones? If not, may residents have phones installed at their own expense?

— Who is responsible if personal items are lost or stolen?

Money   Nursing home residents may need to keep petty cash for newspapers, cosmetics, and sundries.

— What provision is made for safeguarding this money?

— Does the home keep individual accounts for these personal funds?

Restraints   When visiting some nursing homes, you may be upset to see people strapped into wheelchairs, sitting alone and lethargic in their rooms or in a hallway. If physical restraints (called poseys) or chemical restraints (drugs or tranquilizers) are being used, staffing may be insufficient.

— Ask about the home's policy on restraints. Must a doctor order them?

— How often are restrained patients taken to the toilet and helped to exercise? At least every two hours is recommended.

— If restraints aren't used, how does the home deal with severely disturbed patients or those who wander away from their rooms?

Resident Council   Some states require that each nursing home have a resident council or committee to provide a voice for patients. Some administrators decide voluntarily to organize these councils.

— Does the home you're visiting have a resident council? Does it have a relatives' council?

— How often do the councils meet?

— If you have questions, ask to meet the officers of either or both groups.

Privacy and respect Try to determine how committed a home is to respecting the privacy of its residents.
— Are residents addressed by their full names and without condescension?
— Are they listened to, even when they are confused?
— Does the staff talk about residents in their presence, as if they weren't there?
— Do staff members knock on a resident's door before entering?
— What are the visiting hours, and are they flexible?
— Are married couples assigned to the same room and given privacy for lovemaking? (Sex continues to be a major concern in later life, though many people assume that the elderly have no interest in it.)
— What happens when unmarried residents take a romantic interest in each other? Are they given privacy?
— Can rooms be locked for intimate moments?

PHYSICAL PLANT

A good nursing home should maintain up to date medical and nursing practices, but a modern building does not guarantee a caring environment. Safety and cleanliness are important in a nursing home, no matter what its age.

Fire Safety A good home takes federal and state safety regulations seriously.
— How often are fire drills held?
— What evacuation routes are used? Are patients and staff aware of them?
— What exit routes are used for bedfast patients? Can they be evacuated quickly?
— Are there enough fire extinguishers and are they in convenient places?

Building Safety Since falls are one of the greatest health hazards for older people, nursing homes should be well-lighted and free of obstacles.
— Do rooms and hallways have adequate handrails, and are they free of obstructions like throw rugs, chairs, and medical equipment?
— Do bathtubs and toilets have nearby grab bars?
— Are ramps available for wheelchair access?

Cleanliness Use all your senses, especially your sense of smell, to determine whether a home is clean.
— Do you smell strong urine or fecal odors? Either poor housekeeping or poor patient care could be at fault.
— Do you smell strong chemical odors? If so, disinfectants may be masking other smells.

Activities Rooms, Lounges In most nursing homes, officials proudly show visitors recreation areas and activities rooms available for residents.

— Look for signs that these rooms are actually used. (The best-equipped arts and crafts room may stay vacant without a competent and enthusiastic staff.)
— Is the lounge anything more than a glorified TV room?
— Does it have adequate light for reading or playing cards?
— Are drinking fountains, public telephones, or vending machines accessible?
— Does the home provide a beauty and/or barber shop for patients? How often are the beautician and barber on the premises? What does a haircut and/or set cost?
— Is there a snack bar or shop to buy incidentals?

Outdoor Spaces   Many homes have wide porches or lawns to give residents access to the out of doors.
— Are patients, including those in wheelchairs, encouraged to go outside in warm weather?
— Are outdoor activities or barbecues ever held?

Transportation
— Does the home have a van, minibus, or other transportation for residents who want to shop, go to church, or vote?
— Does transportation cost extra?
— Is there a regular schedule?

A Word of Caution

No matter how friendly the staff, most people are upset or at least bewildered by the blizzard of emotions they feel on visiting a nursing home—particularly one where they may place a loved one. What may be most disturbing is the sight of the sickest patients, especially the most profoundly disoriented.

To help you keep your cool, talk to as many people possible who are familiar with the nursing home situation in your area. You might also want to read some of the many good pamphlets and nursing home checklists that are available from state departments of health, the local Area Agency on Aging, the AARP, and other advocacy organizations for the aging.

An excellent checklist is available free from

Nursing Home Information Service
   National Council of Senior Citizens
   925 15th St., N.W.
   Washington, D.C. 20005
   (202) 347-8800

In addition, the American Health Care Association makes available a number of free pamphlets on nursing homes, including *Thinking About A*

Nursing Home. Its series of *Here's Help* brochures cover topics such as sexuality, reactions to nursing home admission, confusion in the elderly, Alzheimer's Disease, and tips on visiting for friends and relatives.

American Health Care Association
1200 15th St., N.W.
Washington, D.C. 20005
(202) 833-2050

Making the Choice and Living With It

Once you collect the available information, you and your family will be prepared to place your parent in the highest quality nursing home available, given his or her individual needs. In the best of all possible worlds, this home would be an excellent facility, providing good care. In some cases, however, older people end up in homes of lesser quality—either because of a shortage of beds in another home or for financial reasons.

If this happens to you and your parent, realize that you have done the best you can. Fight the inevitable feelings of guilt by visiting frequently, or, if you live far away, by finding local surrogates to do so for you. Your visible concern will send a message to the home's staff that you expect good care and will complain if you see it's not being provided.

HELPING YOUR PARENTS ADJUST

Adjusting to a nursing home is understandably difficult for older people, particularly if they did not choose to go there. The move almost always involves a significant loss of one's place in the community.

In the first place, your parents are probably losing much of their independence and the right to make important life decisions. If the move is permanent, they are leaving behind most of the furniture and belongings collected over a lifetime. In some cases, they may have had to give up a beloved pet.

As a result, anger and grief are both normal reactions. Your parents may lash out at family as well as the home's staff. They may also become depressed and agitated. Often new residents are unable to eat—or refuse to eat—and they may lose weight.

In making the adjustment, new residents will have to learn to get along with at least two entirely new groups of people—the staff and other patients—so they may pull away from you and other family members. Having placed your parent in a home, your feelings may be tumultuous as well. Your feelings of relief that they are getting care may be mixed with guilt and doubt.

You can help your parents adjust to a nursing home by encouraging them to bring their personal belongings and family photos. (PHOTO BY ROCHELLE CASSERD)

Here are several suggestions in helping a parent adjust:

1. Encourage older people to take along as many personal belongings as possible, including an easy chair, plants, family photos, paintings, typewriter, even their own beds. Hospital beds are usually required in a skilled care wing but not necessarily for intermediate care.
2. Visit as often as possible, bringing children and other favorite people along. Keep lines of communications open with your parent. Be as honest as possible.
3. If your mother or father is confused and complains that no one visits, consider setting up an informal guestbook. Have visitors sign their names and the date along with a warm message to look at after they leave.
4. Develop a relationship with the nurses and aides on the floor where your parent lives. Especially if you live far away, get the phone number for the nurses' station, and learn when the most cooperative nurses are on duty. Nurses are in daily contact with residents, so they may have better information than the doctor or medical director.
5. Find out how to get in touch with the doctor in case of serious illness or a change in condition.

6. If you live far away from the nursing home, set up a regular schedule of phone calls with your parent. If possible, get the number of a phone near your parent's room, so you can call unexpectedly.

MONITORING CARE

A family's regular visits to a nursing home can do more than boost patient morale. The presence of a watchful outsider can insure that neglect or indifferent treatment will be noted and complained about promptly.

Friends and relatives sometimes hesitate to complain about nursing home problems for fear of retaliation against the elderly person. But organizations that act as advocates for nursing home residents say that well-informed family members can be very effective in improving conditions.

One such organization is Friends and Relatives of the Institutionalized Aged (FRIA), a New York City-based group working to assure quality care for nursing home residents. FRIA officials say patients whose relatives act as their advocate tend to receive better care than those without active relatives.

FRIA's 1982 manual, *A Consumer's Guide to Nursing Home Care in New York City*, outlines a number of steps to take in monitoring nursing home care:

1. Become familiar with your relative's daily routine in the nursing home, so that you'll know when something goes wrong. If a problem arises, begin by asking questions in a friendly manner. Try to identify the staff member most likely to be able to make a change, and consult him or her about the problem.
2. If the problem persists after a reasonable period, speak to the department head, keeping a written record of names, the facts of the case, and what was agreed to. If this fails, contact the home's administrator, owner, or board of directors.
3. You may want to discuss your problem with relatives of other residents. If the home has a relatives' council, talk to council members about your grievances. Residents (and their relatives) may also be able to voice complaints through a residents' council.
4. Contact the Long-Term Care Ombudsman Program by calling the state department on aging or the local Area Agency on Aging. As we have seen, the Ombudsman program is in business to investigate citizens' complaints and assist in finding remedies. You should expect your complaint to be kept confidential.
5. Call the state survey and certification agency, usually the state Department of Health, for information and to lodge complaints. Expect confidentiality here as well.

6. In some areas, private groups like FRIA have been organized to defend the rights of nursing home residents. To find out if such a group exists in your locality, contact

    National Citizens' Coalition for Nursing Home Reform
        1825 Connecticut Ave., N.W., Suite 417B
        Washington, D.C. 20009
        (202) 797-0657

CHAPTER X

If Parents Are Unable to Handle Their Resources

At some point, your parents may not be able to manage their own financial affairs. Paralyzed stroke victims may be unable to sign legal papers or indicate how they want their business handled. Those with Alzheimer's Disease or another organic brain disorder may not be able to understand matters they could have dealt with easily in earlier years.

Families frequently assume that little or nothing can be done to prepare for such incapacity. "To the contrary," wrote New York City attorneys Ellice Fatoullah and David Frazer in their paper, *Money Management and the Cost of Health Care: Options for the Elderly and Disabled.* "Prudent and timely attention to such issues can assure sound money management and provision of care while simultaneously easing the financial burden of uninsured health care on the spouse and family."

The two lawyers, who specialize in problems of the aging, suggest five possible legal options for patients unable to take care of their own resources. Each option has a different implication for Medicaid eligibility.

"I don't advise doing anything unless a disabling illness is diagnosed or the age is 75," Fatoullah said. "Before that time, if you're healthy, there's no reason to give up control of your money. People are relatively young at 65. Many are still vibrant, still working."

Outright Gifts

The easiest way to manage the resources of an incapacitated parent is to have the patient make an outright gift to his or her children or spouse. Fatoullah and Frazer recommend this option for older people with $50,000 or less in assets.

Pros   In most cases, the recipient of the gift assumes responsibility for the assets without charge to the disabled person, so this option is the most inexpensive kind of money management for the incapacitated. Such a gift can be structured to minimize federal and state gift taxes.

Cons   When assets are given freely to another person, there are no formal controls on what the beneficiary can do with the funds. For this obvious reason, an elderly person must trust the recipient of the assets.

If trust breaks down, there are implications for both recipient and donor. Parents may fear their children will turn into King Lear's ungrateful daughters, frittering away resources intended to care for an aged father. Adult children, on the other hand, may do their best in managing a parent's assets, only to find their investment ideas under suspicion.

Even with a relationship of trust, problems may arise. First, assets can be signed over only when the donor is legally competent. If this is in doubt, the gift may be questioned. Second, in case the recipient divorces or dies unexpectedly, the assets may be tied up in the estate or divorce proceedings and diverted away from the parent it was intended to help.

In addition, the assets and resulting income will add to the recipient's income tax bill. If the amounts are substantial, this tax burden may be unacceptable.

Medicaid eligibility   To qualify for Medicaid, an outright gift of assets must be made two years or more before a Medicaid application is made. If the recipient is an adult child, the question of fiscal responsibility for nursing home bills should not arise. If the gift is made to a spouse, however, some of the assets may be claimed for payment of a nursing home bill.

Durable Power of Attorney

A power of attorney is a written, signed, and notarized document, used in every state, in which one person, the "principal," nominates another, often a family member, to act as "attorney-in-fact" on his or her behalf. A power of attorney is "durable" when the language specificies that it should continue even if the principal becomes disabled or incompetent. It can be revoked at any time so long as the principal is competent. Durable powers of attorney can also be used to name a trusted individual to make medical-treatment decisions. When used for financial management, Fatoullah and Frazer recommend it for people with "very small estates."

Pros A power of attorney is easy to draft and execute. It authorizes the nominee to take action in a wide range of financial matters, paying bills, and buying or selling stocks. Under a durable power of attorney, the patient's financial affairs may be managed both before and during incapacity.

Cons As with an outright gift, the attorney-in-fact has few formal controls on his or her actions, especially if the older person becomes incompetent. Therefore, only a trusted individual should be appointed. In addition, a power of attorney may not be recognized by a bank, insurance company, or brokerage house unless a power of attorney form is signed specifically for that company.

Medicaid implications A power of attorney may be used to make business transactions, but it would not affect Medicaid eligibility unless assets were transferred to another person. As with any transfer, Medicaid eligibility would not begin for two years.

Conservatorship

A conservatorship is a court proceeding in which a judge appoints a "conservator" (usually a friend or relative) to care for the property of a person unable to manage his or her own financial affairs because of illness or advanced age. Laws differ state to state, but an actual trial may be held, with a physician testifying as to the mental state of the "conservatee" and a *guardian ad litem* appointed in some cases to represent the disabled person's interests.

Pros The court supervises the management of assets to make sure the older person's needs are being met. As an added protection, the conservator must post a bond and file an annual accounting with the court. A conservatorship may be the only practical way to buy and sell stocks and transfer funds if an elderly person is entirely lacking in mental capacity.

Cons A conservatorship is the most drastic and least desirable money management option, particularly because it involves an open court proceeding to assess the capacity of the individual. Besides the breach of privacy, such a proceeding may be costly because of fees for the lawyer, physician, *guardian* *ad litem,* and conservator. It may take several months to complete, possibly leaving a patient's financial affairs up in the air during the process.

Medicaid eligibility   A conservatorship may make it impossible to transfer assets for Medicaid eligibility because the legal proceeding is designed to protect—not divest—the assets of the conservatee.

Protective Custody

When a frail elderly person is truly alone and without resources, a person paid by the state (usually an attorney or social worker) may be appointed a guardian or conservator. Laws differ in each state, but protective services are usually used for seriously impaired people who have no other source of help. In some states, a protective services order can be used to remove an older person from a home if elderly abuse is found.

Pros   This technique is used when the older person has no family or friends able or willing to serve as conservator or when the amount of resources involved is too small to warrant the private appointment of a conservator.

Cons   Some people may object to being placed under governmental supervision. Since court oversight may be lax, some may fear they will be placed in a nursing home without due process.

Medicaid implications   A protective services order cannot be used to transfer assets to qualify for Medicaid. In many cases, however, the guardian can help an eligible person fill out applications and produce the needed documentation to get on Medicaid quickly.

Trusts

A trust is a legal agreement in which a person or couple transfers resources to a trust fund and orders that the assets and income be used in a particular way. The grantor or grantors designate a trustee, often a relative or friend, to manage the fund in accordance with their wishes.

As a legal entity, a trust must obtain a Social Security (or tax identification) number and pay taxes. Grantors decide whether the trust will be revocable or irrevocable and may direct that it come into being at the time when they become disabled or can no longer take care of themselves.

The trust agreement can specify exactly how to dispose of the assets of the trust (stocks, bonds, real estate, etc.) or the income (dividends, interest, rent), or it can leave the details up to the trustee. The trust may be ended after a particular "term," often the life of the grantor or the life of a disabled beneficiary, or it may cease when the assets have been paid out to a designated group of beneficiaries.

Fatoullah and Frazer regard the trust as the most desirable money management tool for a disabled elderly person. They recommend it "for estates in excess of $100,000 and for persons of 75 years of age and older."

Pros   Trusts are flexible, ordinarily enabling the family to use various estate planning techniques to protect an older person's resources. Banks, insurance companies, and brokerage houses readily recognize a trustee's authority, enabling smooth management of assets and transfers of property. Unlike an outright gift, a trust will not mean added income taxes for a child serving as trustee, since assets and income belong to the trust.

In addition, elderly grantors can specify in a trust agreement how assets will be disbursed after their death, thereby avoiding the process of probating a will.

Cons   Setting up a trust fund is a legal procedure, more complex (and more costly, because of lawyers' fees) than making an outright gift or signing a power of attorney. A trust also places more obligations on the trustee, who must file an annual accounting with the court and an income tax return with the IRS. Also, it may be difficult for an elderly person to find an individual he or she regards as trustworthy enough to handle substantial assets.

Medicaid implications   Congress has criticized the use of trusts to avoid payment of nursing home bills. Current Medicaid implications are under scrutiny and may change.

Not for the Rich Alone

Legal maneuvers to facilitate the transfer of older people's assets are usually thought of as a tactic designed for the very wealthy. Not necessarily so, say legal experts.

"If you have a huge amount of money, you can afford to pay privately or to transfer assets and wait two years," said Fatoullah. "It's the middle class that tends to be hurt. People with estates of $50,000 or less will run out of money very soon with the lack of long-term care financing. I can't believe society wants to bankrupt its elderly people."

CHAPTER XI

Preparing for Death

Making a Will • Living Wills: A Choice Whether to Live • Hospice Programs • Planning the Funeral

As you try to help your parents cope with the increasing aches and pains of old age, you may be haunted by the certain knowledge that death—rather than eventual recovery—lies in the future. But "life and death are intertwined," said Tish Sommers, founder of the Older Women's League, when she was dying of cancer. "We are all terminal cases, and we're all going to die sooner or later."

No one loses a parent casually. You probably expect to feel overwhelmed by emotion, but you may be surprised at the form your grief takes. Many people react with pain, anger, and an unanticipated sense of abandonment at the death of a father, even after years of bitter antagonism. Others may feel relieved—and guilty about it—when the burden of caring for a beloved mother is lifted.

Your parents may be more anxious to discuss their concerns about death and dying than you are. Knowing their wishes can prepare you to help them remain in control of their own destiny as long as possible, since you may have to make decisions for them in case of their incapacity or death.

Your parents, on the other hand, may regard any mention of death as unlucky or taboo and resent the very mention of subjects like living wills or funerals. If they feel this way, you may want to assure them that you do not wish to intrude. But you might also point out that you or some other trusted person should be told the location of their will and which estate lawyer, funeral home, and cemetery they wish to use. If your parents have prepaid for a funeral or a burial plot, it's especially important that the family knows who to contact at the time of death.

MAKING A WILL

A will is a legal declaration of how people want their money, property, and other possessions disposed of after their death. Wills are also used to determine guardianship of minor children and to set up trusts for heirs with an inadequate knowledge of how to manage property and money.

Since most people hate to think about death, many die intestate—that is, without making a will. If so, their belongings are distributed according to the laws of their state, rather than by their own choice.

Other estate-planning strategies have already been discussed. Some people prefer to give their property away during their lifetime, rather than make a will. Others put their estate in trust, assigning a court-supervised trustee to manage it and pass it along to a beneficiary at a given time.

Many married couples expect to pass their resources along through joint ownership. In a marriage where all assets are held jointly, the surviving spouse automatically owns the joint property without the need for a will.

A will is usually the simplest method by which a person can direct what happens to his or her resources at death, however. It's as wise for married people to have wills as those who are single, since almost everyone holds some property, if only a bank account, in his or her own name.

When making a will, it's best to see a lawyer and pay the legal fees, which should not exceed $150 for a pair of simple wills. Handwritten and verbal wills are honored in some states, but they can be challenged more easily than written wills, if some family members feel they were not treated fairly.

Steps to Remember

If your parents ask you for advice, suggest they consider the following points and then see a lawyer:

Make a list of resources   Urge your parents to have a written list of assets and income with them when they visit the lawyer. If they need help in drawing up such a list, use the format in the Financial Planning section of this book.

Clarify and write down their wishes   Before seeing an attorney, your parents should talk honestly with each other about how they want to dispose of their assets and who any treasured belongings should go to.

Choose an executor   In making a will, your parents will be asked to select one or more executors to carry out the will's provisions. Most married people choose their spouses as executor, but you or another trusted individual, a bank, or a lawyer may also be chosen. Depending on the will and the estate size, an executor's work may be demanding, so most are paid a fee, usually a small percentage of the estate. Sometimes the will specifies a lawyer for the estate; in many cases, executors hire the designated attorney, but they are not legally required to do so.

Witnesses   A will must be signed in the presence of witnesses, who generally should not be family members or possible beneficiaries in the estate. The number of witnesses is set by state law.

Where to keep it   A will may be filed for safekeeping by the lawyer who drew it up, though most people want to keep copies themselves. In general, a safety-deposit box is not a good place for a will, since in some states, these boxes are sealed after a renter's death. Some close family member should know where the original is.

Review it periodically   Wills should be reviewed periodically and amended if necessary. If your parents move to another state or if the family situation changes, a new will should be made promptly.

What Happens at the Time of Death

When a person dies, his or her will is presented to the appropriate state court (the probate court in most states), usually after being opened and read by the family. Everyone with an interst in the estate is to be notified—heirs as well as those owed money by the deceased person.

If one of the interested parties believes the will is not valid, a court challenge may be filed. If the challenger wins, a prior will may be found valid or the estate may be divided according to the state's laws.

Most wills are found valid by the probate court without court battles. If so, the executor pays taxes and court fees, distributes the property, and carries out other instructions according to the will's terms. The estate is then closed and the executor discharged.

If Your Parent Has No Will

If your father or mother never made a will, all individually held assets will be divided according to state law, which sets forth what percentage of the estate each family member is entitled to. Jointly held assets, of course, will pass directly to the co-owner.

Without a will appointing an executor, the probate court will appoint you, your surviving parent, or another person as administrator to handle the estate. The court may also appoint a lawyer or a guardian, if children or an incapacitated adult are involved, with the estate becoming responsible for the ensuing fees.

LIVING WILLS: A CHOICE WHETHER TO LIVE

A living will is a document that allows people to state in advance their wishes regarding the use of life-sustaining procedures when they are dying. The living will may also appoint someone else—a relative, friend, or attorney—to direct health care if the person signing it is unable to do so.

In most cases, people who sign living wills want to be sure that they will not receive unwanted or unwarranted treatment if death is near and they have no reasonable expectation of recovering. Others may want to make clear that they would like to spend their last days at home or that they want to donate their organs for transplants.

Living wills are based on the right of competent adults to refuse life-sustaining treatment. With rare exceptions, this legal right has been upheld in the courts at least since the early 1900s. If a patient dies as a result of refusing treatment, the courts have not defined the death as suicide, since the life-threatening illness or condition is not self-inflicted.

In 1981, the American Medical Association officially recognized this legal principle, observing that physicians sometimes face a conflict in trying both to prolong life and to relieve suffering. When such a contradiction arises, the AMA said the problem should be resolved jointly by the physician, the patient, and the patient's family.

Legal Standing of Living Wills

A total of 38 states and the District of Columbia have passed laws making some form of a living will legally binding under certain circumstances. But living wills have been upheld in the other states as well, according to Concern for Dying, an educational council that provides information about living wills.

The organization's legal advisors say the living will is enforceable in all states "as an assertion of the common-law right to bodily self-determination and the constitutional right to privacy." What court cases have arisen have usually been filed by nursing homes or hospitals fearful of withholding treatment because of possible legal recriminations.

When a written living will exists, Concern for Dying contends that such fears may be groundless. "To date, no health-care provider or facility has had to face criminal or civil charges as a result of honoring a living will." In fact, the organization argues that "the living will can provide the basis for legal action against a health-care provider if the living will is *not* honored."

What Does a Living Will Say?

Living wills come in many forms. Some people choose to write a personal letter to their family and doctor about what they would like done in case of severe illness and inability to speak. Others prefer Living Will forms provided by organizations like Concern for Dying:

> Let this statement stand as an expression of my wishes and directions, while I am still of sound mind. If at such a time the situation should arise in which there is no reasonable expectation of my recovery from extreme physical or mental disability, I direct that I be allowed to die and not be kept alive by medications, artificial means or "heroic measures."

Language can be added to specify that cardiopulmonary resuscitation, nasogastric tube feeding, or mechanical respiration not be used or to issue other instructions.

Durable Power of Attorney for Health Care

The living will drafted by Concern for Dying also has an optional provision for a durable power of attorney for health care. With the "durable" power, the attorney-in-fact would be authorized to make decisions about medical treatment even if the person signing became incompetent.

To Be Sure the Living Will Is Enforced

You and your parents will want to make sure that the living will is honored. Concern for Dying makes the following recommendations:

Communication   Once a living will is written, your parents should discuss their wishes with you, their physician, attorney, other relatives, and anyone else who might be called on to make a medical decision in case of their incapacity. Their doctor should put a copy of the living will in their medical file. If the physician objects to doing this, they may want to consider changing doctors.

Durable Power of Attorney   In signing a durable power of attorney for health care, your parents can name any willing person—you or some other close relative or friend—as attorney-in-fact for making medical decisions. They should talk to this person in advance about their wishes and the terms of their living will.

Safekeeping   Living wills should be kept in safe but accessible places. Besides their doctor, your parents should give copies to the person named in the durable power of attorney (if any), close family members, their lawyer, and their clergy person. A safety deposit box is not a good place to keep a living will, since the document might not be found when it is needed.

Witnesses   The signature on a living will should be witnessed by two adults who are not related by blood and who are not designated the attorney-in-fact. As witnesses, these people testify that the living will is being signed voluntarily. If the witnesses were relatives or possible heirs to the estate, the implied conflict of interest could call the living will into question.

Having the living will notarized   A durable power of attorney *must* be notarized, so if your parents want to include this provision in a living will, they must have a notary public witness their signatures. It's a good idea to have a living will notarized in any case, as evidence of the seriousness of a signer's intent.

Updating the living will   Living wills should be redated and initialed periodically, about every five years, to keep the instructions current. In case of confusion about your parents' intentions, a recent date acts as evidence to a doctor or a court that a living will is genuine.

For More Information

Since it was founded in 1967, Concern for Dying has distributed more than seven million copies of its Living Will. Single copies and specific data about requirements in individual states are available free from

> Concern for Dying
> 250 West 57th St.
> New York, NY 10107
> (212) 246-6962

HOSPICE PROGRAMS

Contemporary society gives us little help in coping with a fatal illness like cancer or with the resulting moment of death. Hospice, a program now funded by Medicare, helps dying people retain as much control over their lives as possible in case of terminal illness. It provides a continuum of care, including pain relief and counseling, for patients with six months or less to live and focuses on helping both patient and family come to terms with the imminent death. With hospice, family members provide most of the direct care in the home with the help of an interdisciplinary hospice team.

Historically, most people died at home, cared for by family members. With modern medical technology, however, death now more often occurs in the sterile, clinical environment of a hospital, after the full range of curative measures—from radical surgery to painful chemotherapy—have been tried unsuccessfully. Experimental programs may begin with hope, only to leave patients feeling like guinea pigs.

With hospice, the emphasis is on restoring dignity by relieving pain and offering psychosocial supports not available in a hospital. Once a patient decides on hospice, aggressive techniques like chemotherapy, radiotherapy, or surgery are no longer tried. No attempt is made to prolong life beyond its natural end through resuscitation or special machines. Instead, the interdisciplinary hospice team uses its expertise not for curing but for caring.

"Hospice affirms life and regards dying as a normal process," according to the standards of the National Hospice Organization. "Hospice neither hastens nor postpones death. Hospice believes that through personalized services and a caring community, patients and families can attain the necessary preparation for a death that is satisfactory to them."

History of Hospice

The term "hospice" was first used during the Middle Ages for church-sponsored lodging places where sick and weary travelers could rest and refresh themselves. The relatively short history of the modern hospice movement began in 1967, when Dame Cicely Saunders, a British doctor, opened St. Christopher's Hospice in London. In the homelike atmosphere of St. Christopher's, neither visiting hours nor visitors were limited, so the staff could help the entire family share in the dying experience.

The first American hospice began operations in 1974 in Branford, Connecticut, near New Haven. The Connecticut Hospice has a 44-bed inpatient unit modeled after St. Christopher's, but it led the American hospice tradition away from the idea of hospice as a *homelike place* for dying and emphasized the idea of *care for the dying at home.* By late 1985, the Connecticut facility was treating 1,400 patients a year, about 83% of everyone who died of cancer in the New Haven area.

In 1983, Medicare began offering hospice benefits, making the at-home model primary, in part because home-based hospice care in the final year of life costs significantly less than either conventional care or hospital-based hospices. Medicare pays for inpatient hospice care on a short-term basis only, when the patient needs specific professional services or when the family needs respite.

Hospice Programs Today

Today, the United States has approximately 1,500 hospice programs serving 100,000 dying persons each year, according to the National Hospice Organization. About 65% of the patients are 65 years old or older, and 80% suffer from cancer.

The programs vary in structure. Some are all-volunteer, grassroots groups that offer their services free. Some are, in effect, agencies that provide professional care in the home and in a special inpatient hospice unit, usually in a hospital, if and when the need arises.

A third kind is run by hospitals themselves with a special hospice staff and section for dying patients. And a few other hospices, like Connecticut's, have their own inpatient facilities, entirely separate from hospitals.

Hospice programs have four basic characteristics: the patient and family as the unit of care, a multidisciplinary hospice team, pain control, and counseling.

Patient and Family as the Unit of Care

Hospice programs believe that people who are dying can be cared for best in their own homes with their families acting as the primary caregivers. For that reason, the patient and family together are regarded as the "unit of care," meaning that services and support go to the family as well as to the patient.

Families receive training in the specifics of patient care during regular visits from the hospice staff. They learn how to administer pain-killing drugs in adequate dosages. Equally important, they receive counseling both before the death and afterwards, to help them deal with their grief.

To lighten the load, most hospice programs provide respite workers who stay in the home if the family must be away for a few days. The respite program also allows patients to check into the hospice inpatient unit temporarily.

Some programs insist that a family member or "significant other" be available to act as primary caregiver and the hospice contact. But many programs will accept a patient who lives alone. "We often find ourselves piecing together a significant other from whomever the person has—a neighbor, a friend, or a former spouse," said Sue Buster of the Hospice of Marin in San

Raphael, California. "We need someone to take responsibility and relate to us."

Multidisciplinary Team

Unlike conventional medical care, hospice services are provided by a team of professionals, not a lone physician. This reflects hospice philosophy, which sees a person as a composite of physical, psychological, social, and spiritual elements.

The team begins its work with an assessment of patient needs, usually made after a home visit by the nurse, medical director, and social worker. Then a plan of care is developed, utilizing the following kinds of services to support the individual needs of patient and family.

Physicians   A patient's own primary-care physician generally serves on the hospice team, shifting to a palliative, or pain-relieving, approach once all the curative efforts have been tried. In addition, a hospice must have a doctor as medical director.

Nurses   The hospice nurse coordinates the work of the team. After developing the plan of care, nurses ordinarily make one or two visits of an hour or two a week to each patient on their case list. In addition to providing direct care, they offer counseling to both patient and family. Most hospice programs have a nurse on call 24 hours a day, enabling family members to phone for advice if the patient's symptoms intensify. If an emergency arises, a nurse or aide may be sent immediately to a patient's home.

Social Workers   Social workers help with financial planning, counseling, and assessing family needs. They also provide family support in helping plan funeral arrangements and comforting families during the bereavement period.

Home health aides and homemakers   These nursing aides are usually assigned to visit patients several times a week for periods of an hour or two each. They may bathe patients, do light housekeeping or shopping, cook a meal, give counseling, or, as a hospice director noted, "just hold their hands and befriend them." If a health crisis arises, aides or nurses may be assigned temporarily on a 24-hour basis to supplement family care.

Clergy   Ministers, priests, and rabbis have traditionally been part of hospice. When dying patients need spiritual counseling or support, their own pastor or rabbi may provide it as a team member, though the hospice may also suggest a name from a list of religious counselors available in the community.

Volunteers In most hospice programs, a volunteer is assigned to each patient, not to provide direct care but to be a regular visitor and friend. Volunteers usually undergo extensive training in how to give family support. They also handle practical tasks, like shopping and errands.

Some programs train volunteers to work exclusively in the bereavement process, so families can "tell their story all over again to work through the death experience." These volunteers often never meet the patient.

In other programs, volunteers are utilized only in the office or for transportation duties, sometimes because of the lack of professional liability insurance.

Pain Control

Terminally ill patients often fear pain as much as dying, especially when the diagnosis is cancer, so the hospice team immediately prescribes the most effective medications to relieve pain and symptoms. Dosages are kept at sufficient levels to prevent pain from ever developing or to keep it at the lowest level possible while maintaining the patient's mental alertness.

"In most patients, we can with a mixture of drugs and careful titration eliminate pain completely," said Ira Bates of the National Hospice Organization. Titration is the process of determining how much medication is needed to keep each person's pain just below the sensory threshold. Drugs are prescribed on a continuous basis, rather than "as needed" (when pain recurs).

Families are taught to administer the medications, often orally or by suppository. At the Connecticut Hospice, to minimize pain, only 22% of dosages are given by injection.

Some hospices also teach patients relaxation techniques, like self-hypnosis or the use of visual imaging, to take their minds off pain. "A lot of it is psychic pain," said Becky McDonald of the Hospice of Volusia in Daytona Beach, Florida. "People are anxious and this heightens their symptoms."

Ironically, some patients resist having pain relieved, believing that their agony will somehow stave off death. Patients and families also worry that pain killers will lead to addiction or that patients will end life in a drug-induced trance. "We try to educate them through brochures on pain control and by talking," McDonald said. "The incidence of addiction is less than 1% in hospice patients. We absolutely can control the pain and keep patients alert."

Counseling   Once physical pain is relieved, the hospice team can begin helping patients and families deal emotionally with the subject of death. "Controlling pain and symptoms gives the patients quality of life so they can deal with the other issues," said the NHO's Ira Bates. "They may start to walk again once the pain is gone, and then they may be able to seek counseling."

Three issues seem to trouble families of the dying most—how to tell patients they are dying, what to do if and when the patient dies at home, and how to get over their grief.

Telling the Patient   Participating in a hospice program means, by definition, that a terminal illness is involved, so the difficult task of "telling the patient" is a necessary preliminary. In many cases, family members wonder how to proceed.

Hospice personnel say many patients already know. "If you see yourself getting thinner, while everyone says you're okay, you have probably put two and two together," said William Liss-Levinson, director of the Brooklyn Hospice.

In some cases, the family has more difficulty coping with the news than the patient, so the hospice team may try to set up a meeting to help the family deal with the physical realities or with fears that the act of entering hospice means "giving up" or a loss of hope.

"I don't feel it's a case of the door closing," said Sue Buster of the Hospice of Marin, "because we have discharged patients who have recovered after being in hospice. It doesn't happen often, but the possibility is there."

Facing Death at Home   For caregivers facing the moment of death, the hospice team can help by informing both patient and family what to expect. "With given types of cancers, we can project what may happen, though it's always hard to be accurate," said Liss-Levinson. When caregivers know what the signs of death are, they may be able to spend the final moments with their loved one and remain calm. Since hospice support is available round-the-clock, family members also have the option of having a nurse come to the home at the time of death—to call the funeral director or whoever will handle burial or simply as a source of comfort.

Bereavement Counseling   As part of its commitment to families, hospice programs ordinarily include grief counseling for immediate relatives for a year or more after the death, depending on their reaction. Some of this counseling is done on an individual basis, often in the home, but groups are also used.

The Hospice of Marin invites bereaved relatives every month to an educational program on loss and grief or to a potluck dinner so relatives can socialize with volunteers, staff members, and other alumni of the program.

Medicare's Hospice Benefits

Medicare's hospice program, covered under Part A hospital insurance, is one of its most generous for those eligible. Older people pay no deductibles and are covered for most of the cost of pain-killing drugs and inpatient respite care.

The program pays 100% of the cost of home visits by hospice doctors, nurses, home health aides, medical social workers, and physical, occupational, and speech therapists. It also pays for medical supplies and appliances and for short-term, inpatient care. Round-the-clock coverage by aides or homemakers is possible during a health crisis.

Drugs to relieve pain and control symptoms are covered both in the hospital and out, with patients responsible for only 5% of the cost, or $5 per prescription, whichever is less. Patients also must pay 5% of the cost of inpatient respite care up to the total of the Part A deductible ($520 in 1987).

To qualify, patients must meet the following three conditions:

1. A doctor must certify they are terminally ill (with six months or less to live).
2. They must choose hospice and waive standard Medicare benefits for the terminal illness, a step that means an end to chemotherapy, radiotherapy, and other curative efforts. (Regular Medicare benefits are still in effect for health problems not related to the terminal illness.)
3. The hospice program must be Medicare-certified.

Medicare coverage is limited to 210 days—two 90-day periods plus an additional period of 30 days. For patients who still need and want hospice care after that time, Medicare mandates that services be continued indefinitely. The hospice may bill for the extended services if the family is able to pay.

Patients can opt out of the hospice program at any time and return to regular Medicare, but if they want to return to hospice, they will be limited to the number of days of the 210-day maximum that they didn't use.

Alternatives to Medicare Hospice

Unfortunately, only about 240 hospices nationwide have received Medicare certification, so many terminally ill patients may be out-of-range of a certified program. If this happens to your mother or father, there are several alternatives.

1. Design a hospice-style, home-care arrangement for your parent through regular home health benefits supplied by a Medicare-certified home health agency. If your doctor authorizes it (and other conditions are met), Medicare may pay for regular visits by nurses, therapists, home health aides, and social workers. Specific hospice benefits like respite, outpatient prescription drugs, and counseling will not be included, however.
2. Get help from one of the many hospice programs without Medicare certification. These programs may have no inpatient unit or may offer counseling only, but "that is not to say they are unqualified," according to Ira Bates of the NHO.
3. Some group insurance policies now cover hospice services. So if your parents were able to continue their preretirement group policy, they may be able to get hospice care from a program not certified by Medicare in this way.

Few, if any, hospices reject a patient for inability to pay. Some, especially those run mainly by volunteers or organized by a religious group, don't believe in charging anything for their services. Others have a sliding scale.

When Is Hospice Not Appropriate?

Hospice is not appropriate for every terminally ill person. The reasons may include the following:

1. The patient and the family want to continue to fight the terminal disease. Patients are not accepted in hospice as long as they are undergoing curative treatments, and many cancer patients—and their families—want to try everything, including experimental treatments.
2. The patient lives alone, perhaps in a city far from your home, without a relative or friend nearby who can act as a primary care giver. Some programs will not accept a dying patient who lives alone.
3. You and your family are unable to act as primary care giver, for health or other reasons. For some people, caring for a dying person at home is too intimidating, even with the help of hospice.
4. Your parent suffers from an incurable disease for which a six-month prognosis cannot be established. Severe heart and kidney conditions fall into this category, along with amyotrophic lateral sclerosis (ALS, sometimes called Lou Gehrig's disease) and Alzheimer's Disease. As doctors learn more about the course of these illnesses, biological markers may be developed to make a six-month prognosis easier to determine.
5. You and your parent already get enough support from friends, relatives, and church volunteers and do not need the formal help of hospice.

Selecting a Hospice Program

If you feel hospice could help your mother or father either soon or at sometime in the future, call a local program and talk about your situation. Referrals to hospice are not limited to doctors. Anyone may refer a patient, including clergy, hospital discharge planners, social workers, a relative, or a friend. Many hospices offer family consultations at no cost, and hospice personnel are often able to tell whether the patient has reached a stage appropriate for the program.

In selecting a program, explore the following issues:

Licensing   Eighteen states and the District of Columbia licensed hospice programs as of 1986, though each uses different guidelines. The states are Colorado, Connecticut, Delaware, Florida, Georgia, Illinois, Iowa, Kentucky, Maryland, Massachusetts, Michigan, Montana, New Mexico, New York, North Carolina, Texas, Virginia, and West Virginia. If your parents live in one of these states, check to see that the hospice has a current license. For more information, call the state health department.

Accreditation   The Joint Commission on Accreditation of Hospitals has been evaluating hospice programs since 1984. A total of 100 programs were accredited as of May 1986, 78 of them associated with Commission-accredited hospitals.

Medicare Certification   All 240 Medicare-certified hospices (as of April 1986) provide the full range of services provided by Medicare. Some hospices have chosen not to seek certification because they do not offer all the mandated services or because they say Medicare reimbursement rates are inadequate. Others fear the economic burden of having to continue hospice care for patients who live beyond the 210-day benefit limit if patients cannot afford to pay.

Standards   The National Hospice Organization has drawn up a list of standards for a model hospice, covering such issues as personnel, administration, patient care, and the physical plant. NHO members agree voluntarily to comply with the standards.

Other Questions   Question hospice officials about the specifics of the services offered, including the following:

1. Are team members open to participation by your parent's private, primary-care physician?

2. How would the hospice proceed in controlling your parent's pain and other symptoms? What procedures are ordinarily used?

3. Do team members receive special training? Are aides employed by the hospice or are they supplied by nurses registries or other subcontractors?

4. How does the hospice provide round-the-clock coverage? Is a nurse available to come to your home 24 hours a day, when needed, or only available for advice by telephone?

5. Is counseling available on an individual basis during the bereavement period or is it limited to support groups? How long are bereavement services offered?

6. Does the hospice have its own inpatient unit? Is the unit part of a hospital? Is hospice-type care given from admission through discharge, even in cases of emergency admissions through the emergency room? Does the hospice arrange for "Do Not Resuscitate" orders if patients and families agree?

For Further Information

To find a hospice program near your parents, call the Area Agency on Aging or check the local phone book under "hospice." In addition, information is available from the

> National Hospice Organization
> 1901 North Fort Myer Drive, Suite 901
> Arlington, VA 22209
> (703) 243-5900

In addition, write for *A Consumer Guide to Hospice Care*, from

> National Consumers League
> 600 Maryland Ave., S.W., Suite 202-West
> Washington, D.C. 20024
> (202) 554-1600

PLANNING THE FUNERAL

After the anxiety and pain of a parent's final illness, you still face difficult decisions in preparing for a funeral or cremation. For most families, it's most important to arrange a meaningful and appropriate service for the person who has died.

Cost may not initially seem to be a major concern, but you may begin to worry about the total price as you meet with a funeral director to decide on arrangements. In fact, funerals tend to be very costly. The average cost (not including burial expenses) is $2,500.

Your parents may already have told you what kind of funeral they want for themselves when the time comes, or they may have written down their instructions. If death comes before planning can be done, consider asking a friend, clergy person, or some other non-family member to go with you to the funeral home for emotional support and help in making wise decisions. Otherwise, high-pressure tactics of a salesman can leave you feeling helpless and paralyzed.

Traditional Funerals

Usually the most expensive arrangements, the traditional funeral varies according to religion or culture, but it ordinarily involves embalming the body of the deceased person for a period of mourning and sometimes viewing.

Traditional funeral expenses usually include

— moving the body to the funeral home from the place of death
— use of funeral home facilities and hearse
— embalming and other preparations for the body
— coffin, flowers, guest register, and acknowledgement cards
— newspaper obituary notices
— preparing and filing the death certificate and burial permit

Funeral directors now must disclose the price of all items involved in a funeral, both over the phone and, during a visit, in writing, according to the consumer-oriented funeral rule adopted in 1984 by the Federal Trade Commission. This rule makes it possible for families to comparison shop and choose only the goods and services they want.

Once arrangements are complete, the funeral director must give the family an itemized statement and the total cost of the services they want. If you don't get such a statement, ask for one. The funeral rule also requires morticians to notify the family of any service fee charged for so-called cash advance items, like flowers or obituaries.

Cemetery Burial

Burial in a cemetery plot can be an expensive addition to the cost of funeral arrangements. Earth burial usually includes the following costs:

— the plot, which, at most cemeteries, must be paid for in full before use
— opening and closing the grave, often more costly on weekends
— a vault or grave liner. Many cemeteries require a vault to prevent collapse of the grave site, though it is not required by state or local law

— grave marker or monument, with the price depending on the material, and a fee for installation

Some cemeteries charge a fee for perpetual care of the grave. Others regard this as a part of the purchase price and keep part of the fee in trust for this purpose. Some states require that funds be set aside in this manner.

Above-ground or mausoleum tombs tend to be more expensive than cemetery plots, but some of the costs of an earth burial will be saved.

Before purchasing a cemetery plot or mausoleum tomb, ask for the cemetery association's rules and regulations. If you wish, visit several local cemeteries to compare prices, policies, and maintenance.

Cremation

With cremation, the body is placed in a boxlike container or casket and taken to a crematory where it is exposed to intense heat and reduced to ashes and bone fragments. The "cremains" may be stored in an urn, scattered, or buried in a cemetery or in a niche at a columbarium (a special building designed to hold cremation urns).

Cremation is less expensive than a traditional funeral, because neither embalming nor a casket is necessary. The FTC rule directs funeral directors to notify families that embalming is not legally required for a cremation and that they may buy an unfinished wood box or a simple container of fiberboard or cardboard instead of a casket.

The costs usually include:

— transportation of the body and the ashes
— box or container for the body
— cremation itself
— urn or container for the ashes
— use of a chapel, if desired, and other goods or services provided by a funeral home
— filing of death certificate and other legal documents
— burial or scattering of ashes
— memorial plaque, if desired

Burial of ashes in a cemetery or columbarium would entail expenses, like any other burial. The scattering of cremated remains could be handled through the crematorium or individually by the family, but local laws should be checked. Some states and localities restrict the scattering of ashes over land or water.

Direct Disposition

Direct disposition is less expensive than a traditional funeral and is appropriate when the family wants to proceed quickly. The body is taken from the place of death directly to the cemetery or crematorium for disposition. A graveside service may be held, or a memorial service may be scheduled later.

The usual costs are:

— transportation of body from place of death to cemetery or crematorium
— suitable container for the transfer
— shelter prior to disposition
— filing of death certificate and other legal documents
— burial or cremation expenses
— funeral goods and services, if any

Memorial Service

A memorial service is usually held after a direct cremation or burial, either at a funeral home or in another suitable location. It may be similar to a traditional funeral service, or it may be designed to reflect the values and philosophy of the deceased person, family, or friends. It usually costs less than a traditional funeral and involves:

— use of a chapel or auditorium for the service
— whatever goods and services a funeral home may supply

Prepayment

In recent years, some funeral directors have promoted the idea of paying in advance for funerals and offer contracts on an installment basis. Many older people prepay so they can decide for themselves what kind of funeral they want and protect their families from heavy expenses. Prepayment can also offer peace of mind when there are no close relatives to handle arrangements.

But consumer advocates caution that prepayment carries certain risks, especially if the contract and the individual state's laws do not contain specific consumer protections. Possible disadvantages include the following:

— Family members may not know about the prepayment contract and may not be able to take advantage of it.
— The funeral home may go out of business before the purchaser's death.
— The person may die before completing the payments, invalidating the contract unless there is life insurance or survivors pay the balance.

— Because of financial hardship, purchasers may not be able to pay installments when due or may have to stop paying altogether. Refunds may be substantially less than the total already paid.

— Buyers may move to another area, but there may be no way to transfer the arrangement to another funeral home or get a refund.

— In some states, money paid must be placed in an interest-bearing trust account for the purchaser. In states without such requirements, unscrupulous dealers may spend the funds and the interest, leaving nothing for funeral expenses at the time of death.

Half the states now require a license to sell funerals on preneed basis, and more than half require that the entire contract price be placed in trust. If your parents are considering prepayment, suggest that they consider the above issues in reviewing the contract and that they consult a lawyer before signing. In addition, information is available from the agency in each state that governs the funeral industry.

Cemeteries and mausoleums also offer spaces for sale on a preneed basis. Consumer advocates say this is wise only if buyers are sure the burial site involved will be their final choice and that they are not likely to move to another part of the country. To avoid high costs of transporting a body hundreds of miles for burial, some cemeteries offer exchange programs with cemeteries in other states.

Alternatives to Prepaying

Instead of buying a preneed contract from a funeral home or purchasing a burial plot in advance, your parents may want to consider setting up a specific interest-bearing bank account or buying a standard life insurance policy specifically to cover funeral expenses. If they want to make sure their opinions count in making funeral and disposition arrangements, they should put their intentions in writing in a letter to you or another family member.

For Further Information

For further information on funerals and related issues, contact the state licensing board that regulates the insurance industry in your parents' state. Other organizations that could provide help include the AARP, other aging advocates, and the following:

Continental Association of Funeral and Memorial Societies
2001 S St., N.W., Suite 530
Washington, D.C. 20009
(202) 745-0634

National Funeral Directors Association
135 West Wells St., Suite 600
Milwaukee, WI 53203
(414) 541-2500

Cremation Association of North America
111 East Wacker Drive
Chicago, IL 60601
(312) 644-6610

CHAPTER XII

Listings of State and Area Agencies on Aging

Congress passed the Older Americans Act in 1965 as part of President Lyndon Johnson's Great Society in an effort to provide Americans over 60 with social services beyond those covered by Social Security and Medicare. In 1973, Congress expanded the law and established regional offices called Area Agencies on Aging (AAAs) to coordinate services to the elderly in a given locality.

Today, more than 600 Area Agencies on Aging cover each city and county in the country with a variety of federally funded services. Perhaps the best known of these programs are the senior centers, which provide activities and serve nourishing noon meals to the elderly, both in community dining rooms and at home through Meals on Wheels programs.

Other AAA services that may be available in your parents' community include transportation, home-care workers, counseling, recreation, and information and referral (sometimes nicknamed I & R). In addition, each Area Agency funds a Long-Term Care Ombudsman to investigate complaints about abuse, neglect, or indifference in nursing homes and home health agencies.

Your parents' Area Agency on Aging (or the one in your own community) would be the first office to call if you have specific questions about what local resources are available to help your own parents. Names, addresses, and phone numbers for all AAAs and the state departments on aging are listed here state by state.

(PHOTO BY ROCHELLE CASSERD)

ALABAMA

State Agency on Aging

Alabama Commission on Aging
502 Washington Ave.
Montgomery, AL 36130
(205) 261-5743

Area Agencies on Aging

Northwest Council of Local Governments Area Agency on Aging
(Lauderdale, Colbert, Franklin, Marion, and Winston counties)
P.O. Box L
400 Hamilton St.
Russellville, AL 35653
(205) 332-9173

West Alabama Planning and Development Commission
(Lamar, Fayette, Pickens, Greene, Hale, Bibb, and Tuscaloosa counties)
P.O. Drawer 408
Northport, AL 35476
(205) 345-5545

Birmingham Regional Planning Commission
(Walker, Blount, Saint Clair, Shelby, and Chilton counties)
2112 S. 11th Ave., Suite 220
Birmingham, AL 35205
(205) 251-8139

Jefferson County Office of Senior Citizens' Activities
2611 Highland Ave.
Birmingham, AL 35205
(205) 251-2992

East Alabama Planning and Development Commission
(Cherokee, Etowah, Calhoun, Cleburne, Talladega, Clay, Randolph, Coosa, Tallapoosa, and Chambers counties)
P.O. Box 2186
Anniston, AL 36202
(205) 237-6741

South Central Alabama Development Commission
(Lowndes, Butler, Crenshaw, Pike, Bullock, and Macon counties)
P.O. Box 20028
Montgomery, AL 36120
(205) 281-2196

Alabama Tombigbee Regional Commission
(Sumter, Marengo, Choctaw, Clarke, Washington, Monroe, Wilcox, Conecuh, Dallas, and Perry counties)
P.O. Box 269
Camden, AL 36726
(205) 262-4234

Southeast Alabama Regional Planning and Development Commission
(Barbour, Henry, Houston, Dale, Coffee, Geneva, and Covington counties)
P.O. Box 1406
Dothan, AL 36301
(205) 794-4092

South Alabama Regional Planning Commission Area Agency on Aging
(Mobile, Baldwin, and Escambia counties)
P.O. Box 1665
Mobile, AL 36601
(205) 433-6541

Central Alabama Aging Consortium
(Autauga, Elmore, and Montgomery counties)
2911 Zelda Road, Suite B
Montgomery, AL 36106
(205) 271-2866

Lee County Area Council of Governments
(Lee and Russell counties)
P.O. Box 1072
Auburn, AL 36830
(205) 821-3042

North Central Alabama Regional Council of Governments
(Lawrence, Morgan, and Cullman counties)
P.O. Box C
Decatur, AL 35602
(205) 355-4515

Top of Alabama Council of Governments
(Limestone, Madison, Jackson, Marshall, and DeKalb counties)
115 Washington St., SE
Huntsville, AL 35801
(205) 533-3330

Medicare Peer Review Organization

Alabama Quality Assurance Foundation, Inc.
Twin Towers East
236 Goodwin Crest Drive, Suite 300
Birmingham, AL 35206
(205) 942-0785

ALASKA

State Agency on Aging

(no area agencies)
Older Alaskans Commission
P.O. Box C, Mail Stop 0209
Juneau, Alaska 99811
(907) 465-3250

Medicare Peer Review Organization

Professional Review Organization for Washington
2150 N. 107th St., Suite 200
Seattle, WA 98133
(206) 364-9700

ARIZONA

State Agency on Aging

Aging and Adult Administration
P.O. Box 6123
1400 West Washington St.
Phoenix, AZ 85005
(602) 255-4446

Area Agencies on Aging

Region 1 Area Agency on Aging
(Maricopa County)
1366 East Thomas Rd., Suite 108
Phoenix, AZ 85016
(602) 264-2255

Pima County Council on Aging
100 East Alameda, Suite 406
Tucson, AZ 85701
(602) 624-4419

Northern Arizona Council of Governments
(Yavapai and parts of Coconino, Navajo, and Apache counties)
P.O. Box 57
Flagstaff, AZ 86002
(602) 774-1895

District 4 Council of Governments
Area Agency on Aging
(Mohave and Yuma counties)
1018 South 4th St., Suite 201
Yuma, AZ 85364
(602) 782-1886

Pinal/Gila Council for Senior Citizens
(Pinal and Gila counties)
Area Agency on Aging
P.O. Box 1129
512 East Butte Ave.
Florence, AZ 85232
(602) 868-5400

Southeastern Arizona Governments Organization
Area Agency on Aging
(Greenlee, Graham, Cochise, and Santa Cruz counties)
P.O. Box 204
Bisbee, AZ 85603
(602) 432-5301

Navajo Nation Area Agency on Aging
Division of Health Improvements
Aging Department
P.O. Drawer 1390
Window Rock, AZ 86515
(602) 871-4941

Intertribal Council of Arizona
(All Indian reservations except Navajo)
124 West Thomas Rd., Suite 201
Phoenix, AZ 85013
(602) 248-0071

Medicare Peer Review Organization

Health Services Advisory Group Inc.
P.O. Box 16731
301 E. Bethany Home Rd., Bldg. B, Suite 157
Phoenix, AZ 85012
(602) 264-6382

ARKANSAS

State Agency on Aging

Arkansas Division of Aging and Adult Services
Donaghey Building, Suite 1417
7th and Main Streets
Little Rock, AR 72201
(501) 371-2441

Area Agencies on Aging

Central Arkansas Area Agency on Aging
(Faulkner, Saline, Pulaski, Lonoke, Prairie, and Monroe counties)
P.O. Box 5988
706 West Fourth St.
North Little Rock, AR 72119
(501) 758-2294
(800) 482-6359 (toll-free, within area)

Southeast Arkansas Area Agency on
Aging
(Grant, Jefferson, Arkansas,
Cleveland, Lincoln, Desha,
Bradley, Drew, Chicot, and
Ashley counties)
115 East Fifth St., Suite 301
Pine Bluff, AR 71611
(501) 534-3268
(800) 272-2025 (toll-free, within
area)
Northwest Arkansas Area Agency
on Aging
(Benton, Carroll, Boone, Marion,
Baxter, Washington, Madison,
Newton, and Searcy counties)
P.O. Box 1795
Harrison, AR 72601
(501) 741-1144
(800) 432-9721 (toll-free, within
area)
White River Area Agency on Aging
(Fulton, Izard, Sharp, Stone, Inde-
pendence, Jackson, Van Buren,
Cleburne, White, and Woo-
druff counties)
P.O. Box 2637
617 Virginia Drive
Batesville, AR 72501
(501) 793-4431
East Arkansas Area Agency on
Aging
(Randolph, Clay, Greene,
Lawrence, Craighead, Missis-
sippi, Poinsett, Cross, Critten-
den, St. Francis, Lee, and
Phillips counties)
P.O. Box 5035
Jonesboro, AR 72401
(501) 972-5980
(800) 382-3265 (toll-free, within
area)

West Central Arkansas Area Agency
on Aging
(Johnson, Pope, Conway, Yell,
Perry, Montgomery, Garland,
and Hot Spring counties)
624 Malvern Ave.
Hot Springs, AR 71901
(501) 321-2811
(800) 272-2138 (toll-free, within
area)
Southwest Arkansas Area Agency
on Aging
(Howard, Pike, Clark, Sevier,
Hempstead, Nevada, Ouachita,
Calhoun, Dallas, Miller, Little
River, Lafayette, Columbia, and
Union counties)
P.O. Box 26
Magnolia, AR 71753
(501) 234-7410
Western Arkansas Area Agency on
Aging
(Crawford, Franklin, Logan, Se-
bastian, Scott, and Polk coun-
ties)
P.O. Box 1724
1411 Rogers Ave.
Fort Smith, AR 72902
(501) 783-4500

Medicare Peer Review Organization

Arkansas Foundation for Medical
Care Inc.
P.O. Box 2607
809 Garrison Ave.
Fort Smith, AR 72902
(501) 785-2471

CALIFORNIA

State Agency on Aging

California Department of Aging
1020 19th St.
Sacramento, CA 95814
(916) 322-9566

Area Agencies on Aging

Los Angeles County Department of
Senior Citizens Affairs
1102 Crenshaw Blvd.
Los Angeles, CA 90019
(213) 857-6466

Los Angeles City Department of
Aging
207 S. Broadway, 7th floor
Los Angeles, CA 90012
(213) 485-4685

San Francisco City and County
Commission on Aging
1360 Mission St., 4th floor
San Francisco, CA 94103
(415) 557-5844

San Diego County Area Agency on
Aging
4161 Marlborough Ave.
San Diego, CA 92105
(714) 560-2427

Area 4 Area Agency on Aging
(Sierra, Nevada, Yuba, Placer,
Sutter, Yolo, and Sacramento
counties)
2862 Arden Way, Suite 101
Sacramento, CA 95825
(916) 447-7063

Alameda County Department on
Aging
1755 Broadway, 5th floor
Oakland, CA 94612
(415) 874-7233

Council on Aging of Santa Clara
County
2131 The Alameda
San Jose, CA 95126
(408) 296-8290

Marin County Area Agency on
Aging
Civic Center, Room 279
San Rafael, CA 94903
(415) 499-7396

Contra Costa County Office on
Aging
2425 Bisso Lane, Suite 110
Concord, CA 94520
(415) 671-4233

PSA 3 Area Agency on Aging
(Plumas, Butte, Glenn, and Colusa
counties)
California State University at
Chico
Chico, CA 95929
(916) 895-5961

San Bernardino County Office of
Aging
602 S. Tippecanoe
San Bernardino, CA 92415
(714) 383-3861

Central Coast Commission for Senior Citizens
(Santa Barbara and San Luis Obi-
spo counties)
122-C W. El Camino
Santa Maria, CA 93454
(805) 925-9554

Ventura County Area Agency on
Aging
800 S. Victoria Road, Lower Plaza
Ventura, CA 93003
(805) 654-3660

County of Riverside Office on Aging
On the Mall at 6th St.
P.O. Box 1480
Riverside, CA 92502
(714) 683-7880

County of Orange Area Agency on
Aging
801-C N. Broadway
Santa Ana, CA 92701
(714) 834-6017

Area 1 Area Agency on Aging
(Del Norte and Humboldt counties)
3300 Glenwood St.
Eureka, CA 95501
(707) 442-3763

Area Agency on Aging
(Siskiyou, Modoc, Trinity, Shasta,
Lassen, and Tehama counties)
P.O. Box 1400
Yreka, CA 96097
(916) 842-1687

San Mateo Area Agency on Aging
617 Hamilton St.
Redwood City, CA 94063
(415) 363-4511

San Joaquin County Area Agency
on Aging
222 East Weber Ave., Room 402
Stockton, CA 95202
(209) 944-2448

Central Sierra Area Agency on
Aging
(Amador, Calaveras, Alpine, Tuo-
lumne, and Mariposa counties)
56 N. Washington St.
Sonora, CA 95370
(209) 532-6272

Seniors Council of Santa Cruz and
San Benito Counties
234 Santa Cruz Ave.
Aptos, CA 95003
(408) 688-0400

Fresno-Madera Area Agency on
Aging
(Fresno and Madera counties)
1221 Fulton Mall, Suite 553
Fresno, CA 93721
(209) 455-3278

Kings-Tulare Area Agency on Aging
1920 W. Princeton Drive, Suite A
and B
Visalia, CA 93277
(209) 733-1079

Inyo-Mono Area Agency on Aging
(Inyo and Mono counties)
P.O. Box 1799
Bishop, CA 93514
(714) 873-4248

Imperial County Area Agency on
Aging
654 Main St.
El Centro, CA 92243
(619) 352-8521

Mendocino-Lake Area Agency on
Aging
(Mendocino and Lake counties)
413-A N. Lake St.
Ukiah, CA 95482
(707) 462-1954

Sonoma County Area Agency on
Aging
1488 Guerneville Road
Santa Rosa, CA 95401
(707) 527-3138

Solano/Napa Area Agency on Aging
(Solano and Napa counties)
1814 Capitol St.
Vallejo, CA 94590
(707) 644-6612

El Dorado County Area Agency on
Aging
935-A Spring St.
Placerville, CA 95667
(916) 626-2149

Stanislaus County Area Agency on
Aging
1024 J St., Room 416
Modesto, CA 95354
(209) 385-7550

Merced County Area Agency on
Aging Programs
2150 M St., Suite 3
Merced, CA 95340
(209) 385-7550

Monterey County Area Agency on
Aging
P.O. Box 299
1164 Monroe St., Suite 5
Salinas, CA 93902
(408) 449-1877

Kern County Office on Aging
  1415 Truxton Ave., Suite AB
  Bakersfield, CA 93301
  (805) 861-2445

Medicare Peer Review Organization

California Medical Review Inc.
  1388 Sutter St., Suite 1100
  San Francisco, CA 94109
  (415) 923-2300

COLORADO

State Agency on Aging

Colorado Aging and Adult Services
  Division
  Department of Social Services
  P.O. Box 181000
  717 17th St., 11th floor
  Denver, CO 80218-0899
  (303) 294-5905

Area Agencies on Aging

Denver Regional Aging Services Division
  (Denver, Boulder, Adams, Gilpin,
  Jefferson, Clearcreek, Arapahoe,
  and Douglas counties)
  2480 W. 26th Ave., Suite 200-B
  Denver, CO 80211
  (303) 455-1000
Pikes Peak Area Agency on Aging
  (Park, Teller, and El Paso counties)
  27 Vermijo St.
  Colorado Springs, CO 80903
  (303) 471-7080
Pueblo County Area Agency on
  Aging
  228 N. Union
  Pueblo, CO 81003
  (303) 544-4307

Northeastern Colorado Association
  of Local Governments
  (Logan, Sedgwick, Phillips, Morgan, Washington, and Yuma
  counties)
  300 Main St.
  Fort Morgan, CO 80701
  (303) 867-9409
Larimer County Area Agency on
  Aging
  Department of Human Development
  P.O. Box 1190
  525 S. Oak St.
  Fort Collins, CO 80522
  (303) 221-7440
Weld County Area Agency on
  Aging
  Health Department Building
  1516 Hospital Rd.
  Greeley, CO 80631
  (303) 744-1573, ext. 328
East Central Area Agency on Aging
  (Elbert, Lincoln, Kit Carson, and
  Cheyenne counties)
  Box 28
  Stratton, CO 80836
  (303) 348-5562
Lower Arkansas Valley Area Agency
  on Aging
  (Crowley, Kiowa, Otero, Bent,
  Prowers, and Baca counties)
  456 Carson Ave.
  Las Animas, CO 81054
  (303) 456-0692
Huerfano-Las Animas Area Agency
  on Aging
  (Huerfano and Las Animas counties)
  Council of Governments
  Courthouse, Room 201
  Trinidad, CO 81082
  (303) 846-4401

South Central Community Seniors
 (Saguache, Mineral, Rio Grande,
  Alamosa, Conejos, and Costilla
  counties)
 c/o SLV Nutrition Project
 P.O. Box 896
 Alamosa, CO 81101
 (303) 589-4511
San Juan Basin Area Agency on
  Aging
 (Dolores, Montezuma, San Juan,
  and La Plata counties)
 572 Sixth Ave.
 Durango, CO 81301
 (303) 259-1967
District 10 Regional Planning Com-
  mission
 (Montrose, San Miguel, Delta,
  Ouray, Hinsdale, and Gunnison
  counties)
 Drawer 849
 Montrose, CO 81402
 (303) 249-2436
Associated Governments of North-
  west Colorado
 (Moffat, Rio Blanco, Garfield, and
  Mesa counties)
 P.O. Box 351
 Rifle, CO 81650
 (303) 625-1723
Skyline Six Area Agency on Aging
 (Routt, Jackson, Grand, Eagle,
  Summit, and Pitkin counties)
 Box 739
 Frisco, CO 80443
 (303) 668-5445
Upper Arkansas Area Agency on
  Aging
 (Lake, Chaffee, Fremont, and Cus-
  ter counties)
 1310 E. Rainbow Blvd., No. 17
 Salida, CO 81201
 (303) 275-8350

Medicare Peer Review Organization

Colorado Foundation for Medical
  Care
ct Building 2, Suite 400
 6825 E. Tennessee Ave.
 Denver, CO 80224
 (303) 321-8642

CONNECTICUT

State Agency on Aging

Connecticut Department on Aging
 175 Main St.
 Hartford, CT 06106
 (203) 566-7772

Area Agencies on Aging

North Central Area Agency on
  Aging
 (Hartford County and part of Tol-
  land and Litchfield)
 999 Asylum Ave.
 Hartford, CT 06105
 (203) 278-2044
Southwestern Connecticut Area
  Agency on Aging
 (part of Fairfield County)
 276 Park Ave.
 Bridgeport, CT 06604
 (203) 333-9288
South Central Connecticut Area
  Agency on Aging
 (part of Fairfield and New Haven
  counties)
 201 Noble St.
 West Haven, CT 06516
 (203) 933-5431
Eastern Connecticut Area Agency
  on Aging
 (Middlesex, New London, and
  Windham counties and part of
  Tolland)
 27 Lafayette St.
 Norwich, CT 06360
 (203) 887-3561

Northwestern Area Agency on
Aging
(parts of Litchfield, New Haven,
and Fairfield counties)
c/o Connecticut Department on
Aging
175 Main St.
Hartford, CT 06106
(203) 566-4810

Medicare Peer Review Organization

Connecticut Peer Review Organization Inc.
384 Pratt St.
Meriden, CT 06450
(203) 237-2773

DELAWARE

State Agency on Aging

(no area agencies)
Delaware Division of Aging
1901 N. Dupont Highway
New Castle, DE 19720
(302) 421-6791

Medicare Peer Review Organization

West Virginia Medical Institute
3412 Chesterfield Ave., S.E.
Charleston, WV 25304
(304) 925-0461

DISTRICT OF COLUMBIA

Agency on Aging

D.C. Office on Aging
Office of the Mayor
1424 K St., N.W., 2nd floor
Washington, D.C. 20005
(202) 724-5622

Medicare Peer Review Organization

Delmarva Foundation for Medical
Care Inc.
341B N. Aurora St.
Easton, MD 21601
(301) 822-0697

FLORIDA

State Agency on Aging

Program Office of Aging and Adult
Services
Department of Health and Rehabilitation Services
1317 Winewood Blvd.
Tallahassee, FL 32301
(904) 488-8922

Area Agencies on Aging

Area Agency on Aging of Dade and
Monroe Counties
902 S.W. 2nd Ave.
Miami, FL 33130
(305) 854-8311
Area Agency on Aging for North
Florida
(Holmes, Washington, Bay, Jack-
son, Calhoun, Gulf, Gadsden,
Liberty, Franklin, Wakulla,
Leon, Jefferson, Madison, and
Taylor counties)
Box 12
2639 North Monroe St., Suite
145B
Tallahassee, FL 32303
(904) 488-0055
Northwest Florida Area Agency on
Aging
(Escambia, Santa Rosa, Okaloosa,
and Walton counties)
24 W. Chase St., Suite A
Pensacola, FL 32501
(904) 436-5224
Area Agency on Aging
(Hamilton, Suwannee, Columbia,
Lafayette, Dixie, Gilchrist, Levy,
Alachua, Union, Bradford,
Marion, Citrus, Hernando,
Sumter, Lake, and Putnam
counties)
5700 S.W. 34th St., Suite 222
Gainesville, FL 32608
(904) 378-6649

Northeast Florida Area Agency on
Aging
(Nassau, Baker, Duval, Clay, St.
Johns, Flagler, and Volusia
counties)
2722 College St.
Jacksonville, FL 32205
(904) 388-6495
Tampa Bay Regional Planning
Council
(Pasco and Pinellas counties)
9455 Koger Blvd.
St. Petersburg, FL 33702
(813) 577-5151
Manahill Area Agency on Aging
(Hillsborough and Manatee coun-
ties)
8405 N. Himes Ave., Suite 106
Tampa, FL 33614
(813) 933-5945
East Central Florida Area Agency on
Aging
(Seminole, Orange, Osceola, and
Brevard counties)
1011 Wymore Rd., Room 105
Winter Park, FL 32789
(305) 645-3339
Area Agency on Aging
(Polk, Hardee, Highlands, DeSoto,
Sarasota, Charlotte, Lee, Collier,
Hendry, and Glades counties)
1402 Jackson St.
Fort Myers, FL 33901
(813) 332-4233
Gulfstream Area Agency on Aging
(Indian River, Okeechobee, St.
Lucie, Martin, and Palm Beach
counties)
1115 W. Lantana Rd.
Lantana, FL 33462
(305) 582-3446

Area Agency on Aging of Broward
County
2700 W. Oakland Park Blvd.
Oakland Park, FL 33311
(305) 485-6370

Medicare Peer Review Organization

Professional Foundation for Health
Care Inc.
2907 Bay to Bay Blvd., Suite 100
Tampa, FL 33629
(813) 831-6273

GEORGIA

State Agency on Aging

Georgia Office of Aging
878 Peachtree St., N.E., Room 632
Atlanta, GA 30309
(404) 894-5333

Area Agencies on Aging

Atlanta Regional Commission
(DeKalb, Gwinnett, Fulton, Cobb,
Clayton, Bockdale, and Douglas
counties)
100 Edgewood Ave., N.W., Suite
1801
Atlanta, GA 30305
(404) 656-4000
Altamaha Georgia Southern Area
Planning and Development
Commission
(Bulloch, Candler, Evans, Tattnall,
Toombs, Jeff Davis, Appling,
and Wayne counties)
P.O. Box 328
Baxley, GA 31513
(912) 367-3648

Central Savannah River Area Planning and Development Commission
(Wilkes, Taliaferro, Lincoln, McDuffie, Columbia, Warren, Glascock, Richmond, Jefferson, Burke, Emanuel, Jenkins, and Screven counties)
P.O. Box 2800
Augusta, GA 30904
(404) 737-1823
Chattahoochee Flint Area Planning and Development Commission
(Carroll, Heard, Coweta, Troup, and Meriwether counties)
Box 2308
Newman, GA 30264
(404) 253-8521
Coastal Area Planning and Development Commission
(Effingham, Bryan, Chatham, Liberty, Long, McIntosh, Glynn, and Camden counties)
P.O. Box 1917
Brunswick, GA 31521
(912) 264-7363
South Georgia Area Planning and Development Commission
(Turner, Ben Hill, Irwin, Tift, Berrien, Cook, Lanier, Lowndes, Brooks, and Echols counties)
P.O. Box 1223
Valdosta, GA 31601
(912) 333-5277
Coosa Valley Area Planning and Development Commission
(Dade, Catoosa, Walker, Chattooga, Floyd, Polk, Haralson, Paulding, Bartow, and Gordon counties)
P.O. Drawer H
Rome, GA 30161
(404) 295-6485

Georgia Mountains Area Planning and Development Commission
(Union, Towns, Rabun, Lumpkin, White, Habersham, Stephens, Dawson, Forsyth, Hall, Banks, Franklin, and Hart counties)
P.O. Box 1720
Gainesville, GA 30501
(404) 536-3431
Heart of Georgia Council on Aging
(Laurens, Bleckley, Treutlen, Pulaski, Dodge, Wheeler, Montgomery, Wilcox, and Telfair counties)
P.O. Box 503
McRae, GA 31055
(912) 868-5917
Lower Chattahoochee Area Planning and Development Commission
(Harris, Talbot, Muscogee, Chattahoochee, Stewart, Quitman, Randolph, and Clay counties)
P.O. Box 1908
Columbus, GA 31901
(404) 324-4221
McIntosh Trail Area Planning and Development Commission
(Fayette, Henry, Newton, Spaulding, Butts, Pike, Lamar, and Upson counties)
408 Thomaston St.
P.O. Drawer A
Barnesville, GA 30204
(404) 358-3647
Middle Flint Area Planning and Development Commission
(Taylor, Marion, Macon, Schley, Webster, Dooly, Crisp, and Sumter counties)
P.O. Box 6
Ellaville, GA 31806
(912) 937-2561

Middle Georgia Area Planning and Development Commission
(Monroe, Jones, Crawford, Bibb, Peach, Twiggs, and Houston counties)
711 Grand Bldg.
Macon, GA 31201
(912) 744-6160

North Georgia Area Planning and Development Commission
(Whitfield, Murray, Fannin, Gilmer, Pickens, and Cherokee counties)
503 W. Waugh St.
Dalton, GA 30720
(404) 272-2300

Northeast Georgia Planning and Development Commission
(Jackson, Madison, Elbert, Barrow, Clarke, Oglethorpe, Oconee, Walton, Morgan, and Greene counties)
305 Research Rd.
Athens, GA 30601
(404) 548-3141

Oconee Area Planning and Development Commission
(Jasper, Putnam, Hancock, Baldwin, Washington, Wilkinson, and Johnson counties)
P.O. Box 707
Milledgeville, GA 31601
(912) 453-5327

Southwest Georgia (SOWEGA) Council on Aging
(Terrell, Lee, Worth, Dougherty, Calhoun, Baker, Mitchell, Colquitt, Early, Miller, Seminole, Decatur, Grady, and Thomas counties)
P.O. Box 3149
Albany, GA 31706
(912) 432-1124

Southeast Georgia Planning and Development Commission
(Coffee, Bacon, Atkinson, Ware, Pierce, Brantley, Clinch, and Charlton counties)
P.O. Box 2049
Waycross, GA 31720
(912) 285-6096

Medicare Peer Review Organization

Georgia Medical Foundation
4 Executive Park Drive, N.W., Suite 1300
Atlanta, GA 30329
(404) 881-5600

HAWAII

State Agency on Aging

Hawaii Executive Office on Aging
Office of the Governor
335 Merchant St., Room 241
Honolulu, HI 96813
(808) 548-2593

Area Agencies on Aging

Oahu County Elderly Affairs Division
650 S. King St., 6th floor
Honolulu, HI 96813
(808) 523-4361

Kauai County Office of Elderly Affairs
4396 Rice St.
Lihue, HI 96766
(808) 245-4737

Maui County Office on Aging
200 S. High St.
Wailuku, HI 96793
(808) 244-7837

Hawaii County Office of Aging
34 Rainbow Drive
Hilo, HI 96720
(808) 961-3794

Medicare Peer Review Organization

Hawaii Medical Services Association
  P.O. Box 860
  Honolulu, HI 96808
  (808) 944-2110

IDAHO

State Agency on Aging

Idaho Office on Aging
  Room 114-Statehouse
  Boise, ID 83720
  (208) 334-3833

Area Agencies on Aging

Southeast Idaho Council of Governments
  (Bingham, Power, Bannock, Caribou, Oneida, Franklin, and Bear Lake counties)
  1070 Hilene Rd., Suite 390
  Pocatello, ID 83201
  (208) 233-4032
East Idaho Special Services
  (Lemhi, Custer, Butte, Clark, Jefferson, Bonneville, Fremont, Madison, and Teton counties)
  P.O. Box 1098
  Idaho Falls, ID 83401
  (208) 522-5391
Association for Inner Community Development
  (Boundary, Bonner, Kootenai, Benewah, and Shoshone counties)
  3655 N. Government Way, No. 6
  Coeur d'Alene, ID 83814
  (208) 667-4523
Area 2 Agency on Aging
  (Latah, Clearwater, Nez Perce, Lewis, and Idaho counties)
  1424 Main St.
  Lewiston, ID 83501
  (208) 743-5580

Ida-Ore Planning and Development Association
  (Adams, Valley, Washington, Payette, Boise, Gem, Ada, Canyon, Owyhee, and Elmore counties)
  P.O. Box 311
  Weiser, ID 83672
  (208) 549-2411
College of Southern Idaho
  (Camas, Blaine, Gooding, Lincoln, Twin Falls, Jerome, Cassia, and Minidoka counties)
  P.O. Box 1238
  Twin Falls, ID 83301
  (208) 733-9554, ext. 204

Medicare Peer Review Organization

Professional Review Organization for Washington
  2150 N. 107th St., Suite 200
  Seattle, WA 98133
  (206) 364-9700

ILLINOIS

State Agency on Aging

Illinois Department on Aging
  421 E. Capitol Ave.
  Springfield, IL 62701
  (800) 252-8966 (toll-free, within Illinois)
  (217) 785-3356

Area Agencies on Aging

Chicago Department on Aging and Disability
  510 N. Peshtigo Court, 3rd floor
  Chicago, IL 60611
  (312) 744-5768
Suburban Cook County Area Agency on Aging
  400 W. Madison, Room 400
  Chicago, IL 60606
  (312) 559-0616

Northwestern Illinois Area Agency
on Aging
(Jo Daviess, Stephenson, Winnebago, Boone, Carroll, Ogle, DeKalb, Whiteside, and Lee
counties)
Eastmoore Bldg.
4223 E. State St.
Rockford, IL 61108
(815) 226-4901

Region 2 Area Agency on Aging
(McHenry, Lake, Kane, DuPage,
Kendall, Will, Grundy, and
Kankakee counties)
P.O. Box 809
Kankakee, IL 60901
(815) 939-0727

Western Illinois Area Agency on
Aging
(Rock Island, Henry, Bureau, Putnam, LaSalle, Mercer, Knox,
Warren, Henderson, and
McDonough counties)
4016 Ninth St.
Rock Island, IL 61201
(309) 793-6800

Central Illinois Agency on Aging
(Peoria, Stark, Marshall, Woodford, Fulton and Tazewell counties)
700 Hamilton Blvd.
Peoria, IL 61603
(309) 674-2071

East Central Illinois Area Agency on
Aging
(Champaign, Livingston, Ford,
Iroquois, Vermilion, McLean,
DeWitt, Piatt, Macon, Shelby,
Moultrie, Douglas, Edgar,
Coles, Cumberland, and Clark
counties)
2714 McGraw Drive
Bloomington, IL 61701
(309) 662-9393

West Central Illinois Area Agency
on Aging
(Hancock, Adams, Pike, Calhoun,
Brown, and Schuyler counties)
P.O. Box 428
1125 Hampshire St.
Quincy, IL 62306
(217) 223-7904

Project Life Area Agency on Aging
(Mason, Logan, Cass, Menard,
Morgan, Sangamon, Scott,
Greene, Macoupin, Jersey,
Christian, and Montgomery
counties)
2815 W. Washington St., Suite
310
Springfield, IL 62702
(217) 787-9234

Southwestern Illinois Area Agency
on Aging
(Madison, Bond, St. Clair, Clinton, Monroe, Washington, and
Randolph counties)
Fairview Executive Plaza, Suite
225
Fairview Heights, IL 62208
(618) 632-1323

Midland Area Agency on Aging
(Fayette, Effingham, Clay, Marion,
and Jefferson counties)
P.O. Box 1420
Centralia, IL 62801
(618) 532-1853

Southeastern Illinois Area Agency
on Aging
(Jasper, Crawford, Richland,
Lawrence, Wabash, Edwards,
Wayne, White, and Hamilton
counties)
302 Market St.
Mount Carmel, IL 62863
(618) 262-8001

Egyptian Area Agency on Aging
(Perry, Franklin, Jackson, Williamson, Union, Johnson, Pope, Hardin, Saline, Gallatin, Alexander, Pulaski, and Massac counties)
108 S. Division
Carterville, IL 62918
(618) 985-8311

Medicare Peer Review Organization

Crescent Counties Foundation for Medical Care
350 Shuman Blvd., Suite 240
Naperville, IL 60540
(312) 357-8770

INDIANA

State Agency on Aging

Indiana Department on Aging and Community Services
P.O. Box 7083
251 N. Illinois
Indianapolis, IN 46207-7083
(317) 232-7000

Area Agencies on Aging

Central Indiana Council on Aging
(Boone, Hamilton, Hendricks, Marion, Hancock, Morgan, Johnson, and Shelby counties)
615 N. Alabama St., Suite 336
Indianapolis, IN 46204
(317) 633-6191
Lake County Economic Opportunity Council
(Lake, Porter, Newton, Jasper, Starke, and Pulaski counties)
5518 Calumet Ave.
Hammond, IN 46320
(219) 937-3500

Area 2 Council on Aging
REAL Services of St. Joseph County
(LaPorte, St. Joseph, Elkhart, Marshall, and Kosciusko counties)
P.O. Box 1835
622 N. Michigan St.
South Bend, IN 46634
(219) 233-8205
Northeast Area 3 Council on Aging
(Lagrange, Steuben, Noble, DeKalb, Whitley, Allen, Huntington, Wells, and Adams counties)
5720 St. Joe Road
Fort Wayne, IN 46815
(219) 485-4026
(800) 552-3662 (toll-free, within area)
Area 4 Agency on Aging and Community Services
(Benton, White, Carroll, Tippecanoe, Warren, Fountain, Montgomery, and Clinton counties)
P.O. Box 4727
10 N. Earl Ave.
Lafayette, IN 47903
(317) 447-7683
(800) 382-7556 (toll-free, within area)
Area 5 Council on Aging and Community Services
(Fulton, Cass, Miami, Wabash, Howard, and Tipton counties)
912 W. Market St.
Logansport, IN 46947
(219) 722-4451
Area 6 Council on Aging
(Grant, Blackford, Jay, Madison, Delaware, Randolph, and Henry counties)
1968 W. Main St.
Muncie, IN 47303
(317) 289-1121

West Central Indiana Economic Development District
(Vermillion, Parke, Putnam, Vigo, Clay, and Sullivan counties)
P.O. Box 359
Terre Haute, IN 47808
(812) 238-1561
(800) 742-0804 (toll-free, within area)

Area 9 Agency on Aging
(Wayne, Rush, Fayette, Union, and Franklin counties)
Indiana University East
303 S. A St.
Richmond, IN 47374
(317) 966-1795

Area 10 Agency on Aging
(Owen and Monroe counties)
924 W. 17th St.
Bloomington, IN 47401
(812) 334-1769

Area 11 Agency on Aging
(Brown, Bartholomew, Decatur, Jackson, and Jennings counties)
4340 Jonathon Moore Pike
Columbus, IN 47201
(812) 372-6918

Area 12 Council on Aging
(Ripley, Dearborn, Ohio, Jefferson, and Switzerland counties)
P.O. Box 97
Dillsboro, IN 47018
(812) 432-5000

Area 13-A Agency on Aging
(Greene, Knox, Daviess, Martin, Dubois, and Pike counties)
Vincennes University
Vincennes, IN 47591
(812) 882-6370

Southwest Indiana Council on Aging
(Posey, Gibson, Vanderburgh, Warrick, Spencer, and Perry counties)
7 S.E. Seventh St.
Evansville, IN 47708
(812) 464-7800

South Central Council on Aging and Aged
(Scott, Clark, Harrison, and Floyd counties)
134 E. Main
New Albany, IN 47150
(812) 948-9161

Hoosier Uplands Economic Development Corp.
(Lawrence, Orange, Crawford, and Washington counties)
521 Main St.
Mitchell, IN 47446
(812) 849-4457

Medicare Peer Review Organization

Indiana Peer Review Inc.
501 Congressional Blvd., Suite 200
Carmel, IN 46032
(608) 258-4680

IOWA

State Agency on Aging

Iowa Department of Elder Affairs
914 Grand Ave., Suite 236
Des Moines, IA 50319
(515) 281-5187

Area Agencies on Aging

Crossroads of Iowa Area Agency on Aging
(Boone, Story, Dallas, Polk, Jasper, Madison, Warren, and Marion counties)
1040 Fourth St.
Des Moines, IA 50314
(515) 244-4046

Scenic Valley Area Agency on Aging
(Dubuque, Delaware, and Jackson counties)
801 Davis St.
Dubuque, IA 52001
(319) 588-3970

Area 4 Agency on Aging
(Plymouth, Cherokee, Woodbury, Ida, and Monona counties)
SIMPCO, P.O. Box 447
Sioux City, IA 51102
(712) 279-6286

Heritage Area Agency on Aging
(Benton, Linn, Jones, Iowa, Johnson, Cedar, and Washington counties)
6301 Kirkwood Blvd., S.W.
Cedar Rapids, IA 52406
(319) 398-5559
(800) 332-5934 (toll-free, within area)

Area 1 Agency on Aging
(Howard, Winneshiek, Allamakee, Fayette, and Clayton counties)
808 River St.
Decorah, IA 52101
(319) 382-2941

Elderbridge Area Agency on Aging
(Kossuth, Winnebago, Worth, Mitchell, Hancock, Cerro Gordo, Floyd, Pocahontas, Humboldt, Wright, Franklin, Sac, Calhoun, Webster, Hamilton, Crawford, Carroll, Greene, Audubon, and Guthrie counties)
22 N. Georgia, Suite 216
Mason City, IA 50401
(515) 424-0678
(515) 955-5244 (Fort Dodge)
(712) 792-3512 (Carroll)

Hawkeye Valley Area Agency on Aging
(Chickasaw, Butler, Bremer, Hardin, Grundy, Black Hawk, Marshall, Tama, and Poweshiek counties)
P.O. Box 2576
620 Mulberry St.
Waterloo, IA 50704
(319) 233-5214

Great River Bend Area Agency on Aging
(Clinton, Scott, and Muscatine counties)
Bi-State Metropolitan Planning Commission
1504 Third Ave.
Rock Island, IL 61201
(309) 793-6300

Area 14 Agency on Aging
(Adair, Adams, Union, Clarke, Taylor, Ringgold, and Decatur counties)
228 N. Pine St.
Creston, IA 50801
(515) 782-4040

Area 15 Agency on Aging, SIEDA
(Mahaska, Keokuk, Lucas, Monroe, Wapello, Jefferson, Wayne, Appanoose, Davis, and Van Buren counties)
P.O. Box 658
226 W. Main St.
Ottumwa, IA 52501
(515) 682-8741

Southwest Eight Area 13 Agency on Aging
(Harrison, Shelby, Pottawattamie, Cass, Mills, Montgomery, Fremont, and Page counties)
P.O. Box 368
Council Bluffs, IA 51502
(712) 328-2540

Iowa Lakes Area Agency on Aging
(Lyon, Osceola, Dickinson,
Emmet, Sioux, O'Brien, Clay,
Palo Alto, and Buena Vista
counties)
Box 3010
2 Grand Ave.
Spencer, IA 51301
(712) 262-1775
(800) 242-5033 (toll-free, within
area)
Southeast Iowa Area Agency on
Aging
(Des Moines, Louisa, Henry, and
Lee counties)
510 Jefferson St.
Burlington, IA 52601
(319) 752-5433
(800) 292-1268 (toll-free, within
area)

Medicare Peer Review Organization

Iowa Foundation for Medical Care
3737 Woodland Ave., Suite 500
West Des Moines, IA 50265
(515) 223-2900

KANSAS

State Agency on Aging

Kansas Department on Aging
610 W. Tenth St.
Topeka, KS 66612
(913) 296-4986

Area Agencies on Aging

Wyandotte-Leavenworth County
Area Agency on Aging
9400 State Ave.
Kansas City, KS 66112
(913) 788-7820

Johnson County Human Resources
and Aging Department
130 N. Cherry
Olathe, KS 66061
(913) 782-7188
Central Plains Area Agency on Aging
(Harvey, Butler, and Sedgwick
counties)
510 N. Main St.
Wichita, KS 67203
(316) 268-7298
Jayhawk Area Agency on Aging
(Shawnee, Jefferson, and Douglas
counties)
1195 Buchanan, No. 103
Topeka, KS 66604
(913) 235-1367
Northwest Kansas Area Agency on
Aging
(Cheyenne, Rawlins, Decatur,
Norton, Phillips, Smith, Sher-
man, Thomas, Sheridan, Gra-
ham, Rooks, Osborne, Wallace,
Logan, Gove, Trego, Ellis, and
Russell counties)
208 E. Seventh St.
Hays, KS 67601
(913) 628-8204
Southeast Kansas Area Agency on
Aging
(Woodson, Allen, Bourbon, Wil-
son, Neosho, Crawford, Mont-
gomery, Labette, and Cherokee
counties)
Box 269
1500 W. Seventh St.
Chanute, KS 66720
(316) 431-2980

Southwest Kansas Area Agency on Aging

(Greeley, Wichita, Scott, Lane, Ness, Rush, Barton, Hamilton, Kearny, Finney, Hodgeman, Pawnee, Stafford, Edwards, Pratt, Kiowa, Ford, Gray, Haskell, Grant, Stanton, Morton, Stevens, Seward, Meade, Clark, Comanche, and Barber counties)

P.O. Box 1636
Dodge City, KS 67801
(316) 225-0510

Mid-America Council on Aging

(Osage, Franklin, Miami, Coffey, Anderson, and Linn counties)

1610 S. Main
Ottawa, KS 66067
(913) 242-7200

North Central Flint Hills Area Agency on Aging

(Jewell, Republic, Mitchell, Cloud, Ottawa, Lincoln, Ellsworth, Clay, Riley, Geary, Pottawatomie, Morris, Dickinson, Wabaunsee, Marion, Chase, Lyon, and Saline counties)

2601 Anderson Ave.
Manhattan, KS 66502
(913) 776-9294

Northeast Kansas Area Agency on Aging

(Washington, Marshall, Nemaha, Brown, Doniphan, Jackson, and Atchison counties)

P.O. Box 456
107 Oregon West
Hiawatha, KS 66434
(913) 742-7152

South Central Kansas Area Agency on Aging

(Rice, McPherson, Reno, Kingman, Harper, Sumner, Cowley, Chautauqua, Elk, and Greenwood counties)

P.O. Box 1122
Arkansas, KS 67005
(316) 442-0268

Medicare Peer Review Organization

The Kansas Foundation for Medical Care Inc.
2947 S.W. Wanamaker Drive
Topeka, KS 66614
(913) 273-2552

KENTUCKY

State Agency on Aging

Kentucky Division for Aging Services
Cabinet of Human Resources Building, 6th floor
275 E. Main St.
Frankfort, KY 40621
(502) 564-6930

Area Agencies on Aging

Kentuckiana Regional Planning and Development Agency

(Bullitt, Jefferson, Oldham, Trimble, Henry, Shelby, and Spencer counties)

912 E. Broadway
Louisville, KY 40204
(502) 589-4406

Bluegrass Area Agency on Aging
(Harrison, Nicholas, Bourbon,
Clark, Madison, Scott, Powell,
Estill, Garrard, Lincoln, Boyle,
Mercer, Jessamine, Anderson,
Woodford, Fayette, and Frank-
lin counties)
3220 Nicholasville Road
Lexington, KY 40502
(606) 272-6656

Purchase Area Development District
(Ballard, McCracken, Marshall,
Calloway, Graves, Fulton, Hick-
man, and Carlisle counties)
P.O. Box 588
Mayfield, KY 42066
(502) 247-7171

Pennyrile Area Development Dis-
trict
(Livingston, Crittenden, Caldwell,
Hopkins, Todd, Muhlenberg,
Christian, Trigg, and Lyon
counties)
609 Hammond Plaza Bldg.
Fort Campbell Blvd.
Hopkinsville, KY 42240
(502) 886-9484

Green River Area Agency on Aging
(Union, Henderson, Webster,
McLean, Daviess, Hancock, and
Ohio counties)
3860 U.S. Highway 60 West
Owensboro, KY 42301
(502) 926-4433

Barren River Development District
(Butler, Edmonson, Hart, Met-
calfe, Barren, Monroe, Allen,
Simpson, Warren, and Logan
counties)
P.O. Box 2120
Bowling Green, KY 42101
(502) 781-2381

Lincoln Trail Area Development
District
(Grayson, Breckinridge, Meade,
Hardin, Nelson, Washington,
Marion, and Larue counties)
702 College St. Road
Elizabethtown, KY 42701
(502) 769-2393

Northern Kentucky Area Development District
(Carroll, Gallatin, Boone, Kenton,
Campbell, Pendleton, Grant,
and Owen counties)
7505 Sussex Drive, Suite 8
Florence, KY 41042
(606) 283-1885

Buffalo Trace Area Development
District
(Bracken, Robertson, Mason,
Fleming, and Lewis counties)
327 W. Second St.
Maysville, KY 41056
(606) 564-6894

Gateway Area Development District
(Bath, Rowan, Morgan, Menifee,
and Montgomery counties)
P.O. Box 107
Owingsville, KY 40360
(606) 674-6355

FIVCO Area Agency on Aging
(Greenup, Boyd, Lawrence, Elliott,
and Carter counties)
Box 636
Catlettsburg, KY 41129
(606) 739-5191

Big Sandy Area Development District
(Magoffin, Johnson, Martin, Floyd,
and Pike counties)
Municipal Bldg., 2nd floor
Prestonburg, KY 41653
(606) 886-2374

Kentucky River Area Development
District
(Wolfe, Breathitt, Knott, Letcher,
Perry, Leslie, Owsley, and Lee
counties)
381 Perry Park Rd.
Hazard, KY 41701
(606) 436-3158
Cumberland Valley Area Agency on
Aging
(Rockcastle, Jackson, Clay, Laurel,
Whitley, Knox, and Bell coun-
ties)
CVADD Building
Route 13
London, KY 40741
(606) 864-7391
Lake Cumberland Area Develop-
ment District
(Green, Taylor, Casey, Pulaski,
McCreary, Wayne, Clinton,
Cumberland, Russell, and Adair
counties)
P.O. Box 570
Russell Springs, KY 42642
(502) 343-3154

Medicare Peer Review Organization

Peerview Inc.
501 Congressional Blvd., Suite 200
Carmel, IN 46032
(317) 573-6888

LOUISIANA

State Agency on Aging

Louisiana Office of Elderly Affairs
4528 Bennington Ave.
P.O. Box 80374
Baton Rouge, LA 70898-0374
(504) 925-1700

Area Agencies on Aging

New Orleans Council on Aging
P.O. Box 19067
New Orleans, LA 70179-0067
(504) 821-4121
Capital Area Agency on Aging
(Livingstone, Ascension, Iberville,
West Baton Rouge, Pointe Cou-
pee, West Feliciana, East Feli-
ciana, St. Helena, Tangipahoa,
and Washington parishes)
P.O. Box 66638
Baton Rouge, LA 70896
(504) 343-9278
East Baton Rouge Council on Aging
2905 Fairfields Ave.
Baton Rouge, LA 70802
(504) 389-4916
Caddo Council on Aging
4015 Greenwood Road
Shreveport, LA 71109
(318) 636-7956
Allen Council on Aging
Drawer E-L
600 E. Seventh Ave.
Oakdale, LA 71463
(318) 335-3195
Assumption Council on Aging
P.O. Box 318
Napoleonville, LA 70390
(504) 369-7961
Beauregard Council on Aging
P.O. Drawer 534
112 Jefferson St.
DeRidder, LA 70634
(318) 463-6578
Bienville Council on Aging
P.O. Box 233
Arcadia, LA 71001
(318) 263-8936
Bossier Council on Aging
P.O. Box 5606
Bossier City, LA 71111
(318) 742-8993

Calcasieu Council on Aging
P.O. Box 6403
Lake Charles, LA 70606
(318) 474-5672

Caldwell Council on Aging
P.O. Box 1498
Columbia, LA 71418
(318) 649-2584

Cameron Council on Aging
P.O. Box 421
Cameron, LA 70631
(318) 775-5668

Claiborne Council on Aging
P.O. Box 326
608 E. Fourth St.
Homer, LA 71040
(318) 927-6922

Desoto Council on Aging
P.O. Box 1003
519 Franklin St.
Mansfield, LA 71052
(318) 872-2691

East Carroll Council on Aging
P.O. Box 486
Lake Providence, LA 71254
(318) 559-2774

Jefferson Council on Aging
P.O. Box 6878
Metairie, LA 70009
(504) 888-5880

Jefferson Davis Parish Council on
Aging
P.O. Box 667
Jennings, LA 70546
(318) 824-5504

LaFourche Council on Aging
P.O. Box 187
710 Church St.
Lockport, LA 70374
(504) 532-2381

Lincoln Council on Aging
109 S. Sparta
Ruston, LA 71270
(318) 255-5070

Madison Council on Aging
P.O. Drawer 352
Tallulah, LA 71282
(318) 574-4101

Morehouse Council on Aging
P.O. Box 1471
Bastrop, LA 71221-1471
(318) 281-6127

Natchitoches Council on Aging
P.O. Box 566
Natchitoches, LA 71457-0566
(318) 352-8490

Ouachita Council on Aging
1209 Oliver Road
Monroe, LA 71201
(318) 387-0535

Plaquemines Council on Aging
P.O. Box 992
Port Sulphur, LA 70083
(504) 564-3220

Red River Council on Aging
P.O. Box 688
Coushatta, LA 71019
(318) 932-5419

Sabine Council on Aging
750 Railroad Ave.
Many, LA 71449
(318) 256-5278

St. Bernard Council on Aging
1818 Center St.
Arabi, LA 70032
(504) 279-0444

St. Charles Council on Aging
Angus Drive
Luling, LA 70070
(504) 785-1981

St. James Area Agency on Aging
P.O. Box 87
Convent, LA 70723
(504) 562-2300

St. John Council on Aging
P.O. Drawer H
Laplace, LA 70068
(504) 652-3660

St. Landry Council on Aging
P.O. Box 1596
Opelousas, LA 70570
(318) 942-6579

St. Tammany Council on Aging
P.O. Box 171
Covington, LA 70433
(504) 892-0377

Tensas Council on Aging
P.O. Box 726
St. Joseph, LA 71366
(318) 766-3770

Terrebonne Council on Aging
P.O. Box 1066
Station 1
Houma, LA 70360
(318) 868-7701

Webster Council on Aging
P.O. Box 913
Minden, LA 71055
(318) 377-0141

West Carroll Council on Aging
P.O. Box 1058
Oak Grove, LA 71263
(318) 428-4217

Evangeline Regional Planning and
Development District
(Evangeline, Acadia, Vermilion,
Lafayette, St. Martin, Iberia,
and St. Mary parishes)
P.O. Box 90070
501 St. John St.
Lafayette, LA 70505
(318) 233-3215

Kisatchie Delta Regional Planning
and Development District
(Winn, Grant, LaSalle, Catahoula,
Concordia, Avoyelles, Rapides,
and Vernon parishes)
P.O. Box 8076
Alexandria, LA 71306
(318) 487-5454

North Delta Regional Planning and
Development District
(East Carroll, Franklin, Jackson,
Richland, and Union parishes)
2115 Justice St.
Monroe, LA 71201
(318) 387-2572

Medicare Peer Review Organization

Louisiana Health Care Review Inc.
9337 Interline
Baton Rouge, LA 70809
(504) 926-6353

MAINE

State Agency on Aging

Bureau of Maine's Elderly
Department of Human Services
State House, Station No. 11
Augusta, ME 04333
(207) 289-2561

Area Agencies on Aging

Southern Maine Area Agency on
Aging
(Cumberland and York counties)
P.O. Box 10480
Portland, ME 04104
(207) 775-6503

Central Maine Area Agency on
Aging
(Somerset, Kennebec, Waldo,
Knox, Lincoln, and Sagadahoc
counties)
P.O. Box 510
Augusta, ME 04330
(207) 622-9344

Eastern Area Agency on Aging
(Piscataquis, Penobscot, Washing-
ton, and Hancock counties)
P.O. Box 187
Brewer, ME 04412
(207) 989-6012

Western Area Agency on Aging
  (Franklin, Oxford, and Andro-
    scoggin counties)
  P.O. Box 649
  65 Central Ave.
  Lewiston, ME 04240
  (207) 784-8797
  (207) 784-8797
Aroostock (County) Area Agency on
  Aging
  P.O. Box 1288
  Presque Isle, ME 04769
  (207) 764-3396

Medicare Peer Review Organization

Health Care Review Inc.
  The Weld Bldg.
  345 Blackstone Blvd.
  Providence, RI 02906
  (401) 331-6661

MARYLAND

State Agency on Aging

Maryland Office on Aging
  State Office Bldg.
  301 W. Preston St.
  Baltimore, MD 21201
  (301) 225-1100

Area Agencies on Aging

Baltimore City Area Agency on
  Aging
  1114 Cathedral St.
  Baltimore, MD 21201
  (301) 396-5780
Baltimore County Department of
  Aging
  611 Central Ave.
  Towson, MD 21204
  (301) 494-2107
Montgomery County Area Agency
  on Aging
  3950 Ferrara Drive
  Wheaton, MD 20906
  (301) 468-4430

Garrett County Area Agency on
  Aging
  P.O. Box 449
  360 W. Liberty St.
  Oakland, MD 21550
  (301) 334-9431
Allegany County Area Agency on
  Aging
  19 Frederick St.
  Cumberland, MD 21502
  (301) 777-5970
Washington County Area Agency
  on Aging
  9 Public Square
  Alexander House
  Hagerstown, MD 21740
  (301) 790-0275
Frederick County Commission on
  Aging
  520 N. Market St.
  Frederick, MD 21701
  (301) 694-1604
Carroll County Office on Aging
  West End School
  Schoolhouse Ave.
  Westminster, MD 21157
  (301) 875-3342
  (301) 876-3363 (toll-free, from
    Baltimore)
Harford County Area Agency on
  Aging
  Equitable Bldg., 1st floor
  220 S. Main St.
  Bel Air, MD 21014
  (301) 879-2000, ext. 129
Howard County Office on Aging
  John Carroll Bldg, 1st floor
  3450 Courthouse Drive
  Ellicott City, MD 21043
  (301) 992-2327

Anne Arundel County Area Agency
on Aging
Ann Arundel Center North
101 N. Crain Highway
Glen Burnie, MD 21061
(301) 787-6707
Prince Georges' County Area
Agency on Aging
County Services Bldg.
5012 Rhode Island Ave.
Hyattsville, MD 20781
(301) 699-2797
Calvert County Office on Aging
450 W. Dares Beach Rd.
Prince Frederick, MD 20678
(301) 535-4606
(800) 855-1170 (toll-free, from
Washington, D.C.)
Charles County Aging Services
P.O. Box B
LaPlata, MD 20646
(301) 934-3776
St. Mary's County Office on Aging
Governmental Center
P.O. Box 653
Leonardtown, MD 20650
(301) 475-5621, ext. 474
Upper Shore Aging Inc.
(Cecil, Kent, Talbot, and Caroline
counties)
400 High St., 2nd floor
Chestertown, MD 21620
(301) 778-6000
Queen Anne's County Office on
Aging
County Annex Bldg.
Centreville, MD 21617
(301) 758-0848
MAC Inc. Area Agency on Aging
(Dorchester, Wicomico, Somerset,
and Worcester counties)
1504 Riverside Drive
Salisbury, MD 21801
(301) 742-0505

Medicare Peer Review Organization

Delmarva Foundation for Medical
Care Inc.
341B N. Aurora St.
Easton, MD 21601
(301) 822-0697

MASSACHUSETTS

State Agency on Aging

Massachusetts Executive Office of
Elder Affairs
38 Chauncy St.
Boston, MA 02111
(617) 727-7750

Area Agencies on Aging

Boston Commission on Affairs of
the Elderly
1 City Hall Square, Room 271
Boston, MA 02201
(617) 725-3980
Somerville/Cambridge Home Care
Corp.
1 Davis Square, 2nd floor
Somerville, MA 02144
(617) 628-2601
Baypath Senior Citizens Services
P.O. Box 2625, Center Station
Framingham, MA 01701
(617) 620-0840
North Shore Elder Services
484 Lowell St.
Peabody, MA 01960
(617) 535-6220
Greater Lynn Senior Services
90 Exchange St.
Lynn, MA 01902
(617) 599-0110
Chelsea/Revere/ Winthrop Elder
Services
300 Broadway
P.O. Box 189
Revere, MA 02151
(617) 284-0550

Minuteman Home Care Corp.
 83 Hartwell Ave.
 Lexington, MA 02173
 (617) 862-6200
West Suburban Elder Services
 124 Watertown St.
 Watertown, MA 02172
 (617) 926-4100
Elder Services of Berkshire County
 100 North St.
 Pittsfield, MA 01201
 (413) 499-1353
Franklin County Home Care Corp.
 Central St.
 Turners Falls, MA 01376
 (413) 863-9565
Highland Valley Elder Services Center
 320 Riverdale Dr.
 Northampton, MA 01060
 (413) 586-2000
Holyoke-Chicopee Home Care
 198 High St.
 Holyoke, MA 01040
 (413) 538-9020
Greater Sringfield Senior Services
 66 Industry Ave.
 Springfield, MA 01104
 (413) 781-8800
Region 2 Area Agency on Aging
 1128 Main St.
 Holden, MA 01520
 (617) 829-5364
 (800) 322-3032 (toll-free within
  area)
Senior Home Care Services
 2 Main St.
 Gloucester, MA 01930
 (617) 281-1750
Mystic Valley Elder Services
 661 Main St., Suite 110
 Malden, MA 02148
 (617) 321-7705

King Phillip Elder Services
 IGO Bldg., Carpenter St.
 Foxboro, MA 02035
 (617) 769-7440
 (800) 462-5221 (toll-free in Norfolk only)
South Shore Elder Services
 639 Granite St.
 Braintree, MA 02184
 (617) 749-6832
Old Colony Planning Council
 9 Belmont St.
 Brockton, MA 02401
 (617) 584-1561
Bristol County Home Care for the
  Elderly
 182 N. Main St.
 Fall River, MA 02720
 (617) 675-2101
Coastline Elderly Services
 106 Huttleston Ave.
 Fairhaven, MA 02719
 (617) 999-6400
Elder Services of Cape Cod & Is-
  lands
 68 Route 134
 South Dennis, MA 02660
 (617) 394-4630
 (800) 352-7178 (toll-free within
  area)
Elder Services of the Merrimack
  Valley
 420 Common St.
 Lawrence, MA 01840
 (617) 683-7747
 (800) 892-0890 (toll-free within
  area)
Elder Home Care Services of
  Worcester Area
 1241 Main St.
 Worcester, MA 01603
 (617) 756-1545

Medicare Peer Review Organization

Massachusetts Peer Review Organization Inc.
300 Bearhill Rd.
Waltham, MA 02254
(617) 890-0011

MICHIGAN

State Agency on Aging

Michigan Office of Services to the
Aging
P.O. Box 30026
Lansing, MI 48909
(517) 373-8230

Area Agencies on Aging

Detroit Area Agency on Aging
3110 Book Bldg.
1249 Washington Blvd.
Detroit, MI 48226
(313) 961-6680
The Senior Alliance
3850 Second St., Suite 160
Wayne, MI 48184
(313) 722-2830
Area Agency on Aging 1-B
(St. Clair, Macomb, Oakland, Livingston, Washtenaw, and
Monroe counties)
29508 Southfield Rd., Suite 100
Southfield, MI 48076
(313) 569-0333
Region 2 Commission on Aging
(Jackson, Hillsdale, and Lenawee
counties)
P.O. Box 915
3221 N. Adrian Drive
Adrian, MI 49221
(517) 265-7881

Southcentral Michigan Council on
Aging
(Barry, Kalamazoo, Calhoun, St.
Joseph, and Branch counties)
8135 Cox's Drive, Suite 1-C
Portage, MI 49002
(616) 327-4321
Region 4 Area Agency on Aging
(Van Buren, Cass, and Berrien
counties)
People's State Bank Bldg., Room 8
517 Ship St.
St. Joseph, MI 49085
(616) 983-0177
Valley Area Agency on Aging
(Lapeer, Genesee, and Shiawassee
counties)
110 Old Sears Bldg.
708 Root St.
Flint, MI 48503
(313) 239-7671
Tri-County Office on Aging
(Clinton, Eaton, and Ingham
counties)
500 W. Washtenaw
Lansing, MI 48933
(517) 487-1066
Region 7 Area Agency on Aging
(Roscommon, Ogemaw, Iosco,
Clare, Gladwin, Arenac, Isabella, Midland, Bay, Gratiot,
Saginaw, Tuscola, Sanilac, and
Huron counties)
East Community Center
1200 N. Madison Ave.
Bay City, MI 48706
(517) 893-4506

Area Agency on Aging of Western
Michigan
(Mason, Lake, Osceola, Newaygo,
Mecosta, Montcalm, Kent, Alle-
gan, and Ionia counties)
1108 People's Bldg.
60 Monroe Center, N.W.
Grand Rapids, MI 49503
(616) 456-5664
Northeast Michigan Community
Services
(Cheboygan, Presque Isle, Otsego,
Montmorency, Alpena, Craw-
ford, Oscoda, and Alcona coun-
ties)
P.O. Box 297
2373 Gordon Rd.
Alpena, MI 49707
(517) 356-3474
Northwest Senior Resources Inc.
(Emmet, Charlevoix, Antrim, Lee-
lanau, Benzie, Grand Traverse,
Kalkaska, Manistee, Wexford,
and Missaukee counties)
P.O. Box 2010
1609 Park Drive
Traverse City, MI 49685
(616) 947-8920
Region 11 Area Agency on Aging
(Mackinac, Chippewa, Luce,
Schoolcraft, Alger, Delta, Men-
ominee, Dickinson, Marquette,
Iron, Baraga, Keweenaw,
Houghton, Ontonagon, Goge-
bic, and Isle Royal counties)
UPCAP Services Inc.
118 N. 22nd St.
Escanaba, MI 49829
(906) 786-4701
Area Planning Council on Aging
(Oceana, Muskegon, and Ottawa
counties)
315 W. Webster
Muskegon, MI 49440
(616) 722-7811

Medicare Peer Review Organization

Michigan Peer Review Organization
40500 Ann Arbor Rd., Suite 200
Plymouth, MI 48170
(313) 459-0900

MINNESOTA

State Agency on Aging

Minnesota Board on Aging
204 Metro Square Bldg.
121 E. Seventh St.
St. Paul, MN 55101
(612) 296-2770

Area Agencies on Aging

Aging Metro Council
(Hennepin, Anoka, Ramsey,
Washington, Carver, Scott, and
Dakota counties)
300 Metro Square Bldg.
121 E. Seventh St.
St. Paul, MN 55101
(612) 291-6497
Arrowhead Planning Program on
Aging
(Koochiching, St. Louis, Lake,
Cook, Itasca, Aitkin, and Carl-
ton counties
330 S. First Ave. East
Duluth, MN 55802
(218) 722-5545
Southeastern Minnesota Area
Agency on Aging
(Rice, Goodhue, Wabasha, Steele,
Dodge, Olmsted, Winona, Free-
born, Mower, Fillmore, and
Houston counties)
121 N. Broadway, Room 302
Rochester, MN 55901
(507) 288-6944

Region 9 Area Agency on Aging
(Sibley, Nicollet, Le Sueur,
Brown, Watonwan, Blue Earth,
Waseca, Martin, and Faribault
counties)
Box 3367
410 S. Fifth St.
Mankato, MN 56001
(507) 387-5643
Northwest Regional Development
Commission
(Kittson, Roseau, Marshall, Polk,
Pennington, Norman, and Red
Lake counties)
P.O. Box E
525 Brooks Ave. South
Thief River Falls, MN 56701
(218) 681-2637
Region 2 Area Agency, Headwater
Regional Development Com-
mission
(Lake of the Woods, Beltrami,
Clearwater, and Hubbard coun-
ties)
Box 906
Bemidji, MN 56601
(218) 751-3108
West Central Area Agency on Aging
(Clay, Becker, Wilkin, Otter Tail,
Grant, Douglas, Stevens, Pope,
and Traverse counties)
P.O. Box 726
Fergus Falls, MN 56536
(218) 739-4617
Region 5 Area Agency on Aging
(Cass, Wadena, Crow Wing,
Todd, and Morrison counties)
611 Iowa Ave.
Staples, MN 56479
(218) 894-3233

Region 6 East Regional Develop-
ment Commission
(Kandiyohi, Meeker, Renville, and
McLeod counties)
311 W. Sixth St.
Willmar, MN 56201
(612) 235-8504
Upper Minnesota Valley Area
Agency on Aging
(Big Stone, Swift, Lac Qui Parle,
Chippewa, and Yellow Medi-
cine counties)
323 W. Schlieman
Appleton, MN 56208
(612) 289-1981
Region 7 Area Agency on Aging
(Mille Lacs, Kanabec, Pine, Isanti,
and Chisago counties)
100 S. Park St.
Mora, MN 55051
(612) 679-4065
Central Minnesota Council on
Aging
(Stearns, Benton, Sherburne, and
Wright counties)
26 N. Sixth Ave.
St. Cloud, MN 56301
(612) 253-9349
Southwestern Area Agency on
Aging
(Lincoln, Lyon, Redwood, Pipes-
tone, Murray, Cottonwood,
Rock, Nobles, and Jackson
counties)
Box 265
2524 Broadway
Slayton, MN 56172
(507) 836-8549
Minnesota Chippewa Tribe Area
Agency on Aging
(Tribal areas)
P.O. Box 217
Cass Lake, MN 56633
(218) 335-2252, ext. 145

Medicare Peer Review Organization

Foundation for Health Care Evaluation

Health Associations Center

One Appletree Square

Minneapolis, MN 55420

(612) 854-3306

MISSISSIPPI

State Agency on Aging

Mississippi Council on Aging

301 W. Pearl St.

Jackson, MS 39203-3092

(601) 949-2070

Area Agencies on Aging

Central Mississippi Area Agency on Aging

(Yazoo, Madison, Warren, Hinds, Rankin, Copiah, and Simpson counties)

P.O. Box 4935

Jackson, MS 39216

(601) 981-1511

Southern Mississippi Area Agency on Aging

(Jefferson Davis, Covington, Jones, Wayne, Marion, Lamar, Forrest, Perry, Greene, Pearl River, Stone, George, Hancock, Harrison, and Jackson counties)

1020 32nd Ave.

Gulfport, MS 39501

(601) 868-2311

(800) 222-9504 (toll-free, within state)

Golden Triangle Planning and Development District, Aging Division

(Webster, Clay, Choctaw, Oktibbeha, Lowndes, Winston, and Noxubee counties

P.O. Drawer DN

Mississippi State, MS 39762

(601) 325-3855

South Delta Area Agency on Aging

(Bolivar, Washington, Sunflower, Humphreys, Sharkey, and Issaquena counties)

P.O. Box 1776

Greenville, MS 38702-1776

(601) 378-3831

North Central Planning and Development District, Aging Division

(Yalobusha, Grenada, Montgomery, Carroll, Leflore, Holmes, and Attala counties)

P.O. Box 668

Winona, MS 38967

(601) 283-2675

North Delta Area Agency on Aging

(DeSota, Tunica, Tate, Panola, Quitman, Coahoma, and Tallahatchie counties)

P.O. Box 1244

Clarksdale, MS 38614

(601) 627-3401

Three Rivers Planning and Development District, Aging Division

(Lafayette, Union Pontotoc, Lee, Itawamba, Monroe, Chickasaw, and Calhoun counties)

P.O. Box B

Pontotoc, MS 38863

(601) 489-2415

North East Planning and Development District, Aging Division

(Marshall, Benton, Tippah, Alcorn, Prentiss, and Tishomingo counties)

P.O. Box 6D

Booneville, MS 38829

(601) 728-6248

East Central Planning and Development District
(Leake, Neshoba, Kemper, Scott, Newton, Lauderdale, Smith, Jasper, and Clarke counties)
P.O. Box 499
Newton, MS 39345
(601) 683-2007

Southwest Mississippi Area Agency on Aging
(Claiborne, Jefferson, Lincoln, Lawrence, Walthall, Pike, Amite, Wilkinson, Adams, and Franklin counties)
P.O. Box 429
Meadville, MS 39653
(601) 384-5881

Medicare Peer Review Organization

Mississippi Foundation for Medical Care Inc.
P.O. Box 4665
1900 N. West St.
Jackson, MS 39216
(601) 948-8894

MISSOURI

State Agency on Aging

Missouri Division on Aging
Department of Social Services
Broadway State
P.O. Box 570
Jefferson City, MO 65102
(314) 751-3082

Area Agencies on Aging

St. Louis Department of Human Services
10 N. Tucker, 12th floor
Civil Courts Bldg.
St. Louis, MO 63101
(314) 622-3381

Mid-America Regional Council
(Platte, Clay, Ray, Jackson, and Cass counties)
20 W. Ninth St., 7th floor
Kansas City, MO 64105
(816) 474-4240

Mid-East Area Agency on Aging
(St. Louis, St. Charles, Franklin, and Jefferson counties)
2510 S. Brentwood, Room 315
Brentwood, MO 63144
(314) 962-0808

Southwest Missouri Area Agency on Aging
(Dade, Lawrence, Barry, Polk, Greene, Christian, Stone, Taney, Ozark, Douglas, Webster, Dallas, Wright, Texas, Howell, Shannon, and Oregon counties)
P.O. Box 1805
Park Central East
Springfield, MO 65805
(417) 862-0762

Region 10 Area Agency on Aging
(Barton, Jasper, Newton, and McDonald counties)
705 Illinois, Suite 126
Joplin, MO 64801
(417) 781-8562

Southeast Missouri Area Agency on Aging
(Iron, St. Francois, Ste. Genevieve, Perry, Cape Girardeau, Bollinger, Madison, Reynolds, Wayne, Carter, Ripley, Butler, Stoddard, Scott, Mississippi, New Madrid, Pemiscot, and Dunklin counties)
1301 N. Kings Highway
Cape Girardeau, MO 63701
(314) 335-3331

District 3 Area Agency on Aging
(Bates, Vernon, Cedar, St. Clair, Henry, Johnson, Lafayette, Carroll, Chariton, Saline, Pettis, Benton, and Hickory counties)
P.O. Box 556
604 N. McGuire
Warrensburg, MO 64093
(816) 747-3107

Northwest Missouri Area Agency on Aging
(Atchison, Nodaway, Holt, Andrew, Buchanan, Clinton, DeKalb, Gentry, Worth, Harrison, Daviess, Caldwell, Linn, Livingston, Grundy, Mercer, Putnam, and Sullivan counties)
P.O. Drawer G
401 W. Jackson
Albany, MO 64402
(816) 762-3800

Northeast Missouri Area Agency on Aging
(Schuyler, Scotland, Clark, Adair, Knox, Lewis, Macon, Shelby, Marion, Ralls, Monroe, Randolph, Pike, Lincoln, Montgomery, and Warren counties)
P.O. Box 1067
705 E. LaHarpe St.
Kirksville, MO 63501
(816) 665-4682

Central Missouri Area Agency on Aging
(Howard, Boone, Audrain, Callaway, Osage, Cole, Moniteau, Cooper, Morgan, Miller, Camden, Maries, Phelps, Dent, Pulaski, Laclede, Crawford, Washington, and Gasconade counties)
609 Nebraska Ave., Room 9
Columbia, MO 65201
(314) 443-5823

Medicare Peer Review Organization

Missouri Patient Care Review Foundation
311A Ellis Blvd.
Jefferson City, MO 65101
(314) 634-4441

MONTANA

State Agency on Aging

Montana State Unit on Aging
Community Services Division
Department of Social and Rehabilitation Services
P.O. Box 4210
Helena, MT 59604
(406) 444-5650

Area Agencies on Aging

Rocky Mountain Development Council, Area 4 Agency on Aging
(Lewis and Clark, Meagher, Jefferson, Broadwater, Gallatin, and Park counties)
P.O. Box 721
Helena, MT 59624
(406) 442-1552

Missoula County Council on Aging, Area 11
333 N. Washington
Missoula, MT 59802
(406) 728-7682

Cascade County Area 8 Agency on Aging
1601 Second Ave. North, Room 225
Great Falls, MT 59401
(406) 761-1919

Area 1 Agency on Aging, Action for Eastern Montana
(Phillips, Valley, Daniels, Sheridan, Garfield, McCone, Richland, Dawson, Prairie, Wibaux, Fallon, Custer, Rosebud, Treasure, Carter, Roosevelt, and Powder River counties)
123 N. Merrill
Glendive, MT 59330
(406) 365-3364

Area 2 Agency on Aging
(Judith Basin, Fergus, Petroleum, Musselshell, Golden Valley, Wheatland, Sweet Grass, Stillwater, Yellowstone, Big Horn, and Carbon counties)
236 Main St.
Roundup, MT 59072
(406) 323-1320

North Central Area 3 Agency on Aging
(Glacier, Pondera, Toole, Liberty, Chouteau, Blaine, and Teton counties)
323 S. Main St.
Conrad, MT 59425
(406) 278-5662

Area 5 Agency on Aging
(Powell, Granite, Deer Lodge, Silver Bow, Madison, and Beaverhead counties)
115 E. Pennsylvania Ave.
Anaconda, MT 59711
(406) 563-3110

Western Montana Area 6 Agency on Aging
(Ravalli, Sanders, Mineral, Lake, and Lincoln counties)
Box 4027
Polson, MT 59860
(406) 833-6211, ext. 289

Tribal Elders Program, Area 7 Agency on Aging
(all Indian reservations)
2303 Grand Ave., Suite 5
Billings, MT 59102
(406) 652-3113

Flathead County Council on Aging, Area 9
723 Fifth Ave. East
Kalispell, MT 59901
(406) 752-5300, Ext. 322

Hill County Council on Aging, Area 10
2 W. Second St.
Havre, MT 59501
(406) 265-5464

Medicare Peer Review Organization

Montana-Wyoming Foundation for Medical Care
P.O. Box 5117
21 N. Main
Helena, MT 59604
(406) 443-4020

NEBRASKA

State Agency on Aging

Nebraska Department on Aging
P.O. Box 95044
301 Centennial Mall South
Lincoln, NE 68509
(402) 471-2306

Area Agencies on Aging

Eastern Nebraska Office on Aging
(Dodge, Washington, Douglas, Sarpy, and Cass counties)
885 S. 72nd St.
Omaha, NE 68114
(402) 444-6536

Lincoln Area Agency on Aging
(Polk, Butler, Saunders, Lancaster, Seward, York, Fillmore, and Saline counties)
129 N. 10th St., Room 241
Lincoln, NE 68508
(402) 471-7022

Northeast Nebraska Area Agency on Aging
(Cherry, Keya Paha, Boyd, Brown, Rock, Holt, Knox, Cedar, Dixon, Dakota, Thurston, Wayne, Pierce, Antelope, Boone, Burt, Madison, Stanton, Cuming, Colfax, Platte, and Nance counties)
North Stone Bldg.
P.O. Box 1447
Norfolk, NE 68701
(402) 371-7454

South Central Nebraska Area Agency on Aging
(Blaine, Loup, Garfield, Wheeler, Custer, Valley, Greeley, Sherman, Buffalo, Phelps, Kearney, Furnas, Harlan, and Franklin counties)
124 W. 46th St.
Kearney, NE 68847
(308) 234-1851

Midland Area Agency on Aging
(Howard, Merrick, Hamilton, Hall, Adams, Clay, Webster, and Nuckolls counties)
P.O. Box 905
Hastings, NE 68901
(402) 463-4565

Blue Rivers Area Agency on Aging
(Gage, Otoe, Thayer, Jefferson, Johnson, Nemaha, Pawnee, and Richardson counties)
Gage County Courthouse, Room 24
Beatrice, NE 68310
(402) 223-3124

West Central Nebraska Area Agency on Aging
(Grant, Hooker, Thomas, Arthur, McPherson, Logan, Keith, Perkins, Lincoln, Perkins, Chase, Hayes, Frontier, Dundy, Hitchcock, Gosper, and Red Willow counties)
200 S. Silber Ave.
North Platte, NE 69101
(308) 534-6780, ext. 190

Aging Office of Western Nebraska
(Sioux, Dawes, Sheridan, Box Butte, Scotts Bluff, Morrill, Garden, Deuel, Cheyenne, Kimball, and Banner counties)
4502 Avenue I
Scottsbluff, NE 69361
(308) 635-0851

Medicare Peer Review Organization

Iowa Foundation for Medical Care
3737 Woodland Ave., Suite 500
West Des Moines, IA 50265
(515) 223-2900

NEVADA

State Agency on Aging
(no area agencies)

Nevada Division for Aging Services
Department of Human Resources
Kinkead Bldg., Room 101
505 E. King St.
Carson City, NV 89710
(702) 885-4210

Medicare Peer Review Organization

Nevada Physicians Review Organization
Bldg. A, Suite 108
4600 Kietzke Lane
Reno, NV 89502
(702) 826-1996

NEW HAMPSHIRE

State Agency on Aging

(no area agencies)

New Hampshire State Council on
    Aging
    Bldg. 3
    105 Loudon Rd.
    Concord, NH 03301
    (603) 271-2751
    (800) 351-1888 (toll-free, within
    state)

Medicare Peer Review Organization

New Hampshire Foundation for
    Medical Care
    P.O. Box 578
    110 Locust St.
    Dover, NH 03820
    (603) 749-1641

NEW JERSEY

State Agency on Aging

New Jersey Division on Aging
    Department of Community Af-
    fairs
    363 W. State St., CN 807
    Trenton, NJ 08625-0807
    (609) 292-0921

Area Agencies on Aging

Atlantic County Division on Aging
    1333 Atlantic Ave., 3rd floor
    Atlantic City, NJ 08401
    (609) 345-6700, Ext. 3471
Bergen County Office on Aging
    355 Main St.
    Hackensack, NJ 07601-5875
    (201) 646-2625
Burlington County Office on Aging
    49 Rancocas Rd.
    Mount Holly, NJ 08060
    (609) 261-5069

Camden County Office on Aging
    120 White House Pike, Suite 103
    Haddon Heights, NJ 08035
    (609) 546-6404
Cape May County Office on Aging
    P.O. Box 222
    Social Services Bldg.
    Rio Grande, NJ 08242
    (609) 886-2784
Cumberland County Office on Aging
    Administration Bldg.
    790 E. Commerce St.
    Bridgeton, NJ 08302
    (609) 451-8000, Ext. 357
Essex County Office on Aging
    86 Washington St.
    East Orange, NJ 07017
    (201) 678-9700
Gloucester County Department on
    Aging
    44 Delaware St.
    Woodbury, NJ 08096
    (609) 853-3312
Hudson County Office on Aging
    114 Clifton Place
    Jersey City, NJ 07304
    (201) 434-6900
Hunterdon County Office on Aging
    6 Gauntt Place
    Flemington, NJ 08822
    (201) 788-1362
Mercer County Office on Aging
    P.O. Box 8068
    640 S. Broad St.
    Trenton, NJ 08650
    (609) 989-6661
Middlesex County Office on Aging
    841 Georges Rd.
    North Brunswick, NJ 08902
    (201) 745-3293
Monmouth County Office on Aging
    Hall of Records Annex
    East Main St.
    Freehold, NJ 07728
    (201) 431-7450

Morris County Office on Aging
Court House, CN 900
Morristown, NJ 07960
(201) 829-8539

Ocean County Office on Aging
CN-2191
Toms River, NJ 08754
(201) 244-2121

Passaic County Office on Aging
675 Goffle Rd.
Hawthorne, NJ 07506
(201) 881-4950

Salem County Office on Aging
c/o Lakeview Complex
R.D. 2, Box 348
Woodstown, NJ 08098
(609) 769-4150

Somerset County Office on Aging
Box 3000
North Bridge and High Streets
Somerville, NJ 08876
(201) 231-7175

Sussex County Office on Aging
175 High St.
Newton, NJ 07860
(201) 383-5098

Union County Division on Aging
County Administration Bldg., 4th
Floor
Elizabethtown Plaza
Elizabeth, NJ 07201
(201) 527-4866

Warren County Office on Aging
Wayne Dumont Jr. Administra-
tion Bldg.
Route 519
Belvidere, NJ 07823
(201) 475-8000, ext. 591

Medicare Peer Review Organization

The Peer Review Organization of
New Jersey Inc.
Central Division
Brier Hill Court, Bldg. J
East Brunswick, NJ 08816
(201) 238-5570

NEW MEXICO

State Agency on Aging

New Mexico State Agency on Aging
La Villa Rivera Bldg.
224 E. Palace Ave., 4th floor
Santa Fe, NM 87501
(505) 827-7640

Area Agencies on Aging

City of Albuquerque Area Agency
on Aging
P.O. Box 1293
Albuquerque, NM 87103
(505) 766-7550

District 2 Area Agency on Aging
(Santa Fe, San Juan, Rio Arriba,
Taos, Colfax, Mora, San Mi-
guel, Los Alamos, McKinley,
Torrance, Sandoval, and Valen-
cia counties)
c/o New Mexico State Agency on
Aging
La Villa Rivera Bldg.
224 E. Palace Ave., 4th floor
Santa Fe, NM 87501
(505) 827-7640

Eastern New Mexico Area Agency
on Aging
(Guadalupe, Union, Harding,
Quay, Curry, Roosevelt, De
Baca, Lea, Chaves, Eddy, and
Lincoln counties)
901 W. 13th St.
Clovis, NM 88101
(505) 769-1613

Southwestern New Mexico Area
Agency on Aging
(Catron, Socorro, Grant, Sierra,
Otero, Dona Ana, Luna, and
Hidalgo counties)
P.O. Box 833
Mesilla, NM 88046
(505) 525-0352

Medicare Peer Review Organization

New Mexico Medical Review Association
Box 9900
Albuquerque, NM 87119-9900
(505) 842-6236

NEW YORK

State Agency on Aging

New York State Office for the Aging
Agency Bldg. 2
Nelson A. Rockefeller Empire
State Plaza
Albany, NY 12223-0001
(518) 474-5731
(800) 342-9871 (toll-free, within
state)

Area Agencies on Aging

New York City Department for the
Aging
2 Lafayette St.
New York, NY 10007-1392
(212) 577-0848
Westchester County Office for the
Aging
214 Central Ave.
White Plains, NY 10606-3307
(914) 682-3000
Nassau County Department of Senior Citizen Affairs
222 Willis Ave.
Mineola, NY 11501-2676
(516) 535-5990

Suffolk County Office for the Aging
65 Jetson Lane
Central Islip, NY 11722-1298
(516) 348-5313
Albany County Department for the
Aging
112 State St., Room 710
Albany, NY 12207-2005
(518) 447-7180
Erie County Department of Senior
Services
Erie County Office Bldg.
95 Franklin St.
Buffalo, NY 14202-3963
(716) 846-8522
Monroe County Office for the Aging
375 Westfall Rd.
Rochester, NY 14620-4678
(716) 442-6350
Metropolitan Commission on Aging
(Onondaga County)
Civic Center, 10th floor
421 Montgomery St.
Syracuse, NY 13202-2911
(315) 425-2362
Rockland County Office for the
Aging
Bldg. B, Health & Social Services
Complex
Pomona, NY 10970-1000
(914) 354-0200, ext. 2100
Dutchess County Office for the
Aging
488 Main St.
Poughkeepsie, NY 12601-3489
(914) 431-2465
Schenectady County Office for the
Aging
101 Nott Terrace
Schenectady, NY 12308-3111
(518) 382-8481

Sullivan County Office for the Aging
New County Government Bldg.
100 North St.
Monticello, NY 12701-1024
(914) 794-3000

Chemung County Office for the
Aging
425 Pennsylvania Ave.
Elmira, NY 14904-1794
(607) 737-5520

Tompkins County Office for the
Aging
225 S. Fulton St.
Ithaca, NY 14850-3392
(607) 272-2825

Ulster County Office for the Aging
Box 1800
240-44 Fair St.
Kingston, NY 12401-2903
(914) 331-9300, ext. 578

Putnam County Office for the Aging
Bldg. A
110 Old Route 6
Carmel, NY 10512-2196
(914) 225-1034

Saratoga County Office for the
Aging
South Street School
South St.
Ballston Spa, NY 12020-1002
(518) 885-5381, ext. 270

Orange County Office for the Aging
60 Erie St., 3rd floor
Goshen, NY 10924-1531
(914) 294-5151, ext. 1560

Allegany County Office for the
Aging
17 Court St.
Belmont, NY 14813-1099
(716) 268-9390

Broome County Office for the Aging
County Office Bldg., Government
Plaza
Binghamton, NY 13902-1766
(607) 772-2411

Cattaraugus County Department for
the Aging
255 N. Union St.
Olean, NY 14760-2663
(716) 375-4114

Cayuga County Office for the Aging
County Office Bldg.
160 Genesee St.
Auburn, NY 13021-3483
(315) 253-1226

Chautauqua County Office for the
Aging
Hall R. Clothier Bldg.
Mayville, NY 14757-1007
(716) 753-4471

Chenango County Area Agency on
Aging
County Office Bldg.
5 Court St.
Norwich, NY 13815-1794
(607) 335-4624

Clinton County Office for the Aging
137 Margaret St.
Plattsburgh, NY 12901-1394
(518) 565-4620

Columbia County Office for the
Aging
71 N. Third St.
Hudson, NY 12534-1727
(518) 828-4258

Cortland County Office for the
Aging
P.O. Box 1172
County Office Bldg.
60 Central Ave.
Cortland, NY 13045-2795
(607) 753-5060

Delaware County Office for the
Aging
6 Court St.
Delhi, NY 13753-1066
(607) 746-6333

Essex County Office for the Aging
Elizabethtown, NY 12932-0217
(518) 873-6301, ext. 370

Franklin County Office for the Aging
County Court House
89 W. Main St.
Malone, NY 12953-1119
(518) 483-6767

Fulton County Office for the Aging
1 E. Montgomery St.
Johnstown, NY 12095-2534
(518) 762-8288

Genesee County Office for the Aging
Batavia-Genesee Senior Center
2 Bank St.
Batavia, NY 14020-2299
(716) 343-1611

Green County Department for the
Aging
19 S. Jefferson Ave.
Catskill, NY 12414-1307
(518) 943-5332

Herkimer County Office for the
Aging
County Office Bldg.
Mary St.
Herkimer, NY 13350-0267
(315) 867-1121

Jefferson County Office for the
Aging
1240 Coffeen St. (Lower Level)
Watertown, NY 13601-2544
(315) 782-1075

Lewis County Office for the Aging
Lewis County Courthouse
Lowville, NY 13367-1397
(315) 376-5313

Livingston County Office for the
Aging
Livingston County Campus, Bldg. 1
Mount Morris, NY 14510-1694
(716) 658-2881, ext. 18, 29, 41

Madison County Office for the
Aging
Box 250
Route 20
Morrisville, NY 13408-0250
(315) 684-9424

Montgomery Countywide Office for
the Aging
21 New St.
Amsterdam, NY 12010-5627
(518) 843-2300

Niagara County Office for the Aging
Switzer Bldg.
100 Davison Rd.
Lockport, NY 14094-3396
(716) 439-6044

Oneida County Office for the Aging
County Office Bldg.
800 Park Ave.
Utica, NY 13501-2979
(315) 798-5771

Ontario County Office for the Aging
120 N. Main St.
Canandaigua, NY 14424-1296
(716) 394-7070, ext. 2240

Orleans County Office for the Aging
Orleans County Administrative
Bldg.
14016 Route 31
Albion, NY 14411-9362
(716) 589-5673, ext. 191

Oswego County Office for the Aging
P.O. Box 3080
County Office Complex
70 Brunner St.
Oswego, NY 13126-3080
(315) 349-3231

Otsego County Office for the Aging
County Office Bldg.
Cooperstown, NY 13326-1129
(607) 547-4233

Rensselaer County Department for
the Aging
1700 Seventh Ave.
Troy, NY 12180-3497
(518) 270-2730

St. Lawrence County Office for the
Aging
County Office Bldg.
Canton, NY 13617-1194
(315) 379-2204

Schoharie County Office for the
  Aging
  122 E. Main St.
  Cobleskill, NY 12043-1223
  (518) 234-4219
Schuyler County Office for the Aging
  336-8 W. Main St.
  Montour Falls, NY 14865-0838
  (607) 535-7108
Seneca County Office for the Aging
  P.O. Box 480
  Seneca Falls, NY 13148-0810
  (315) 568-5893
Steuben County Office for the Aging
  County Route 113
  Bath, NY 14810-1616
  (607) 776-7651
Tioga County Office for the Aging
  231 Main St.
  Owego, NY 13827-1690
  (607) 687-4120
Warren/Hamilton Counties Office
  for the Aging
  Warren County Municipal Center
  Lake George, NY 12845-9791
  (518) 761-6347
Washington County Office for the
  Aging
  P.O. Box 58
  Whitehall, NY 12887-0058
  (518) 499-2468
Wayne County Office for the Aging
  P.O. Box 7336
  Route 31W
  Lyons, NY 14489-9152
  (315) 946-4163
Wyoming County Office for the
  Aging
  76 N. Main St.
  Warsaw, NY 14569-1329
  (716) 786-3144
Yates County Office for the Aging
  5 Collins Ave.
  Penn Yan, NY 14527-1396
  (315) 536-2368

St. Regis Mohawk Office for the
  Aging
  St. Regis-Mohawk Indian Reservation
  Hogansburg, NY 13655-9704
  (518) 358-2272, ext. 221
Seneca Nation of Indians Office for
  the Aging
  1500 Route 438
  Irving, NY 14081-9505
  (716) 532-4900

Medicare Peer Review Organization

Empire State Medical, Scientific, and
  Educational Foundation Inc.
  Box 5434
  420 Lakeville Rd.
  Lake Success, NY 11042
  (516) 488-6100

NORTH CAROLINA

State Agency on Aging

North Carolina Division of Aging
  1985 Umstead Drive
  Raleigh, NC 27603
  (919) 733-3983

Area Agencies on Aging

Southwestern North Carolina Planning and Economic Development Commission
  (Cherokee, Clay, Macon, Jackson,
  Graham, Swain, and Haywood
  counties)
  P.O. Box 850
  Bryson City, NC 27603
  (919) 733-3983
Land of Sky Regional Council (Region B)
  (Madison, Buncombe, Henderson,
  and Transylvania counties)
  25 Heritage Drive
  Asheville, NC 28806
  (704) 254-8131

Isothermal Planning and Development Commission
(McDowell, Rutherford, Polk, and Cleveland counties)
P.O. Box 841
Rutherfordton, NC 28129
(704) 287-2281

Region D Council of Governments
(Ashe, Alleghany, Avery, Mitchell, Yancey, Watauga, and Wilkes counties)
P.O. Box 1820
Executive Arts Bldg.
Furman Rd.
Boone, NC 28607
(704) 264-5558

Western Piedmont Council of Governments, Region E
(Caldwell, Burke, Alexandeer, and Catawba counties)
30 Third St. N.W.
Hickory, NC 28601
(704) 322-9191

Centralina Council of Governments, Region F
(Iredell, Rowan, Lincoln, Gaston, Mecklenburg, Cabarris, Stanly, and Union counties)
P.O. Box 35008
Charlotte, NC 28235
(704) 372-2416

Piedmont Triad Council of Governments
(Rockingham, Caswell, Guilford, Alamance, Davidson, and Randolph counties)
2120 Pinecroft Rd.
Greensboro, NC 27407
(919) 294-4950

Pee Dee Council of Governments, Region H
(Montgomery, Moore, Anson, and Richmond counties)
P.O. Box 728
Troy, NC 27371
(919) 576-6261

Triangle J Council of Governments
(Durham, Orange, Wake, Chatham, Johnston, and Lee counties)
P.O. Box 12276
100 Park Drive
Research Triangle Park, NC 27709
(919) 549-0551

Kerr Tar Council of Governments, Region K
(Person, Granville, Vance, Warren, and Franklin counties)
P.O. Box 709
Henderson, NC 27536
(919) 492-8561

Region L Council of Governments
(Halifax, Northampton, Nash, Edgecombe, and Wilson counties)
P.O. Box 2748
Rocky Mount, NC 27801
(919) 446-0411

Region M Council of Governments
(Harnett, Sampson, and Cumberland counties)
P.O. Box 1510
Fayetteville, NC 28302
(919) 323-4191

Lumber River Council of Governments
(Hoke, Scotland, Robeson, and Bladen counties)
P.O. Drawer 1529
111 W. Fifth St.
Lumberton, NC 28358
(919) 738-8104

Cape Fear Council of Governments,
Region O
(Columbus, Brunswick, New Hanover, and Pender counties)
P.O. Box 1491
Wilmington, NC 28402
(919) 763-0191

Neuse River Council of Governments, Region P
(Wayne, Greene, Lenoir, Duplin, Jones, Onslow, Craven, Pamlico, and Carteret counties)
P.O. Box 1717
New Bern, NC 28560
(919) 638-3185

Mid-East Development Commission, Region Q
(Hertford, Bertie, Martin, Pitt, and Beaufort counties)
P.O. Drawer 1787
Washington, NC 27889
(919) 946-8043

Albemarle Regional Planning and Development Commission, Region R
(Hyde, Dare, Tyrrell, Washington, Chowan, Perquimans, Pasquotank, Camden, Currituck, and Gates counties)
P.O. Box 646
Hertford, NC 27944
(919) 426-5753

Northwest Piedmont Council of Governments, Region I
(Surry, Stokes, Yadkin, Forsyth, and Davie counties)
280 S. Liberty St.
Winston-Salem, NC 27101
(919) 722-9346

Medicare Peer Review Organization

Medical Review of North Carolina Inc.
P.O. Box 37309
1011 Schaub Drive, Suite 200
Raleigh, NC 27627
(919) 851-2955

NORTH DAKOTA

State Agency on Aging

(no area agencies)
North Dakota Aging Services
Department of Human Services
State Capitol Bldg.
Bismarck, ND 58505
(701) 224-2577
(800) 472-2622 (toll-free, within state)

Medicare Peer Review Organization

North Dakota Health Care Review Inc.
900 N. Broadway, Suite 212
Minot, ND 58701
(701) 852-4231

OHIO

State Agency on Aging

Ohio Department of Aging
50 W. Broad St., 9th floor
Columbus, OH 43215
(614) 466-5500

Area Agencies on Aging

Western Reserve Area Agency on Aging
(Cuyahoga, Lorain, Medina, Lake, and Geauga counties)
Marion Bldg., Room 512
1276 W. Third St.
Cleveland, OH 44113
(216) 443-7560

Council on Aging of the Cincinnati
Area
(Butler, Warren, Clinton, Hamilton, and Clermont counties)
601 Provident Bank Bldg.
7th and Vine
Cincinnati, OH 45202
(513) 721-1025

Area Agency on Aging
(Darke, Preble, Shelby, Miami, Montgomery, Logan, Champaign, Clark, and Greene counties)
184 Salem Ave.
Dayton, OH 45406
(513) 225-3027

Area Agency on Aging of Northwestern Ohio
(Williams, Fulton, Lucas, Wood, Ottawa, Sandusky, Erie, Paulding, Defiance, and Henry counties)
Executive Office Bldg.
2155 Arlington Ave.
Toledo, OH 43609
(419) 382-0624

Central Ohio Area Agency on Aging
(Union, Delaware, Licking, Madison, Franklin, Fairfield, Pickaway, and Fayette counties)
272 S. Gift St.
Columbus, OH 43215
(614) 222-7250

Area Agency on Aging
(Van Wert, Mercer, Auglaize, Allen, Putnam, Hancock, and Hardin counties)
311 Bldg., Suite 201
311 E. Market St.
Lima, OH 45801
(419) 222-7723

Area Office on Aging
(Portage, Summit, Stark, and Wayne counties)
470 Grant St.
Akron, OH 44311
(216) 376-9172

District 5 Area Agency on Aging
(Seneca, Huron, Wyandot, Crawford, Richland, Ashland, Marion, Morrow, and Knox counties)
P.O. Box 966
50 Blymer Ave.
Mansfield, OH 44901
(419) 524-4114

Area Agency on Aging, District 7
(Ross, Vinton, Highland, Pike, Jackson, Gallia, Lawrence, Scioto, Adams, and Brown counties)
P.O. Box 978
Rio Grande College
Rio Grande, OH 45674
(614) 245-5306

Buckeye Hills-Hocking Valley Regional Development District
(Perry, Hocking, Athens, Meigs, Morgan, Washington, Noble, and Monroe counties)
St. Clair Bldg., Suite 410
216 Putnam St.
Marietta, OH 45750
(614) 374-9436

Area Agency on Aging, Region 9
(Holmes, Coshocton, Muskingum, Guernsey, Tuscarawas, Carroll, Harrison, Belmont, and Jefferson counties)
Box 429
117 S. 11th St.
Cambridge, OH 43725
(614) 439-4478

District 11 Area Agency on Aging
(Ashtabula, Trumbull, Mahoning,
and Columbiana counties)
Ohio One Bldg.
25 E. Boardman St.
Youngstown, OH 44503
(216) 746-2938

Medicare Peer Review Organization

Peer Review Systems Inc.
3720-J Olentangy River Rd.
Columbus, OH 43214
(614) 451-3600

OKLAHOMA

State Agency on Aging

Oklahoma Special Unit on Aging
Department of Human Services
P.O. Box 25352
Oklahoma City, OK 73125
(405) 521-2281

Area Agencies on Aging

Areawide Agency on Aging
(Oklahoma, Logan, Canadian, and
Cleveland counties)
P.O. Box 1474
125 N.W. Fifth St.
Oklahoma City, OK 73102
(405) 236-2426
Tulsa Area Agency on Aging
(Tulsa, Osage, and Creek coun-
ties)
200 Civic Center, Room 1025
Tulsa, OK 74103
(918) 529-7688
NECO Area Agency on Aging
(Washington, Nowata, Craig, Ot-
tawa, Rogers, Mayes, and Dela-
ware counties)
P.O. Box 330
Vinita, OK 74301-0330
(918) 256-6478

EODD Area Agency on Aging
(Wagoner, Cherokee, Adair, Se-
quoyah, Muskogee, McIntosh,
and Okmulgee counties)
P.O. Box 1376
800 W. Okmulgee
Muskogee, OK 74402-1367
(918) 682-7891
KEDDO Area Agency on Aging
(Haskell, Pittsburg, Latimer, Le-
Flore, Pushmatawa, McCurtain,
and Choctaw counties)
P.O. Box 638
Wilburton, OK 74578
(918) 465-2367
SODA Area Agency on Aging
(Garvin, Pontotoc, Coal, Atoka,
Carter, Murray, Johnston, Love,
Marshall, and Bryan counties)
P.O. Box 848
16 E St., S.W.
Ardmore, OK 73402
(405) 226-2250
COEDD Area Agency on Aging
(Pawnee, Payne, Lincoln, Pottawa-
tomie, Okfuskee, Seminole, and
Hughes counties)
400 N. Bell
Shawnee, OK 74801
(405) 273-6410
NODA Area Agency on Aging
(Alfalfa, Grant, Kay, Major, Gar-
field, Noble, Blaine, and King-
fisher counties)
3201 Sante Fe Trail
Enid, OK 73701
(405) 237-4810
ASCOG Area Agency on Aging
(Caddo, Grady, Comanche, Ste-
phens, Tillman, Cotton,
McClain, and Jefferson coun-
ties)
P.O. Box 1647
802 Main St.
Duncan, OK 73533
(405) 252-0595

SWODA Area Agency on Aging
   (Roger Mills, Custer, Beckham,
   Washita, Kiowa, Greer, Har-
   mon, and Jackson counties)
   P.O. Box 569
   Burns Flat, OK 73624
   (405) 562-4886
OEDA Area Agency on Aging
   (Cimarron, Texas, Beaver, Harper,
   Woods, Ellis, Woodward, and
   Dewey counties)
   P.O. Box 668
   Beaver, OK 73932
   (405) 625-4531

Medicare Peer Review Organization

Oklahoma Foundation for Peer Review
   5801 Broadway Extension, Suite
   400
   Oklahoma City, OK 73118
   (405) 840-2891

OREGON

State Agency on Aging

Oregon Senior Services Division
   313 Public Service Bldg.
   Salem, OR 97310
   (503) 378-4728

Area Agencies on Aging

Multnomah County Area Agency on
   Aging
   426 S.W. Stark, 6th floor
   Portland, OR 97204
   (503) 248-3646
Washington County Aging Program
   Administration Bldg.
   150 N.E. Third
   Hillsboro, OR 97123
   (503) 640-3489

Mid-Willamette Valley Senior Services Agency
   (Yamhill, Polk, and Marion coun-
   ties)
   410 Senator Bldg.
   220 High St., N.E.
   Salem, OR 97301
   (503) 371-1313
Senior and Disabled Adult Services
   (Lincoln, Benton, and Linn coun-
   ties)
   155 S.W. Madison, No. 5
   Corvallis, OR 97333
   (503) 757-6851
District 5 Area Agency on Aging
   Lane County Council of Govern-
   ments
   Lane County Public Service Bldg.
   125 Eighth Ave. East
   Eugene, OR 97401
   (503) 687-4283
District 1 Area Agency on Aging
   (Clatsop and Tillamook counties)
   P.O. Box 488
   Cannon Beach, OR 97110
   (503) 436-1156
Clackamas County Area Agency on
   Aging
   Social Services Division
   821 Main St.
   Oregon City, OR 97045
   (503) 655-8200
Columbia County Council of Senior
   Citizens
   P.O. Box 141
   St. Helens, OR 97051
   (503) 397-4000
Douglas County Senior Services
   621 W. Madrone
   Roseburg, OR 97470
   (503) 440-3601

Area Agency on Aging, Coos/Curry
  Council of Governments
(Coos and Curry counties)
170 S. Second St., Suite 204
Coos Bay, OR 97420
(503) 267-6500

District 8 Area Agency on Aging,
  Rouge Valley Council of Gov-
  ernments
(Josephine and Jackson counties)
155 S. Second St., Room 200
P.O. Box 3275
Central Point, OR 97502
(503) 664-6674

Mid-Columbia Area Agency on
  Aging
(Hood River, Wasco, and Sherman counties)
700 Union St., Room 233
The Dalles, OR 97058
(503) 298-4114

Central Oregon Council on Aging
(Jefferson, Deschutes, and Crook
  counties)
1345 N.W. Wall St.
Bend, OR 97701
(503) 389-3311

Klamath Basin Senior Citizens
  Council
(Klamath and Lake counties)
2045 Arthur St.
Klamath Falls, OR 97601
(503) 882-4098

East Central Oregon Association of
  Counties Area Agency on
  Aging
(Gilliam, Morrow, Umatilla,
  Grant, and Wheeler counties)
P.O. Box 1207
Pendleton, OR 97801
(503) 276-6732

Eastern Oregon Community Development Council
(Wallowa, Union, and Baker
  counties)
104 Elm
LaGrande, OR 97850
(503) 963-3186

Malheur County Council on Aging
Box 937
Ontario, OR 97914
(503) 889-7651

Harney County Senior Citizens
17 S. Alder St.
Burns, OR 97720
(503) 573-6024

Medicare Peer Review Organization

Oregon Peer Review Organization
1220 S.W. Morrison, Suite 300
Portland, OR 97205
(503) 243-1151

PENNSYLVANIA

State Agency on Aging

Pennsylvania Department of Aging
231 State St., Barto Bldg.
Harrisburg, PA 17101-1195
(717) 787-2177

Area Agencies on Aging

Philadelphia Corporation for Aging
111 N. Broad St.
Philadelphia, PA 19107
(215) 496-0520

Allegheny County Adult Services
  Area Agency on Aging
1440 Arrot Bldg.
401 Wood St.
Pittsburgh, PA 15222
(412) 355-4234

Dauphin County Area Agency on
  Aging
25 S. Front St.
Harrisburg, PA 17101-2025
(717) 255-2790

York County Area Agency on Aging
141 W. Market St.
York, PA 17401
(717) 771-9610

Lancaster County Office on Aging
50 N. Duke St.
Lancaster, PA 17603-1881
(717) 299-7979

Cumberland County Office on Aging
35 E. High St.
Carlisle, PA 17013
(717) 243-8442

Erie County Area Agency on Aging
Greater Erie Community Action
    Committee
18 E. Ninth St.
Erie, PA 16501
(814) 459-4581

Lackawanna County Area Agency
    on Aging
Lackawanna County Office Bldg.
200 Adams Ave.
Scranton, PA 18503
(717) 963-6740

Luzerne/Wyoming Counties Bureau
    for Aging
111 N. Pennsylvania Blvd.
Wilkes-Barre, PA 18701
(717) 822-1158

Montgomery County Office on
    Aging and Adult Services
Montgomery County Court
    House
Norristown, PA 19404
(215) 278-3601

Berks County Area Agency on Aging
15 S. Eighth St.
Reading, PA 19602-1105
(215) 378-8808

Lehigh County Area Agency on
    Aging
Court House Annex
523 Hamilton St.
Allentown, PA 18101
(215) 820-3248

Blair County Office of Services for
    the Aging
1320-24 12th Ave.
Altoona, PA 16601
(814) 946-1237

Cambria County Area Agency on
    Aging
R.D. 3, Box 614
Ebensburg, PA 15931
(814) 472-5580

Centre County Office of Aging
Willowbank Bldg.
Holmes & Valentine Streets
Bellefonte, PA 16823
(814) 355-6716

Northumberland County Area
    Agency on Aging
905 Juniper St.
Shamokin, PA 17872
(717) 648-6828

Union/Snyder County Office on
    Aging
116 N. Second St.
Lewisburg, PA 17837
(717) 524-2100

Mifflin/Juniata Area Agency on
    Aging
P.O. Box 750
Lewistown, PA 17044
(717) 242-0315

Franklin County Office for the
    Aging
Franklin County Farm Lane
Chambersburg, PA 17201
(717) 263-2153

Adams County Area Agency on
    Aging
100 N. Stratton St.
Gettysburg, PA 17325
(717) 334-9296

Perry County Office for the Aging
Court House Annex
South Carlisle St.
New Bloomfield, PA 17068
(717) 582-2131, ext. 223

Lebanon County Area Agency on
Aging
710 Maple St., Room 209
Lebanon, PA 17042
(717) 273-9262
Active Aging
1034 Park Ave.
Meadville, PA 16335
(814) 336-1792
North Central Office of Human Services
(Cameron, Elk, and McKean
counties)
P.O. Box A
Ridgway, PA 15853
(814) 776-2191
Clearfield County Area Agency on
Aging
P.O. Box 550
211 Ogden Ave.
Clearfield, PA 16830
(814) 765-2696
Jefferson County Area Agency on
Aging
Jefferson County Service Center
R.D. 5
Brookville, PA 15825
(814) 849-3096
Experience, Inc., Area Agency on
Aging
(Forest and Warren counties)
P.O. Box 886
514 W. Third Ave.
Warren, PA 16365
(814) 726-1700
Venango County Area Agency on
Aging
P.O. Box 1130
Franklin, PA 16323
(814) 437-6871

Mercer County Area Agency on
Aging
Human Services Complex
120 S. Diamond St.
Mercer, PA 16137
(412) 662-3800, ext. 538
Clarion County Area Agency on
Aging
12 Grant St.
Clarion, PA 16214
(814) 226-4640
Potter County Area Agency on Aging
Mapleview Health Center
Route 872
Coudersport, PA 16915
(814) 274-8843
Lycoming/Clinton Bi-County Office
of Aging
P.O. Box 770
352 Water St.
Lock Haven, PA 17745
(717) 748-8665
Columbia/Montour Area Agency on
Aging
243 W. Main St.
Bloomsburg, PA 17815
(717) 784-9272
Wayne/Pike Area Agency on Aging
Pike County Program Office
400 Broad St.
Milford, PA 18337
(717) 296-7813
Area Agency on Aging for
Tioga/Bradford/Susque-
hanna/Sullivan Counties
701 Main St.
Towanda, PA 18848
(717) 265-6121
(800) 982-4346 (toll-free, within
area)
Carbon County Area Agency on
Aging
P.O. Box 251
Jim Thorpe, PA 18229
(717) 325-2726

Schuylkill County Area Agency on
Aging
13-15 N. Centre St.
Pottsville, PA 17901
(717) 622-3103
Monroe County Area Agency on
Aging
62 Analomink St.
East Stroudsburg, PA 18301
(717) 424-5290
Beaver County Office on Aging
599 Market St., W.B.
Beaver, PA 15009
(412) 728-5700, ext. 406
Aging Services of Indiana County
Airport Offices & Professional
Center
R.D. 3
Indiana, PA 15701
(412) 349-4500
Westmoreland County Office of
Aging
2482 S. Grande Blvd.
Greensburg, PA 15601
(412) 836-1111
Southwestern PA Area Agency on
Aging
(Washington, Fayette, and Greene
counties)
Eastgate 8
Monessen, PA 15062
(412) 684-9000
Area Agency on Aging of Somerset
County
P.O. Box 960
147 E. Union St.
Somerset, PA 15501
(814) 443-2681
Huntingdon/Bedford/Fulton Area
Agency on Aging
P.O. Box 46
406 E. Pitt St.
Bedford, PA 15522
(814) 623-8149

Armstrong County Area Agency on
Aging
125 Queen St.
Kittanning, PA 16201
(412) 548-3290
Lawrence County Area Agency on
Aging
Catholic Charities of the Diocese
of Pittsburgh
20 S. Mercer St.
New Castle, PA 16101
(412) 658-5661
Butler County Area Agency on Aging
165 Brugh Ave.
Butler, PA 16001
(412) 282-3008
Chester County Services for Senior
Citizens
14 E. Biddle St.
West Chester, PA 19380
(215) 431-6350
Bucks County Area Agency on Aging
30 E. Oakland Ave.
Doylestown, PA 18901
(215) 348-0510
Delaware County Services for the
Aging
Second and Orange Streets, Gov-
ernment Center
Media, PA 19063
(215) 891-4455
Northampton County Area Agency
on Aging
Gracedale-Southwest Ground
Gracedale Ave.
Nazareth, PA 18064
(215) 759-7970

Medicare Peer Review Organization

Keystone Peer Review Organization
Inc.
P.O. Box 618
645 N. 12th St.
Lemoyne, PA 17043
(717) 763-7151

RHODE ISLAND

State Agency on Aging

(no area agencies on aging)

Rhode Island Department of Elderly
Affairs
79 Washington St.
Providence, RI 02903
(401) 277-2858

Medicare Peer Review Organization

Health Care Review Inc.
The Weld Bldg.
345 Blackstone Blvd.
Providence, RI 02906
(401) 331-6661

SOUTH CAROLINA

State Agency on Aging

South Carolina Commission on
Aging
915 Main St.
Columbia, SC 29201
(803) 734-3203

Area Agencies on Aging

Trident United Way
(Charleston, Berkeley, and Dor-
chester counties)
P.O. Drawer 2696
Charleston, SC 29403
(803) 723-1676
Central Midlands Regional Planning
Council
(Fairfield, Newberry, Richland,
and Lexington counties)
800 Dutch Square Blvd., No. 155
Columbia, SC 29210
(803) 798-1243

Appalachian Council of Govern-
ments
(Greenville, Pickens, Oconee, and
Anderson counties)
P.O. Drawer 6668
Greenville, SC 29606
(803) 242-9733
Santee-Lynches Council for Govern-
ments
(Kershaw, Lee, Sumter, and
Clarendon counties)
Box 1837
Sumter, SC 29150
(803) 775-7382
Pee Dee Regional Council of Gov-
ernments
(Chesterfield, Marlboro, Dar-
lington, Dillon, Florence, and
Marion counties)
P.O. Box 5719
Florence, SC 29502
(803) 669-3138
Abbeville County Council on Aging
P.O. Box 117
Abbeville, SC 29620
(803) 459-4511
Edgefield County Senior Citizens
Council
P.O. Box 510
400 Church St.
Edgefield, SC 29824
(803) 637-5326
Greenwood County Council on
Aging
P.O. Box 997
123 Bailey Circle
Greenwood, SC 29646
(803) 223-0164
Laurens County Service Council for
Senior Citizens
P.O. Box 777
Laurens, SC 29360
(803) 984-4572

McCormick County Council on
Aging
P.O. Box 684
Augusta St.
McCormick, SC 29835
(803) 465-2626
Saluda County Council on Aging
P.O. Box 507
104 Church St.
Saluda, SC 29138
(803) 445-2175
Catawba Regional Planning Council
(York, Union, Chester, and Lan-
caster counties)
P.O. Box 862
100 Dave Lyle Blvd., Suite 300,
SCN Center
Rock Hill, SC 29730
(803) 327-9041
Lower Savannah Council of Govern-
ments
(Aiken, Calhoun, Orangeburg,
Barnwell, Bamberg, and Allen-
dale counties)
P.O. Box 850
Aiken, SC 29801
(803) 649-7981
Waccamaw Regional Planning and
Development Council
(Horry, Williamsburg, and
Georgetown counties)
P.O. Drawer 419
Georgetown, SC 29440
(803) 546-8502
Low Country Council of Govern-
ments
(Beaufort, Jasper, Hampton, and
Colleton counties)
P.O. Box 98
Yemassee, SC 29945
(803) 726-5536

Medicare Peer Review Organization
South Carolina Professional Review
Organization
Division of Metrolina Medical
Peer Review
1 Charlotte Center, Suite 150
Charlotte, NC 28204
(704) 373-1545

SOUTH DAKOTA
State Agency on Aging
(no area agencies)
South Dakota Office of Adult Services and Aging
Department of Social Services
700 Governor's Drive
Pierre, SD 57501-2291
(605) 773-3656

Medicare Peer Review Organization
South Dakota Foundation for Medical Care
608 West Ave., North
Sioux Falls, SD 57104
(605) 336-3505

TENNESSEE
State Agency on Aging
Tennessee Commission on Aging
715 Tennessee Bldg.
535 Church St.
Nashville, TN 37219
(615) 741-2056

Area Agencies on Aging

Mid-Cumberland Development District
(Williamson, Stewart, Montgomery, Robertson, Sumner, Houston, Humphreys, Dickson, Cheatham, Davidson, Wilson, Troosdale, and Rutherford counties)
501 Union Bldg., L-100
501 Union St.
Nashville, TN 37219
(615) 244-1212

Office of Planning and Development, Delta Commission on Aging
(Shelby, Fayette, Tipton, and Lauderdale counties)
City Hall, Room 419
125 N. Main St.
Memphis, TN 38103
(901) 528-2600

East Tennessee Human Resource Agency
(Scott, Campbell, Claiborne, Grainger, Hamblen, Cooke, Jefferson, Union, Sevier, Knox, Blount, Monroe, Loudon, Roane, Anderson, and Morgan counties)
P.O. Box 14428
6712 Deane Hill Drive
Knoxville, TN 37939
(615) 691-2551

Southeast Tennessee Development District
(McMinn, Meigs, Polk, Bradley, Rhea, Bledsoe, Hamilton, Sequatchie, Grundy, and Marion counties)
Carroon & Black Bldg., Suite 300
216 W. Eighth St.
Chattanooga, TN 37402
(615) 266-5781

First Tennessee-Virginia Development District
(Hancock, Hawkins, Sullivan, Johnson, Carter, Unicoi, Washington, and Greene counties)
207 N. Boone, Suite 800
Johnson City, TN 37601
(615) 928-0224

Upper Cumberland Development District
(Cumberland, Macon, Clay, Pickett, Fentress, Overton, Jackson, Smith, DeKalb, Putnam, White, Cannon, Warren, and Van Buren counties)
1225 Burgess Falls Rd.
Cookeville, TN 38501
(615) 432-4111

South Central Tennessee Development District
(Perry, Hickman, Lewis, Wayne, Lawrence, Giles, Maury, Marshall, Bedford, Lincoln, Moore, Franklin, and Coffee counties)
P.O. Box 1346
Columbia, TN 38402-1346
(615) 381-2040

Northwest Tennessee Development District
(Lake, Obion, Dyer, Gibson, Crockett, Weakley, Henry, Carroll, and Benton counties)
P.O. Box 63
Weldon Drive
Martin, TN 38237
(901) 587-4215

Southwest Tennessee Development District
(Haywood, Madison, Henderson, Decatur, Hardin, McNairy, Chester, and Hardeman counties)
416 E. Lafayette St.
Jackson, TN 38301
(901) 422-4041

Medicare Peer Review Organization

Mid-South Foundation for Medical
Care
   6401 Poplar Ave., Suite 400
   Memphis, TN 38119
   (901) 682-0381

TEXAS

State Agency on Aging

Texas Department on Aging
   1949 Interstate Highway 35 South
   Austin, TX 78741-3702
   (512) 444-2727
   (800) 252-9240 (toll-free, within
     state)

Area Agencies on Aging

Harris County Office on Aging
   806 Main, 3rd floor
   P.O. Box 1562
   Houston, TX 77251
   (713) 222-5693
Houston-Galveston Area Agency on
   Aging
   (Matagorda, Brazoria, Fort Bend,
     Wharton, Colorado, Austin,
     and Waller counties)
   P.O. Box 22777
   3555 Timmons, Suite 500
   Houston, TX 77227
   (713) 627-3200
Dallas County Area Agency on
   Aging
   2121 Main St., Suite 500
   Dallas, TX 75201-4321
   (214) 741-5851
Tarrant County Area Agency on
   Aging
   201 E. Ninth St.
   Fort Worth, TX 76102
   (817) 335-3473

Capital Area Agency on Aging
   (Burnet, Llano, Blanco, William-
     son, Travis, Lee, Fayette, Bas-
     trop, Hays, and Caldwell
     counties)
   2520 Interstate Highway 35 South,
     Suite 100
   Austin, TX 78704
   (512) 443-7653
Alamo Area Agency on Aging
   (Gillespie, Kerr, Kendall, Bandera,
     Medina, Frio, and Atascosa
     counties)
   118 Broadway, Suite 400
   San Antonio, TX 78205
   (512) 225-5201
Bexar County Area Agency on
   Aging
   118 Broadway, Suite 400
   San Antonio, TX 78205
   (512) 225-5201
Panhandle Area Agency on Aging
   (Dallam, Sherman, Hansford,
     Ochiltree, Lipscomb, Hemphill,
     Roberts, Hutchinson, Moore,
     Hartley, Oldham, Potter, Car-
     son, Gray, Wheeler, Deaf
     Smith, Randall, Armstrong,
     Donley, Collingsworth, Hall,
     Briscoe, Swisher, Castro, and
     Parmer counties)
   P.O. Box 9257
   801 S. Jackson, Briercroft Bldg.,
     Suite 200
   Amarillo, TX 79105
   (806) 372-3381
South Plains Area Agency on Aging
   (Lubbock, Bailey, Lamb, Hale,
     Floyd, Motley, King, Dickens,
     Crosby, Hockley, Cochran,
     Yoakum, Terry, Lynn, and
     Garza counties)
   P.O. Box 3730, Freedom Station
   Lubbock, TX 79452
   (806) 762-8721

North Texas Area Agency on Aging
(Childress, Cottle, Hardeman,
Foard, Wilbarger, Baylor,
Wichita, Archer, Young, Clay,
Jack, and Montague counties)
P.O. Box 5144
2101 Kemp Blvd.
Wichita Falls, TX 76307
(817) 322-5281

North Central Texas Area Agency
on Aging
(Wise, Denton, Collin, Hunt,
Rockwall, Kaufman, Parker,
Palo Pinto, Erath, Hood, Somer-
vell, Johnson, Ellis, and Navarro
counties)
P.O. Drawer COG
Centerpoint Two, 2nd floor
616 Six Flags Drive
Arlington, TX 76005-5888
(817) 640-3300

Ark-Tex Area Agency on Aging
(Lamar, Red River, Bowie, Cass,
Morris, Titus, Franklin, Hop-
kins, and Delta counties)
P.O. Box 5307
Texarkana, TX 75505
(214) 832-8636

East Texas Area Agency on Aging
(Rains, Wood, Camp, Upshur,
Marion, Harrison, Gregg, Rusk,
Panola, Cherokee, Anderson,
Henderson, Smith, and Van
Zandt counties)
3800 Stone Rd.
Kilgore, TX 75662
(214) 984-8641

West Texas Area Agency on Aging
(El Paso, Hudspeth, Culberson,
Jeff Davis, Presidio, and Brew-
ster counties)
2 Civic Center Plaza, 8th floor
El Paso, TX 79999
(915) 541-4972

West Central Texas Area Agency on
Aging
(Knox, Kent, Stonewall, Haskell,
Throckmorton, Stephens,
Shackelford, Jones, Fisher,
Scurry, Mitchell, Nolan, Taylor,
Callahan, Eastland, Comanche,
Brown, Coleman, and Runnels
counties)
P.O. Box 3195
1025 E. North 10th St.
Abilene, TX 79604
(915) 672-8544

Permian Basin Area Agency on
Aging
(Gaines, Dawson, Borden, An-
drews, Martin, Howard, Loving,
Winkler, Ector, Midland, Glas-
scock, Upton, Crane, Ward,
Reeves, Pecos, and Terrell
counties)
P.O. Box 6391
2514 Pliska Drive
Midland, TX 79711
(915) 563-1061

Concho Valley Area Agency on
Aging
(Sterling, Coke, Tom Green, Con-
cho, Irion, Reagan, Crockett,
Schleicher, Menard, Mason,
McCulloch, Sutton, and Kimble
counties)
P.O. Box 60050
5002 Knickerbocker Rd.
San Angelo, TX 76906
(915) 944-9666

Heart of Texas Area Agency on
Aging
(Bosque, Hill, Limestone, McLen-
nan, Falls, and Freestone counties)
320 Franklin Ave.
Waco, TX 76701
(817) 756-6631

Brazos Valley Area Agency on
Aging
(Robertson, Leon, Madison,
Brazos, Grimes, Burleson, and
Washington counties)
P.O. Drawer 4128
3006 E. 29th St.
Bryan, TX 77805-4128
(409) 776-2277

Deep East Texas Area Agency on
Aging
(Nacogdoches, Shelby, San Au-
gustine, Sabine, Newton, Jasper,
Tyler, Angelina, Houston, Trinity, Polk, and San Jacinto counties)
P.O. Drawer 1170
274 E. Lamar St.
Jasper, TX 75951
(409) 384-5704

South Texas Area Agency on Aging
(Webb, Zapata, Jim Hogg, and
Starr counties)
P.O. Box 2187
600 S. Sandman, Laredo Interna-
tional Airport
Laredo, TX 78044-2187
(512) 722-3995

South East Texas Area Agency on
Aging
(Hardin, Orange, and Jefferson
counties)
P.O. Drawer 1387
Nederland, TX 77627
(409) 727-2384

Golden Crescent Regional Planning
Commission Area Agency on
Aging
(Gonzales, Lavaca, DeWitt, Jack-
son, Victoria, Calhoun, and Go-
liad counties)
P.O. Box 2028
115 S. Main
Victoria, TX 77902
(512) 578-1587

Coastal Bend Area Agency on Aging
(McMullen, Live Oak, Bee, Refu-
gio, Aransas, Nueces, San Patri-
cio, Jim Wells, Duval, Kleberg,
Kenedy, and Brooks counties)
P.O. Box 9909
2910 Leopard St.
Corpus Christi, TX 78469
(512) 883-5743

Lower Rio Grande Valley Area
Agency on Aging
(Willacy, Cameron, and Hidalgo
counties)
Texas Commerce Bank Bldg.,
Suite 707
1701 W. Business Highway 83
McAllen, TX 78501
(512) 682-3481

Texoma Area Agency on Aging
(Cooke, Grayson, and Fannin
counties)
10000 Grayson Drive
Denison, TX 75020
(214) 786-2955

Central Texas Area Agency on
Aging
(Hamilton, Mills, San Saba, Lam-
pasas, Coryell, Bell, and Milam
counties)
P.O. Box 729
302 E. Central
Belton, TX 76513
(817) 939-1886

Middle Rio Grande Area Agency on
Aging
(Val Verde, Edwards, Real,
Uvalde, Kinney, Maverick, Za-
vala, Dimmit, and LaSalle coun-
ties)
P.O. Box 1199
403 E. Nopal
Carrizo Spring, TX 78834
(512) 876-3533

Medicare Peer Review Organization

Texas Medical Foundation
Barton Oaks Plaza Two
901 Mopac Expressway South,
Suite 200
Austin, TX 78746
(512) 329-6610

UTAH
State Agency on Aging

Utah Division of Aging and Adult
Services
Department of Social Sciences
Box 45500
150 W. North Temple
Salt Lake City, UT 84110-2500
(801) 533-6422

Area Agencies on Aging

Salt Lake County Aging Services
134 E. 2100 South, No. 3
Salt Lake City, UT 84115
(801) 488-5454
Bear River Area Agency on Aging
(Box Elder, Cache, and Rich counties)
170 N. Main
Logan, UT 84321
(801) 752-7242
Weber County Area Agency on
Aging
(Weber and Morgan counties)
Human Services Bldg.
2650 Lincoln Ave.
Ogden, UT 84401
(801) 625-3770
Mountainland Area Agency on
Aging
(Summit, Wasatch, and Utah
counties)
160 E. Center St.
Provo, UT 84601
(801) 377-2262

Davis County Council on Aging
Courthouse Annex
P.O. Box 618
Farmington, UT 84025
(801) 451-3370
Tooele County Area Agency on
Aging
c/o Gary Dalton
47 S. Main, No. 300
Tooele, UT 84074
(801) 882-2870
Six-County Area Agency on Aging
(Wayne, Piute, Juab, Sanpete,
Millard, and Sevier counties)
P.O. Box 788
Richfield, UT 84701
(801) 896-9222
(801) 896-9226
Five-County Area Agency on Aging
(Beaver, Garfield, Iron, Kane, and
Washington counties)
P.O. Box O
St. George, UT 84770
(801) 673-3548 (St. George, Tues.
and Thurs.)
(801) 586-6513 (Cedar City, Mon.,
Wed., and Fri.)
Uintah Basin Area Agency on Aging
(Daggett and Duchesne counties)
P.O. Box 1449
Roosevelt, UT 84066
(801) 722-4519
Uintah County Area Agency on
Aging
155 S. 100 West
Vernal, UT 84078
(801) 789-2169
Southeastern Utah Area Agency on
Aging
(Carbon, Emery, and Grand counties)
P.O. Drawer 1106
Price, UT 84501
(801) 637-4268

San Juan County Area Agency on
  Aging
P.O. Box 9
Monticello, UT 84535
(801) 587-2231

Medicare Peer Review Organization

Utah Professional Standard Review
  Organization
540 E. Fifth South St., Suite 200
Salt Lake City, UT 84102-2707
(801) 532-7545

VERMONT

State Agency on Aging

Vermont Office on Aging
  103 S. Main St.
  Waterbury, VT 05676
  (802) 241-2400
  (800) 642-5119 (toll-free, within
    state)

Area Agencies on Aging

Champlain Valley Area Agency on
  Aging
  (Addison, Chittenden, Franklin,
    and Grand Isle counties)
  110 E. Spring St.
  Winooski, VT 05404
  (802) 655-0084
Central Vermont Council on Aging
  (Washington, Lamoille, and parts
    of Windsor, Orange, Addison,
    and Rutland counties)
  18 S. Main St.
  Barre, VT 05641
  (802) 479-0531
Area Agency on Aging for North-
  eastern Vermont
  (Orleans, Essex, and Caledonia
    counties)
  P.O. Box 640
  St. Johnsbury, VT 05819
  (802) 748-5182

Southwestern Vermont Area Agency
  on Aging
  (most of Rutland and Bennington
    counties)
  142 Merchants Row
  Rutland, VT 05701
  (802) 775-0486
Council on Aging for Southeastern
  Vermont
  (Windham and parts of Windsor
    and Orange counties)
  P.O. Box 818
  139 Main St.
  Brattleboro, Vt. 05301
  (802) 257-0569

Medicare Peer Review Organization

New Hampshire Foundation for
  Medical Care
  (both Vermont and New Hamp-
    shire)
  P.O. Box 578
  110 Locust St.
  Dover, NH 03820
  (603) 749-1641

VIRGINIA

State Agency on Aging

Virginia Department for the Aging
  101 N. 14th St., 18th floor
  Richmond, VA 23219-2797
  (804) 225-2271

Area Agencies on Aging

Alexandria Department of Human
  Services Office on Aging
  2525 Mount Vernon Ave., Unit 5
  Alexandria, VA 22301-1119
  (703) 838-0920
Arlington Area Agency on Aging
  1801 N. George Mason Drive
  Arlington, VA 22207-1999
  (703) 558-2341

Fairfax County Area Agency on
  Aging
  11212 Waples Mill Rd.
  Fairfax, VA 22030-6036
  (703) 691-3384
Capital Area Agency on Aging
  (Hanover, Goochland, Henrico,
    Powatan, New Kent, Charles
    City, and Chesterfield counties)
  316 E. Clay St.
  Richmond, VA 23219-1496
  (804) 648-8381
Southeastern Virginia Areawide
  Model Program
  (Norfolk, Isle of Wight, South-
    ampton, Suffolk, Portsmouth,
    Chesapeake, and Virginia Beach
    counties)
  7 Koger Executive Center, Suite 100
  Norfolk, VA 23502-4121
  (804) 461-9481
Peninsula Agency on Aging
  (James City and York counties)
  13195 Warwick Blvd., Bldg. 2,
    Suite F
  Newport News, VA 23602
  (804) 874-2495
League of Older Americans
  (Roanoke, Craig, Botetourt, and
    Alleghany counties)
  P.O. Box 14205
  Roanoke, VA 24038
  (703) 345-0451
Jefferson Area Board for Aging
  (Albemarle, Greene, Louisa, and
    Fluvanna counties)
  423 Lexington Ave.
  Charlottesville, VA 22901-4711
  (804) 977-3444
Mountain Empire Older Citizens
  (Lee, Wise, and Scott counties)
  P.O. Box 1097
  330 Norton Road
  Wise, VA 24293-1097
  (703) 328-2302

Appalachian Agency for Senior Citi-
  zens
  (Buchanan, Dickenson, Tazewell,
    and Russell counties)
  Box S.V.C.C.
  Richlands, VA 24641-1510
  (703) 783-8158
District 3 Governmental Cooperative
  (Bland, Wythe, Smith, Washing-
    ton, Grayson, and Carroll coun-
    ties)
  305 S. Park St.
  Marion, VA 24354-2999
  (703) 783-8158
New River Valley Agency on Aging
  (Giles, Pulaski, Montgomery, and
    Floyd counties)
  143 Third St., N.W.
  Pulaski, VA 24301-4999
  (703) 980-8888
Valley Program for Aging Services
  (Augusta, Highland, Bath, Rock-
    ingham, and Rockbridge coun-
    ties)
  P.O. Box 817
  Waynesboro, VA 22980-0603
  (703) 949-7141
Shenandoah Area Agency on Aging
  (Shenandoah, Frederick, Clarke,
    Warren, and Page counties)
  15 N. Royal Ave.
  Front Royal, VA 22530-2611
  (703) 635-7141
Loudoun County Area Agency on
  Aging
  115 Harrison St., N.E.
  Leesburg, VA 22075
  (703) 777-0257
Prince William County Area Agency
  on Aging
  9252 Lee Ave.
  Manassas, VA 22110
  (703) 335-6400

Rappahannock-Rapidan Area
Agency on Aging
(Fauquier, Rappahannock, Madison, Culpeper and Orange
counties)
401 S. Main St.
Culpeper, VA 22701
(703) 825-6494

Central Virginia Commission on
Aging
(Amherst, Bedford, Campbell, and
Appomattox counties)
Forest Hill Center
2820 Linkhorne Drive
Lynchburg, VA 24503
(804) 384-0372

Piedmont Seniors of Virginia
(Pittsylvania, Franklin, Patrick,
and Henry counties)
827 Starling Ave.
Martinsville, VA 24112-4228
(703) 632-6442

Lake Country Commission on Aging
(Mecklenburg, Halifax, and
Brunswick counties)
1105 W. Danville St.
South Hill, VA 23970-3501
(804) 447-7661

Piedmont Senior Resources
(Prince Edward, Charlotte, Lunenburg, Nottoway, Amelia, Cumberland, and Buckingham
counties)
P.O. Box 398
Burkeville, VA 23922-0398
(804) 767-5588

Rappahannock Area Agency on
Aging
(Stafford, King George, Spotsylvania, and Caroline counties)
1612 Tidewater Trail, Suite 1
Fredericksburg, VA 22405
(703) 371-3375

Northern Neck—Middle Peninsula
Area Agency on Aging
(Westmoreland, Essex, King and
Queen, King William, Richmond, Middlesex, Gloucester,
Mathews, Northumberland, and
Lancaster counties)
P.O. Box 610
Urbana, VA 23175
(804) 758-2386

Crater District Area Agency on
Aging
(Prince George, Surry, Dinwiddie,
Sussex, and Greensville counties)
120 W. Bank St.
Petersburg, VA 23803-3216
(804) 732-7020

Eastern Shore Community Development Group
(Accomack and Northampton
counties)
P.O. Box 8
54 Market St.
Onancock, VA 23417
(804) 787-3532

Medicare Peer Review Organization

Medical Society of Virginia Review
Organization
1904 Byrd Ave., Room 120
Richmond, VA 23230
(804) 289-5320

WASHINGTON

State Agency on Aging

Washington Bureau of Aging and
Adult Services
Department of Social and Health
Services
OB-43G
Olympia, WA 98504
(206) 753-2502

Area Agencies on Aging

King County Area Agency on Aging
400 Yesler Bldg.
Seattle, WA 98104
(206) 625-4711

Pierce County Area Agency on
Aging
2401 S. 35th St., Room 5
Tacoma, WA 98409
(206) 593-4828

Lewis-Mason-Thurston (counties)
Area Agency on Aging
529 W. Fourth Ave.
Olympia, WA 98501
(206) 786-5579

Southwest Washington Area Agency
on Aging
(Wahkiakum, Cowlitz, Clark,
Skamania, and Klickitat coun-
ties)
P.O. Box 425
Vancouver, WA 98666
(206) 694-6577

Northwest Washington Area
Agency on Aging
(Whatcom, Skagit, and San Juan
Island counties)
Courthouse Annex
1000 Forest St.
Bellingham, WA 98225
(206) 676-6749

Snohomish County Office on Aging
County Courthouse, 1st floor
Everett, WA 98201
(206) 259-9586

Eastern Washington Area Agency
on Aging
(Spokane, Ferry, Stevens, Whit-
man, and Pend Oreille counties)
West 1101 College Ave., Room
365
Spokane, WA 99201
(509) 458-2509

Kitsap County Area Agency on
Aging
Kitsap County Courthouse
614 Division St.
Port Orchard, WA 98366
(206) 876-7068

Olympic Area Agency on Aging
(Clallam, Jefferson, Grays Harbor,
and Pacific counties)
2109 Sumner Ave., Room 203
Aberdeen, WA 98520
(206) 533-9385

North Central Area Agency on
Aging
(Okanogan, Chelan, Douglas, Lincoln, Adams, and Grant counties)
1300 Fifth St.
Wenatchee, WA 98801
(509) 662-1651, ext. 276

Yakima-Southeast Washington Area
Agency on Aging
(Yakima, Kittitas, Benton, Frank-
lin, Walla Walla, Columbia,
Garfield, and Asotin counties)
2009 S. 64th Ave.
Yakima, WA 98903
(509) 575-4226

Yakima Indian Nation Area Agency
on Aging
P.O. Box 151
Toppenish, WA 98948
(509) 865-5121, ext. 484

Colville Indian Area Agency on
Aging
P.O. Box 150
Nespelem, WA 99155
(509) 634-4761

Medicare Peer Review Organization

Professional Review Organization
for Washington
2150 N. 107th St., Suite 200
Seattle, WA 98133
(206) 364-9700

WEST VIRGINIA

State Agency on Aging

West Virginia Commission on
   Aging
   State Capitol
   Charleston, WV 25305
   (304) 348-3317

Area Agencies on Aging

Community Council of Kanawha
   Valley
   (Kanawha, Putnam, Boone, and
      Clay counties)
   Box 2711
   Charleston, WV 25330
   (304) 342-5107

Northern Panhandle Area Agency
   on Aging
   (Hancock, Brooke, Ohio, Mar-
      shall, and Wetzel counties)
   2177 National Rd.
   Wheeling, WV 26003
   (304) 242-1800

Eastern Highlands Area Agency on
   Aging
   (Greenbrier, Pocahontas, Webster,
      Nicholas, and Fayette counties)
   500-B Main St.
   Summersville, WV 26651
   (304) 872-4970

Region 1 Planning and Development
   Commission
   (Summers, Monroe, Mercer, Ra-
      leigh, Wyoming, and McDowell
      counties)
   P.O. Box 1442
   Princeton, WV 24740
   (304) 425-9508

Mid-Ohio Valley Regional Council
   (Tyler, Pleasants, Ritchie, Wood,
      Wirt, Calhoun, Roane, and
      Jackson counties)
   P.O. Box 247
   Parkersburg, WV 26101
   (304) 422-0522

Region 6 Area Agency on Aging
   (Monongalia, Preston, Marion,
      Taylor, Harrison, and Dod-
      dridge counties)
   200 Adams St.
   Fairmont, WV 26554
   (304) 366-5693

Southwestern Area Agency on
   Aging
   (Mason, Cabell, Wayne, Lincoln,
      Logan, and Mingo counties)
   540 Fifth Ave.
   Huntington, WV 25701
   (304) 525-5151

Central West Virginia Area Agency
   on Aging
   (Barbour, Tucker, Randolph, Up-
      shur, Lewis, Gilmer, and Brax-
      ton counties)
   P.O. Box 186
   Buckhannon, WV 26201
   (304) 472-0395

Upper Potomac Area Agency on
   Aging
   (Jefferson, Berkeley, Morgan,
      Hampshire, Mineral, Grant,
      Hardy, and Pendleton counties)
   P.O. Box 866
   Petersburg, WV 26847
   (304) 257-1221

Medicare Peer Review Organization

West Virginia Medical Institute Inc.
   3412 Chesterfield Ave., S.E.
   Charleston, WV 25304
   (304) 925-0461

WISCONSIN

State Agency on Aging

Wisconsin Office on Aging
   1 W. Wilson St., Room 472
   Madison, WI 53707
   (608) 266-2536

Area Agencies on Aging

Milwaukee Area Agency on Aging
  1442 N. Farwell Ave.
  Milwaukee, WI 53202
  (414) 272-8606

Southern Area Agency on Aging
  (Jefferson, Dane, Dodge, Columbia, Sauk, Richland, Grant, Iowa, Lafayette, Green, and Rock counties)
  3601 Memorial Drive
  Madison, WI 53704
  (608) 249-0441

Southeastern Area Agency on Aging
  (Waukesha, Racine, Kenosha, Washington, Ozaukee, and Walworth counties)
  W255 N499 Grandview Blvd., Suite 209
  Waukesha, WI 53188
  (414) 521-5420

Lake Michigan—Winnebago Area Agency on Aging
  (Marinette, Oconto, Menominee, Shawano, Waupaca, Door, Outagamie, Kewaunee, Brown, Manitowoc, Sheboygan, Calumet, Fond du Lac, Winnebago, Green Lake, Waushara, and Marquette counties)
  850-C Lombardi Ave.
  Green Bay, WI 54304
  (414) 432-2935

Western Wisconsin Area Agency on Aging
  (Burnett, Washburn, Polk, Barron, St. Croix, Dunn, Rusk, Chippawa, Eau Claire, Clark, Jackson, Pierce, Pepin, Buffalo, Trempealeau, Monroe, La-Crosse, Vernon, and Crawford counties)
  505 Dewey St. South, Room 207
  Eau Claire, WI 54701
  (715) 836-4105

Northern Area Agency on Aging
  (Juneau, Adams, Portage, Wood, Marathon, Taylor, Price, Lincoln, Langlade, Florence, Forest, Oneida, Sawyer, Douglas, Bayfield, Ashland, Iron, and Vilas counties)
  P.O. Box 1028
  1853 N. Stevens St.
  Rhinelander, WI 54501
  (715) 362-7800

Medicare Peer Review Organization

Wisconsin Peer Review Review Organization
  2001 W. Beltline Highway
  Madison, WI 53713
  (608) 274-1940

WYOMING

State Agency on Aging

(no area agencies)

Wyoming Commission on Aging
  130 Hathaway Bldg.
  Cheyenne, WY 82002
  (307) 777-7986
  (800) 442-2766 (toll-free, within state)

Medicare Peer Review Organization

Montana-Wyoming Foundation for Medical Care
  P.O. Box 5117
  21 N. Main
  Helena, MT 59604
  (406) 443-4020

BIBLIOGRAPHY

BOOKS

Berland, Theodore. *Fitness for Life: Exercises for People Over 50.* American Association of Retired Persons; Glenview, IL: Scott, Foresman & Co., 1986.

Bierbrier, Doreen. *Living With Tenants: How to Happily Share Your House With Renters for Profit and Security.* New York: McGraw-Hill, 1986.

Browne, Colette, and Roberta Onzuka-Anderson, eds. *Our Aging Parents: A Practical Guide to Eldercare.* Honolulu: University of Hawaii Press, 1985.

Brown, Judith N., and Christina Baldwin. *A Second Start: A Widow's Guide to Financial Survival at a Time of Emotional Crisis.* New York: Simon & Schuster, 1987.

Burger, Sarah. *Living in a Nursing Home.* New York: Continuum Publishing Co., 1976.

Butler, Robert N., M.D. *Why Survive? Being Old in America.* San Francisco: Harper & Row, 1981.

Butler, Robert N., M.D., and Myrna I. Lewis. *Aging & Mental Health.* 3d ed. St. Louis: C.V. Mosby Co., 1982.

Cadmus, Robert R., M.D. *Caring for Your Aging Parents: A Concerned, Complete Guide for Children of the Elderly.* Englewood Cliffs, NJ: Prentice-Hall, 1984.

Caine, Lynn. *Widow.* New York: Bantam Books, 1975.

Carr, Rachel. *Arthritis: Relief Beyond Drugs.* New York: Barnes & Noble Books, 1981.

Duvoisin, Robert C. *Parkinson's Disease: A Guide for Patient and Family.* New York: Raven Press, 1978.

Flint, Margaret M. *A Consumer's Guide to Nursing Home Care in New York City.* New York: Friends and Relatives of Institutionalized Aged, 1982.

Freese, Arthur S. *Stroke: The New Help and the New Life.* New York: Random House, 1980.

Friedman, Jo-Ann. *Home Health Care: A Complete Guide for Patients and Their Families.* New York: W.W. Norton & Co., 1986.

Fries, James F., M.D. *The Arthritis Handbook.* Reading, MA: Addison-Wesley, 1980.

————. *Arthritis: A Comprehensive Guide.* Reading, MA: Addison-Wesley, 1981.

Gross, Zenith. *And You Thought It Was All Over!: Mothers and Their Adult Children.* New York: St. Martin's Press, Marek Press, 1985.

Gwyther, Lisa P. *Care of Alzheimer's Patients: A Manual for Nursing Home Staff.* Chicago: American Health Care Association and Alzheimer's Disease and Related Disorders Association, 1985.

Hanaway, Lorraine, ed. *The Three-In-One House: A Guide to Organizing and Operating a House for Three Older Persons.* Frederick, MD: Home Care Research, 1981.

Hemmings, Susan. *A Wealth of Experience: The Lives of Older Women.* London: Pandora Press, 1985.

Hess, Lucille J., and Robert E. Baker. *What Every Family Should Know About Strokes.* Norwalk, CT: Appleton-Century-Crofts, 1981.

Horne, Jo. *Caregiving: Helping An Aging Loved One.* American Association of Retired Persons. Glenview, IL: Scott, Foresman & Co., 1985.

Kübler-Ross, Elisabeth. *On Death and Dying.* New York: Macmillan, Collier Books, 1969.

LaBuda, Dennis R. *The Gadget Book: Ingenious Devices for Easier Living.* American Association for Retired Persons. Glenview, IL: Scott, Foresman & Co., 1985.

Mace, Nancy L., and Peter V. Rabins, M.D. *The 36 Hour Day.* Baltimore: The Johns Hopkins University Press, 1981.

Maurer, Janet M., M.D. *How to Talk to Your Doctor: The Questions to Ask.* New York: Simon & Schuster, Fireside Books, 1986.

Mongeau, Sam, ed. *National Directory of Retirement Facilities.* Phoenix: Oryx Press, 1985.

Munley, Anne. *The Hospice Alternative: A New Context for Death and Dying.* New York: Basic Books, 1986.

Murphy, Lois Barclay. *The Home Hospital: How a Family Can Cope With Catastrophic Illness.* New York: Basic Books, 1982.

Nassif, Janet Zhun. *The Home Health Care Solution: A Complete Consumer Guide.* New York: Harper & Row, 1985.

Nelson, Thomas C. *It's Your Choice: The Practical Guide to Planning a Funeral.* American Association for Retired Persons. Glenview, IL: Scott, Foresman & Co., 1983.

Older Women's League and American Bar Association's Commission on Legal Problems of the Elderly. *Taking Charge of the End of Your Life: Proceedings of a Forum on Living Wills and Other Advance Directives.* Washington, D.C.: 1985.

Persico, J. E. with George Sunderland. *Keeping Out of Crime's Way: The Practical Guide for People Over Fifty.* American Association for Retired Persons. Glenview, IL: Scott, Foresman & Co., 1984.

Powell, Lenore S., and Katie Courtice. *Alzheimer's Disease: A Guide for Families.* Reading, MA: Addison-Wesley, 1983.

Raper, Ann Trueblood, ed. *National Continuing Care Directory.* American Association for Retired Persons. Glenview, IL: Scott, Foresman & Co., 1984.

Reisberg, Barry, M.D. *A Guide to Alzheimer's Disease.* New York: Macmillan, Free Press, 1981.

Richards, Marty, Nancy Hooyman, Mary Hansen, Wendy Brandts, Kathy Smith-DiJulio, and Lynn Dahm. *Choosing a Nursing Home: A Guidebook for Families.* rev. ed. Seattle University of Washington Press, 1985.

Roach, Marion. *Another Name for Madness.* Boston: Houghton Mifflin, 1985.

Schiff, Harriet Sarnoff. *Living Through Mourning: Finding Comfort and Hope When a Loved One Has Died.* New York: Viking, 1986.

Sessler, G. J. *Stroke: How to Prevent It/ How to Survive It.* Englewood Cliffs, NJ: Prentice-Hall. 1981.

Silverstone, Barbara, and Helen Kandel Hyman. *You and Your Aging Parent: The Modern Family's Guide to Emotional, Physical, and Financial Problems.* 2d ed. New York: Pantheon Books, 1982.

Soled, Alex J. *The Essential Guide to Wills, Estates, Trusts and Death Taxes.* American Association for Retired Persons. Glenview, IL: Scott, Foresman & Co., 1984.

Upson, Norma S. *When Someone You Love Is Dying.* New York: Simon & Schuster, Fireside Books, 1986.

Vicker, Ray. *The Dow Jones-Irwin Guide to Retirement Planning.* Homewood, IL: Dow Jones-Irwin, 1985.

Weaver, Peter, and Annette Buchanan. *What to Do with What You've Got.* Washington, D.C.: American Association for Retired Persons. Glenview, IL: Scott, Foresman & Co., 1984.

Winklevoss, Howard E., and Alwyn V. Powell. *Continuing Care and Retirement Communities: An Empirical, Financial, and Legal Analysis.* Homewood, IL: Richard D. Irwin Inc., 1984.

Zarit, Steven H., Nancy K. Orr, and Judy M. Zarit. *The Hidden Victims of Alzheimer's Disease.* New York: New York University Press, 1985.

PAMPHLETS, PAPERS, AND ARTICLES

American Association of Retired Persons. *Your Retirement Anticrime Guide.* Washington, D.C.: 1978.

———.*Have You Heard? Hearing Loss and Aging,* by M. Barbara Laufer. Washington, D.C.: 1984

———. *Housing Options for Older Americans.* Washington, D.C.: 1984.

———. *Your Home, Your Choice.* In cooperation with the Federal Trade Commission. Washington, D.C.: 1984.

———. *Knowing Your Rights: Medicare's Prospective Payment System.* Washington, D.C.: 1985.

———. *Medicare & Health Insurance for Older People.* Washington, D.C.: 1985.

Carroll Center for the Blind. "Aids for Elderly Persons with Impaired Vision," *Aids and Appliances Review* 13 (Summer 1984):1–31.

Connecticut Community Care and Blue Cross & Blue Shield of Connecticut. *Families Who Care for Older Relatives: The Problems, The Solutions.* North Haven, CT: 1986.

Fatoullah, Ellice, and David E. Frazer. *Money Management and the Cost of Health Care: Options for the Elderly and Disabled.* New York: 1985.

Hare, Patrick H., with Susan Conner and Dwight Merriam. *Accessory Apartments: Using Surplus Space in Single-Family Houses.* Planning Advisory Service Report 365. Chicago: American Planning Association, 1981.

Hiatt, Lorraine G. "Environmental Design and the Frail Older Person at Home." *Pride Institute Journal of Long Term Home Health Care* 2, no. 1 (1983): 13–22.

———. "Understanding the Physical Environment." *Pride Institute Journal of Long Term Home Health Care* 4, no. 2 (1985): 12–22.

Lidoff, Lorraine, and Patricia Harris. *Idea Book on Caregiver Support Groups.* Washington, D.C.: The National Council on the Aging Inc., 1985.

Medicine in the Public Interest. *Learning to Live with Osteoarthritis.* Boston (65 Franklin St., 02110): 1983.

National Consumers League. *A Consumer Guide to Life-Care Communities,* by Laura Spitz and Shelah Leader. Washington, D.C.: 1983.

————. *A Consumer Guide to Home Health Care,* by Barbara Coleman. Washington, D.C.: 1985.

————. *A Consumer Guide to Hospice Care,* by Barbara Coleman. Washington, D.C.: 1985.

National Institute on Aging. *Age Pages.* Washington, D.C.: U.S. Government Printing Office, 1984.

National Senior Citizens Law Center. *Shoppers' Guide to Supplemental Medicare Insurance.* Los Angeles.

Scholen, Ken. *Home-Made Pension Plans: Converting Home Equity into Retirement Income.* 3d ed. Madison, WI: National Center for Home Equity Conversion, 1985.

U.S. Consumer Product Safety Commission. *Safety for Older Consumers.* Washington, D.C.: 1985.

U.S. Department of Housing and Urban Development. *Questions About Condominiums: What to Ask Before You Buy.* Washington, D.C.: 1980.

————. *Let's Consider Cooperatives.* Washington, D.C.: 1984.

U.S. Department of Justice, Office of Justice Assistance, Research, and Statistics. *Senior Citizens Against Crime: Take a Bite Out of Crime.* Washington, D.C.: 1979.

Index

About the Author

Jean Crichton is a free-lance writer living in New York City. Born in Johnstown, Pennsylvania, she graduated from Wellesley College, got a Master of Arts in Teaching from Reed College, and taught on the Gila River Indian Reservation in Arizona during the 1960s before getting a start in journalism. Since then, she has reported for the Associated Press and several newspapers and has written numerous magazine articles. This is her first book.